VICTORY IN SHANGHAI

VICTORY IN SHANGHAI

A Korean American Family's Journey to
the CIA and the Army Special Forces

ROBERT S. KIM

POTOMAC BOOKS
An imprint of the University of Nebraska Press

For customers in the EU with safety/GPSR concerns, contact:
gpsr@mare-nostrum.co.uk
Mare Nostrum Group BV
Mauritskade 21D
1091 GC Amsterdam
The Netherlands

LIBRARY OF CONGRESS CATALOGING-IN-PUBLICATION DATA
Names: Kim, Robert S., author.
Title: Victory in Shanghai: a Korean American family's journey to the CIA and the Army Special Forces / Robert S. Kim.
Description: Lincoln: Potomac Books, an imprint of the University of Nebraska Press, 2025. | Includes bibliographical references and index.
Identifiers: LCCN 2024042397
ISBN 9781640126329 (hardback)
ISBN 9781640126602 (epub)
ISBN 9781640126619 (pdf)
Subjects: LCSH: World War, 1939–1945—Secret service—China—Shanghai. | World War, 1939–1945—Military intelligence—China—Shanghai. | World War, 1939–1945—Participation, Korean. | Refugees—China—Shanghai—History— 20th century. | United States. Central Intelligence Agency—History. | Special forces (Military science)—United States—History. | Kim family. | Korean Americans— Biography.
Classification: LCC D810.S7 K49 2025 | DDC 940.54/8673092 [B]—dc23/ eng/20250214
LC record available at https://lccn.loc.gov/2024042397

Designed and set in Garamond Premier Pro by Katrina Noble.

CONTENTS

ILLUSTRATIONS

PREFACE

THERE ARE MILLIONS of stories of people coming to America and millions more of serving the nation in wartime. Among them, some tell of earning a place among the American people through extraordinary deeds during national emergencies. They begin with Lafayette and von Steuben in the Revolutionary War and continue to the recent wars in Iraq and Afghanistan. During the Second World War, an entire family blazed a unique trail from Asia to America by fighting in defense of the nation from both sides of the Pacific as civilians in Japanese-occupied China and as soldiers in the U.S. Army. Their story, hidden after the war for three quarters of a century until few of the family members remained to remember it, is told here for the first time.

The Kim family (no relation to the author) strove to become Americans at a time when people from their former homeland were unwelcome. Originally from Korea, they lived in the United States for years until forced out by changes in the country's immigration laws. They ended up settling in Shanghai, living with the international city's American community—the closest that they could come to the life they had sought in the United States.

The outbreak of the Second World War in Asia ended the family's quiet life in Shanghai but gave its sons opportunities to join the American struggle for victory. From both sides of the Pacific, in situations so dire that they imposed tests of loyalty that few would have passed, the sons stepped forward to join the fight. Their actions would be unique among those of the millions of Americans who went to war.

One, a U.S. citizen by birth and repatriated to the United States by the fortunes of war, overcame discrimination to become a U.S. Army officer who fought across the Pacific. He had enlisted voluntarily but after the attack on Pearl Harbor found himself assigned to a segregated group of Japanese American draftees, classified as one of them because his parents were from a country Japan had conquered decades earlier. He succeeded in persuading the army that he was not one of them, and he went to war as an officer leading infantrymen sent to fight the Japanese in the Pacific theater. He would end the war on the Asian mainland with the U.S. forces sent to liberate his parents' homeland of Korea.

His brothers, trapped in Shanghai when Japanese forces occupied the international settlements, became an American underground in the city. They resisted the Japanese occupation, working with diplomats from neutral Switzerland and then with U.S. military intelligence. When the Japanese herded white Western civilians into internment camps, the brothers became the lifeline to the outside world for their imprisoned compatriots, using their position in the city outside of Japanese barbed wire to aid those they regarded as their fellow Americans.

In 1944 two brothers escaped Shanghai and trekked hundreds of miles through Japanese-occupied territory to join the U.S. Army in China. The army welcomed them and, at the end of the war in August 1945, made one an officer whom it sent back to Shanghai to lead a mission to liberate the internment camps. This intelligence operation freed the seven thousand American, British, and Allied civilians remaining in the internment camps, a quiet victory for those whom the enemy had conquered and persecuted for four years.

With their undivided loyalty to the United States, their perseverance in the face of seemingly insuperable obstacles, and their contributions to victory, these sons earned the Kim family its place as part of the American people that they had sought for so many years. The grateful commanders of the U.S. Army in China went to Washington to fight for the Kim family members who had served the nation, and Congress passed a special law granting U.S. citizenship to the leader of the mission to Shanghai. Then the brothers themselves fought for years for two further laws admitting the rest of the family into the United States. Two decades after having to leave the country, they had gone to war for it and won their right to return.

The nascent intelligence and military special operations communities soon chose the Kim brothers as some of their earliest members. During and after the Korean War, four of the brothers served with U.S. Army intelligence, the Central Intelligence Agency, and the U.S. Army Special Forces. They each blazed a unique trail defending the nation's interests in far-flung parts of the world—Asia, Europe, and Africa—during the decades of the Cold War.

The history of the Kim family belongs among the heroic stories of coming to America, with lessons for all Americans on how their country has been peopled and defended since the Second World War, yet it has barely survived to be recorded and told. Only two of the brothers who were part of the struggle during the Second World War remained alive in 2018. I met them that year, completely fortuitously through a series of unlikely coincidences that began after I published a book in 2017 about Koreans in the U.S. intelligence service of the Second World War, the Office of Strategic Services. I was fortunate that the Kims accepted me as a friend of their family, entrusted me with their story, and allowed me to attempt to convey it in these pages.

All credit for preserving the memories of this unique American story goes to them. Any inaccuracies that may exist in these pages are the result of limitations in the records available to confirm the details of events more than three quarters of a century after they occurred.

VICTORY IN SHANGHAI

PART 1

Americans in Exile

1

Victory

AS THE SUN set over the city of Shanghai in the evening of August 28, 1945, a few men clad in the khaki uniforms of the U.S. armed forces of the Second World War looked down at its streets and waterfront from a dozen stories above. A new world was coming to life before them.

Across the waters to the east, thousands of American soldiers, sailors, airmen, and marines were completing the first day of airborne and amphibious landings on the home islands of Japan. Four years of merciless warfare were ending with the defeated Japanese nation allowing the victorious U.S. forces to occupy its homeland without firing a shot, ready for the official surrender ceremony that would come in a few days. The Second World War was about to come to a close, bringing an end to the bloodiest conflict in the history of humanity.

In Shanghai, a few intelligence officers were the sole Americans in uniform in a city of millions. This team of only ten men represented every U.S. intelligence organization in China: the Office of Strategic Services (OSS); the intelligence branches of the U.S. Army, Navy, and Marine Corps; and the top secret air rescue service in China, the Air Ground Aid Section (AGAS), commanding the mission.

Just over a week earlier, the team had boldly descended from the sky to confront the undefeated forces of the Imperial Japanese Army occupying the city. They had demanded the release of thousands of civilians from the

Allied nations imprisoned for years in Japanese internment camps, the final remnant of the international community that had once thrived in Shanghai. Their world came to an end on the day Japan attacked Pearl Harbor, and its forces had marched into the International Settlement to claim it for the Empire of Japan. For years these civilians had languished behind barbed wire, waiting for the day of their liberation.

The once-arrogant generals of the Empire of Japan, with their thousands of soldiers, had yielded to the ten Americans who had landed in their midst. Now this small team was responsible for the care of thousands of people of many nations and struggled to obtain food and medicines that had been in short supply in the city for months. Relief would not come until U.S. forces hundreds of miles away arrived by air from deep in China's interior or by sea from the Pacific.

The Japanese had surrendered to the team entire floors of the twenty-two-story Park Hotel—the tallest building in Shanghai or anywhere in Asia—to use as its headquarters. The Imperial Japanese Army still controlled Shanghai, its soldiers standing fast in their bases and patrolling the streets, but it granted the Americans a multistory safe house far above the city. In what little time they had between their tasks that day, the team's members had set up the VIP apartment suites on the fifteenth floor as their office space and occupied the hotel rooms of the thirteenth floor as their living quarters.

On the floor in between was the hotel's ballroom, decorated with ornate stained glass skylights in the ceiling. Once it had been a gathering place for Shanghai's community of British and European expatriates who were the heirs of a century-long foreign colonization of China. Now the Americans had come to usher the last living remnants of colonialism out of Shanghai and return the city to an independent and free China.

The American relief mission to Shanghai had accomplished a historic task, and its members had every reason to believe that their actions would live forever in the annals of U.S. intelligence and special operations.

Most of them wore the bars or oak leaf rank badges of U.S. military officers on their collars. With the single silver bar of a first lieutenant on the collar of his army uniform, one man stood out from the others for an obvious reason: he was the only Asian among them.

His name was Peter Kim, and he was a mystery to the other members of the team. Most of them had met a couple of weeks earlier when their hastily assembled task force had formed, and none of them really knew this man, who had been the last addition to their group in the final days before their flight to Shanghai. They only knew that he had spent most of his life in Shanghai and possessed unique knowledge of the city and its internment camps that none of them or anyone else in all the U.S. military and intelligence organizations in China had. He was their guide to Shanghai and the officer supervising their mission's ultimate task—the care of the thousands of liberated Allied civilians in the internment camps—under orders issued directly from the commanding general of the U.S. forces in China.

None of the team knew that Kim was not really a lieutenant. He was not even a U.S. citizen, yet, and therefore not lawfully eligible to be an officer at all. They did not know that senior commanders of the U.S. Army in China had decided, with the lives of thousands of American and Allied nation civilians at stake, that sidestepping their nation's laws and military regulations was the correct course of action. The risk of being revealed and disgraced hung over Peter Kim and these officers throughout the chain of command, all the way up to Lt. Gen. Albert Wedemeyer, the commanding general.

Whether success or embarrassment would follow remained to be learned. So would the fate of Peter Kim's family members. Some of them had been living in Shanghai when he left them more than a year earlier, not knowing whether he was abandoning them to a grim future at the hands of the Japanese authorities who had persecuted them for many years. Some of the Kims were soldiers in the U.S. Army, scattered across China and the Pacific. When, or even whether, they would see each other again—alive or dead—was unknown.

No one could have imagined then that eventually Peter Kim's name would be acclaimed in the halls of the U.S. Congress and that his actions in Shanghai in August 1945 would help win his entire family's admission to the United States, prevailing against racist immigration laws that had denied them entry for a quarter of a century. Equally unimaginable then was that the Kims would become a founding family of modern U.S. intelligence and special operations, being involved in all of America's armed conflicts of the Cold

War and rising to leadership positions in the Central Intelligence Agency (CIA) and the U.S. Army Special Forces.

Peter Kim, the man whom America needed at this pivotal point in history, helped to shatter the barriers created by prejudice and to enrich the nation with his long-excluded family, who in their hearts had always been Americans. After toiling on a decades-long and difficult path, this man was ready for the moment.

2

From Korea to America

IN THE BEGINNING, a family in Korea received word of a great nation on the far side of the world.

The father, Kim Chang Sei, and the mother, Lee Chung Sil, were Christians living in the Pyongyang area in the early years of the twentieth century. The city now known as the capital of North Korea was then the center of thriving communities of Korean Christians, started by American missionaries who had first arrived in 1895. American clergymen had made thousands of converts and founded churches all over the city and the region around it, creating one of the leading Christian communities on the mainland of Asia. By 1910 Pyongyang was home to more than sixty thousand Christians and had become known as the "Jerusalem of the East," renowned for the zeal of its converts and their eagerness to spread their new religion.[1]

Along with their religion, American missionaries brought science and education, which the people of Korea had lacked up to then. In a country regularly ravaged by epidemics of cholera and other infectious diseases, and without a single modern hospital, American doctors sponsored by the churches contained the epidemics and built Korea's first hospitals. Educational missionaries also began the first schools open to the entire people. Previously only a few privileged families had access to education for their children, through tutors teaching the Chinese classics. Americans founded the first modern schools in Korea, including Korea's first four-year college, Union Christian College, founded in Pyongyang in 1905.

Americans led the growth of Christian communities in Korea as the Empire of Japan conquered and colonized the country. Japan had invaded Korea and defeated Chinese forces to establish Japanese hegemony in 1894–95; then it eliminated Korea's ruling monarchy, assassinating its queen and reducing its king to a puppet. A decade later, Japan fought and defeated Russia in a war for control of Korea, establishing uncontested domination of the country. On August 22, 1910, Japan formally annexed Korea, ending its existence as an independent nation. For the first time in their more than two-thousand-year-long history, the Koreans were a conquered people, subjects of a foreign empire intent on erasing their identity from the world.

Kim Chang Sei and Lee Chung Sil, who married a month later on September 25, 1910, saw their destiny elsewhere. Raised by families of Christian converts and educated in American missionary schools, they had seen a glimpse of the American people and their ideals, enough to know that the United States of America was where they wanted to be. The nation across the Pacific whose people had brought enlightenment to theirs was where the Kims felt they belonged.

International politics blocked their way, however. The United States was then in a phase of its history when its western states opposed immigration from Asia, and it had recently made a deal with Japan, called the Gentleman's Agreement of 1907, to stop emigrants from its empire. In this informal pact, never formalized in a treaty or a law enacted by the U.S. Congress, Japan agreed to restrict emigration to the United States by not issuing passports to its subjects who wanted to move there, including the Koreans. Japanese authorities granted few exceptions, and the Kim family would have to find one.

The medical profession offered the Kims a path to America, and Kim Chang Sei was fortunate to find a mentor to guide him through it. Educated professionals were among the few people permitted to emigrate from Japan's territories to the United States, and the colleges and medical schools that Americans had founded in Korea offered Kim Chang Sei a chance to join the Western profession of medicine. Dr. Riley Russell, a missionary doctor who had come to Korea in 1908, arranged for him to attend the medical school of Severance Hospital in Seoul.[2]

Founded in 1885 by the American medical missionary Horace Allen, Severance Hospital was the first modern Western hospital in Korea. Its medical school, started in 1886, was likewise the first in Korea. Kim Chang Sei enrolled in the medical school in 1911, a few years before it merged with Seoul's first institution of higher education, Chosun Christian College, which American Presbyterian missionary Horace Grant Underwood founded in 1915. Today the college is known as Yonsei University, one of South Korea's leading private institutions.

Lee Chung Sil accompanied her husband to Seoul and enrolled in Ewha College. A school for women founded by American Presbyterians in 1886, Ewha became the first and foremost women's college in Korea and is well known today as one of South Korea's most prestigious universities, educating many of Korea's leaders in business, law, science, and other fields. Lee Chung Sil did not graduate because she soon left school and went home to Pyongyang to have the Kims' first child.

Lee Chung Sil gave birth to their first-born son in Pyongyang on June 10, 1912. The attending physician was Dr. Russell, Kim Chang Sei's mentor.[3] The Kims' dreams were evident in the name they chose for the child—Peter, an American Christian name for a child who was destined to be an American. It was the name of the first among the twelve apostles, the rock upon whom the church was built. Their first-born son would establish the foundation of their future in America.

Kim Chang Sei received his medical degree in 1916 with the first graduating class of Chosun Christian College's medical school. In the commencement ceremony, he was the class valedictorian, and he made the occasion a first in another way. With numerous American dignitaries attending the ceremony, he delivered his valedictory speech entirely in English, speaking without any notes. This display of his language skills made a statement to the American visitors about the young Koreans whose graduation they were witnessing, and it thrilled the Korean audience and made a lasting impression on the school. The moment went down in the annals of the college and Yonsei University and is remembered in its history more than a century later.[4]

With his medical training complete, Kim Chang Sei returned to Pyongyang and practiced medicine at a hospital there. He and his wife also brought a second child into the world, another boy, in March 1917. They named him David, another name fit for an American.

Their quest to find a path to America continued, and again Dr. Russell paved the way for them. The Seventh-day Adventist medical missionary arranged for his protégé to do an internship at a newly founded hospital in Shanghai—the Shanghai Adventist Sanitarium and Hospital.[5] There Kim Chang Sei could start to practice medicine and look for opportunities to move his medical practice and family to the United States.

The family left Korea for Shanghai later that year, traveling by ship with documents falsely identifying them as Chinese. Concerned that Japanese authorities would not allow them to leave Korea for Shanghai, where many Korean independence activists were living in exile, Kim Chang Sei obtained from a Chinese friend in Seoul a set of official documents from China declaring the family to be Chinese and the friend's relatives. Five-year-old Peter, too young to understand the cover story, had to spend the voyage locked in the closet of their cabin to avoid the risk that anyone would overhear him speaking Korean. After these precautions, the family arrived safely in Shanghai to begin their new lives free of the Empire of Japan.[6]

In the international city of Shanghai, Kim Chang Sei and Lee Chung Sil settled down temporarily and planned to find a way to America. He began his internship at Shanghai Adventist Sanitarium and Hospital, specializing in tuberculosis and infectious diseases, while looking for opportunities at medical schools and hospitals in the United States. They used their residence in Shanghai to change their citizenship, obtaining Chinese citizenship papers that they hoped would ease their entry into the United States. The family also grew further when in 1919 they had a third son, whom they named William.

The opportunity that they sought finally came in 1920. The General Conference of Seventh-day Adventists decided to sponsor Kim Chang Sei's move to the United States for additional medical training, supported by the Seventh-day Adventist mission in Shanghai. Higher education was an exception to U.S. immigration restrictions, so he received a student visa, and the rest of the family received visas to accompany him. In November 1920 they boarded a passenger liner in Shanghai and sailed across the Pacific to San Francisco, with Lee Chung Sil pregnant with the family's fourth child.[7]

From there the family took a train to Los Angeles to join Lee Chung Sil's sister Helen, who was married to the historic figure Ahn Chang Ho, the Korean independence activist and leader of the city's Korean American immigrant community. Ahn would go down in history as one of the foremost heroes of the Korean independence movement and as a Korean pioneer in the United States. Memorials bear his name in numerous places in Seoul and Los Angeles, as does Atlanta's International Civil Rights Walk of Fame at the Martin Luther King Jr. National Historic Site, which recognizes Ahn as a leading contributor to the worldwide struggle for civil rights.[8]

Helen Ahn's house at 106 North Figueroa Street became the Kim family's temporary home until they found their own place in Los Angeles. In this house, on March 15, 1921, was born the Kim family's fourth son and first American, a U.S. citizen by birth. His mother and father named him James.

James and his brothers grew up as Americans in their new home in Los Angeles. English was the only language that they learned and spoke both in and outside their home. Peter, eight years old when he arrived, went to a regular public school, and his younger brothers would follow as they reached the age for elementary school. The sons of Kim Chang Sei and Lee Chung Sil were on their way to becoming Americans only, as their father and mother wanted.

While his wife and children lived in Los Angeles, Kim Chang Sei went to medical school apart from them. He started at the Loma Linda School of Medicine, the medical school of the Seventh-day Adventists in Loma Linda, California, sixty miles east of Los Angeles. In 1922 he enrolled at Jefferson Medical College in Philadelphia. To attend this distinguished medical school and teaching hospital, founded in 1824 and now called the Sidney Kimmel Medical College at Thomas Jefferson University, he had to live all the way across the country. So began a long period of separation from his wife and children, whom he rejoined only in periodic visits, each time departing to resume his career elsewhere.[9]

He was away when life-changing events happened to his family in Los Angeles. With his father on the opposite side of the country, William died in 1923 at the age of four, run over by a car on an LA street. Soon afterward arrived another Kim child, conceived during a previous visit. Born in April 1923, this child was a daughter, who received the name Betty Marie. Like her brother James, Betty was a U.S. citizen from birth.[10]

The family's sacrifices seemed not to be in vain as Kim Chang Sei rose in the medical profession. In America, a new world opened to him as he thrived in the country that he had admired from afar since his childhood. In the medical schools of the United States, he became a leading expert in his field and met influential people who were shaping the development of his profession worldwide.

Soon after he arrived at Jefferson Medical College, he met Dr. Victor Heiser, a Jefferson graduate who had become a renowned expert in combating infectious diseases and a leader in the emerging field of public health. Dr. Heiser had built the public health system of the U.S. colonial government in the Philippines; then he worked for the Rockefeller Foundation, which sought to use the endowment from its founder's industrial fortune to eradicate disease worldwide, much as the Gates Foundation would a century later. His example and advice helped direct the path of the young doctor from Korea.[11]

Influenced by Dr. Heiser, Kim Chang Sei enrolled in the Johns Hopkins University School of Hygiene and Public Health, the world's first school of public health, founded only seven years earlier in 1916. He moved to Baltimore to begin his graduate studies there in 1923. At Johns Hopkins he became a star pupil of Dr. William H. Welch, the founder of the School of Hygiene and Public Health and one of the founders of the Johns Hopkins School of Medicine in 1884. Welch also served as president of the National Academy of Sciences, the American Medical Association, and numerous other medical and scientific organizations. In 1925 Kim Chang Sei was awarded his second doctorate, becoming a doctor of public health.

An even wider world opened up to Kim Chang Sei after his graduation. The new doctor of public health embarked almost immediately on a tour of Europe, North Africa, and South America. For several weeks, he traveled by steamship to Sweden, Denmark, Italy, Greece, Egypt, Brazil, and numerous other countries to study public health conditions. During his travels in a variety of nations across the world, he made numerous new connections and friends, even befriending Crown Prince Gustaf Adolf of Sweden, who later became King Gustaf VI Adolf. Kim Chang Sei toured Stockholm with the crown prince, and afterward they traveled to Copenhagen together.[12]

Kim Chang Sei's rising American life immediately came to a tragic end, however, when the country's immigration laws closed the door for him and his family. In 1924 Congress passed a new immigration act that drastically reduced the number of immigrants allowed into the country and completely banned all immigration from Asia. The exclusion of Asians would last for more than forty years, easing only slightly in 1952, and did not end until 1965, when a new immigration law finally ended all racial preferences. When the 1924 Immigration Act went into effect, no path to staying in the United States existed any more, not even for the parents of U.S. citizens. The family had no choice but to leave the country after the expiration of Kim Chang Sei's student visa and start their lives over again somewhere else.

They decided to return to Korea for the first time in almost a decade. Chosun Christian College's medical school had offered Kim Chang Sei an opportunity to become a faculty member heading a new department of public health, and he had accepted it before departing for his international tour. Immediately after returning to the States, he traveled across the country to Los Angeles to reunite with his family and prepare for their return to Asia.[13]

The family departed the United States in August 1926, sailing from Los Angeles to Hawaii, to Japan, and on to Korea. They crossed the Pacific in steerage, unable to afford better accommodations. Only a few weeks earlier, Kim Chang Sei had socialized with European royalty, but now he, his wife, and their four children traveled in a passenger liner's oily, noisy lower deck with only a straw mat to sleep on.[14]

Back in Seoul, Kim Chang Sei began a new life as a Korean subject in a Japanese-dominated world. His doctorate from the prestigious Johns Hopkins University made him the leading expert in his field in the country. At the medical school of Chosun Christian College, he founded Korea's first public health program, the Department of Hygiene, now known as the Department of Preventive Medicine at the Yonsei University College of Medicine. His status was precarious as one of the few Koreans in positions of importance in a Japanese-ruled country, however, and he never stopped looking beyond Korea. Within two weeks of his arrival, he went to Beijing to participate in a September public health conference sponsored by the Rockefeller Foundation, after which he resumed his correspondence with Dr. Heiser.[15]

A reminder of his past life soon came to him when Gustav Adolf visited Seoul in October 1926. The crown prince came to Korea with his wife Princess Louise, born Louise Mountbatten, on a royal visit during which he participated in archaeological excavations that discovered one of Korea's ancient royal crowns, now a Korean national treasure.[16] When they arrived at the Seoul train station to an official reception, Gustav Adolf recognized Kim Chang Sei in the crowd and greeted him in front of the assembled Japanese officials.[17] The happy moment ended with the departure of the royal visitors, however, and his life as a subject of Japan resumed immediately afterward.

There was cause for celebration when in June 1927 the family brought another child into the world. The child was a son, their fifth. They named him Richard.

The world that Kim Chang Sei had briefly glimpsed during his years in America pulled at him too strongly, and he soon left Korea and his respected medical school position for an opportunity to go there again. Shanghai was once more the way station on his journey. In early 1928 he moved there to accept a position as the field director of the Council on Health Education, an American organization spreading knowledge of modern medicine in China. His wife and children followed in August. They moved into a house in Shanghai's French Concession, a district located in a long strip of land south of the International Settlement.

From his professional base in Shanghai, Kim Chang Sei traveled all over China, spreading his expertise. He lectured on public health at Peking Union Medical College, a medical school in Beijing founded by Christian missionary organizations and supported by the Rockefeller Foundation, and at the medical school of Lingnan University in Canton (now Guangzhou). He went to Hangzhou to build a tuberculosis sanitarium and then spent several months in the Philippines, a U.S. territory, to found a tuberculosis sanitarium in Baguio, the summer capital of the U.S. governor-general.

Another Kim child arrived in Shanghai in January 1930, a son, whom Kim Chang Sei and Lee Chung Sil named Arthur. Their family now numbered eight, with six surviving children: Peter, David, James, Betty, Richard, and Arthur.

An opportunity for Kim Chang Sei to go to the United States emerged late in 1929. He received an invitation from Dr. Heiser, his mentor in the public health field, to participate in a medical conference in New York. With his wife in the final weeks of pregnancy with Arthur and due to deliver after his departure date, he was uncertain whether he should go, but his wife and his eldest son, Peter, talked him into it. Peter, now seventeen years old, insisted that he would drop out of school and get a job to help support the family during his father's absence. So on January 3, 1930, Kim Chang Sei boarded the passenger liner *President Madison* for the first leg of his journey to New York. He landed at San Francisco on January 22, 1930, four days after Arthur's birth.[18]

Kim Chang Sei's visit to New York for a conference led to an extended stay in the United States when he came to the attention of the National Tuberculosis Association, an organization founded in 1904 to fight the spread of tuberculosis and today is known as the National Lung Association. The association's New York office sponsored him to remain in the United States to conduct a nationwide study of American tuberculosis clinics. He was supposed to take the findings of his study and return to Shanghai to resume his work combating tuberculosis in China, but he prolonged his research to the end of 1930 and on into 1931. His temporary presence eventually became a period of residence lasting for years.

He spent this second stint in the United States traveling from coast to coast, visiting the nation's leading medical facilities and seeing the vast expanse of the country. Late in 1930 he left New York and crossed the country to examine the renowned Pottenger Sanatorium in Monrovia, California. Its founder, Dr. Francis Marion Pottenger, allowed him to use the sanatorium as his temporary residence on the West Coast and became another of his sponsors, providing an affidavit supporting his application for a one-year extension of his visa in December 1930.[19] His visa extension granted, in 1931 Kim Chang Sei returned to Baltimore to continue his work on the East Coast and again applied for a visa extension in December 1931.[20] Granted another visa extension, he again crossed the country in 1932, this time going to San Francisco.[21]

Bringing the family to the United States, always his and his wife's desire, became urgently necessary in 1932. The Imperial Japanese Army had invaded and occupied Manchuria in September 1931, starting a decade of Japanese aggression in China that would ultimately lead to war with the United States in 1941. In January 1932 Japanese troops, warships, and aircraft attacked Nationalist Chinese forces in Shanghai, starting a battle for the city that lasted two months. Thousands of civilians died and many more became homeless as the fighting raged across Shanghai.

The conflict hit the family personally after April 29, when Korean nationalists detonated a bomb at a Japanese victory ceremony in Shanghai on Emperor Hirohito's birthday, killing or wounding many of Japan's senior military commanders and diplomats.[22] A Japanese manhunt for Korean independence activists in Shanghai ensued. Its victims included Ahn Chang Ho, who was arrested in Shanghai and sent back to Korea to spend the rest of his life in prison, where he would die six years later. As relatives of Ahn Chang Ho, Lee Chung Sil and her children were prime targets for the Japanese dragnet.

The family had to hide from the Japanese police until the crisis ended, and they were fortunate to get shelter in the home of American friends, the McNairs. The two families had met on the passenger liner that had brought them all across the Pacific in 1926, and when they met again in Shanghai in 1928, Lee Chung Sil and Mrs. McNair became close friends, as did Peter Kim and Roy McNair Jr. As Americans, the McNairs could defy the Japanese police as they searched the French Concession and the International Settlement for Koreans, so the family protected Lee Chung Sil and her children until they could safely return to their own house.[23]

With the lives of his wife and children now at stake, Kim Chang Sei invoked all of the professional connections that he could in support of their cause. Letters of recommendation from Dr. Heiser at the Rockefeller Foundation, Dean Frost of the Johns Hopkins School of Hygiene and Public Health, and the director of the National Tuberculosis Association went to Shanghai in support of an application for a temporary visitor visa that Lee Chung Sil submitted to the U.S. Consul in June 1932.[24] None of this support made a difference. The family was refused visas and had to remain in Shanghai and at risk of arrest by the Japanese police.[25]

As well as his own family, Kim Chang Sei tried to help Ahn Chang Ho. In early May 1932, he went to Washington DC to plead with members of Congress to pressure Japan for Ahn's release from captivity. He went on behalf of the Korean National Association, a U.S.-based organization that he had been associated with since the 1920s and that Ahn had founded to unite Koreans worldwide in opposition to Japanese colonial rule. Kim Chang Sei met members of Congress including Senator William Borah of Idaho, chairman of the Senate Foreign Relations Committee, and Representative John Linthicum of Maryland, chairman of the House Foreign Relations Committee. His efforts were fruitless. Ahn's imprisonment continued with no official U.S. statement against it.[26]

Powerless to help his family or Ahn Chang Ho, Kim Chang Sei continued to live alone in the United States. His work continued for another year, taking him from California to New York. Mayor of New York Jimmy Walker commissioned him to establish a medical facility in downtown Manhattan's Chinatown. On the side, he also served as the health commissioner for the Boy Scouts in Manhattan.[27]

In February 1934 everything suddenly seemed to change when a telegram arrived at the family's house in Shanghai from their father in New York. It announced that he had finally worked out a way for them to enter the United States to join him, and the family should prepare to travel to America in March on the passenger liner *President Lincoln*. After four years apart and six years in Shanghai, a life-changing reunion in their adopted homeland finally appeared within reach.[28]

For Peter there was further life-changing news about his future. His father informed him that he would be enrolled in the Horace Mann School, an exclusive college preparatory school in New York that sends many of its graduates to prestigious Ivy League colleges. After years of working to support his mother and siblings in Shanghai, he could look ahead to a clear path to higher education and success in America.[29]

The Kims joyfully prepared for their departure from Shanghai and return to the United States. Lee Chung Sil renewed her Chinese passport, which included her minor children, and James and Betty obtained new U.S. passports. Peter looked into booking passage on a different ship, the *President Wilson*, that would take them directly from Shanghai to New York. He was in the process of working out the details with his father when stunning news arrived from New York.

Kim Chang Sei had committed suicide. He had done so on March 15, 1934, the birthday of his American-born son, James.[30]

The family would never learn why their father had taken his own life. Far away in Shanghai, all they knew for certain was that he had committed suicide by inhaling oven gas and that no one had expected it. Even a brother-in-law who also lived in New York, a block away from Columbia University in the Upper West Side of Manhattan, had been taken by surprise. Perhaps Kim Chang Sei's arrangement to bring the family to America had fallen through, plunging him into despair. Perhaps the arrangement had been no more than a fantasy, the last desperate thoughts of a man overwhelmed by feelings that he had failed his distant family, whom he had not seen for years.[31] Newspaper stories about his death reported threats against him and attempts at extortion, indicating that something had gone wrong with his life in New York. His wife and children would never know for certain.[32]

Kim Chang Sei's passing at the age of only forty-one ended a remarkable life that had begun in the rural outskirts of Pyongyang, ascended to prominence in the profession of medicine, and for a few years lived the dream of going to the United States to become an American. He had the misfortune of living in an era too early for his dream to be attainable, making his path a difficult and lonely one. When he gave up and took his own life, he left his wife alone to raise their six children in Shanghai. They were Americans in spirit but would have to grow up in the American community of Shanghai, far from the country that they considered to be theirs.

3

Exile in Shanghai

IN SHANGHAI, LEE Chung Sil and her six children had to live between two separate worlds. By blood they were part of the city's Korean community and one of its most respected families, being related closely to Ahn Chang Ho, the philosophical leader of Korea's independence movement whom the Japanese had taken from Shanghai and imprisoned in Korea in 1932. In spirit, though, Lee Chung Sil and her children were Americans in exile. Their identities and the lives that they lived were with the city's American community.

Lee Chung Sil remained true to the course that she and her late husband had chosen a quarter century earlier in Korea. She continued to raise their children as English speakers and to educate them in American schools with friends who were Americans. Their Korean heritage was something from their past, even though Korean remained her first language, and she never mastered English as her husband had. Peter, David, James, Betty, Richard, and Arthur grew up as Americans of the expatriate community in Shanghai.[1]

She struggled to raise them, living in poverty on the fringe of Shanghai's foreign communities. In the French Concession, a popular residential area for people of many nationalities, the family lived for years in a rented row house at 260 Route Vallon (now Nanchang Street), named after a French aviator who had died in a crash during an exhibition flight over the Shanghai Racecourse in 1916. Many of their neighbors were White Russians who had arrived in Shanghai as refugees after the Russian Revolution. In the mid-1930s, unable to afford the rent, the Kim family moved to a smaller house at 198 Route Père Robert (now Ruijin Road).

Peter, twenty-one years of age when his father took his own life, assumed the role of leader of the family. He had been prepared for it by the family's years of wandering and living for long periods, beginning when he was five years old, apart from their father, and by the four years that he had been working to support the family. He had started working in 1929 as a rental property manager at a real estate company. When his father's suicide made him the family's sole breadwinner, he was working as a purchasing agent at an electrical equipment manufacturing business called the Asia Electric Company. In 1935 he went to work for Getz Brothers & Company, a San Francisco–based import-export company. He managed the company's sales of American-made building materials in Shanghai for the rest of the decade.[2]

Beyond working, he also set an example for his younger siblings as an American. Korean had been his first language in his early childhood in Korea, but after the family's arrival in the United States in 1920, he had mastered the English language and identified entirely as an American. In Shanghai, he went to American schools, and his closest friends were Americans. After he quit school to work and support the family, he continued to educate himself in his spare time, including by joining the amateur theatrical group of the Lyceum Theater.[3] There he acted on stage in English-language productions, further developing the persona that had been evolving since his American journey had begun.

Peter's hiring by Getz Brothers in 1935 showed how far he had come. The job was supposed to go to an American hired stateside, who of course would have been white, as was practically everyone in the Western business communities of Shanghai. Getz's manager in Shanghai, Anker Henningsen, recognized Peter as an American and hired him, overcoming the resistance of his superiors. Peter and Henningsen were friends from then onward.[4]

Joining an American military organization defending the American community of Shanghai further showed who Peter had become. In 1932, at the age of nineteen, he had enlisted in the American company of the Shanghai Volunteer Corps, the multinational military organization that protected the Shanghai International Settlement. The Shanghai Volunteer Corps consisted of units recruited from the city's various communities—American, British, Chinese, Eurasian, Filipino, Jewish, Portuguese, Scottish, White Russian—under the command of the settlement's governing body, the Shanghai Municipal Council. They protected the International Settlement from incursions by Japanese forces during the assault on Shanghai in 1932 and continued to stand guard on the settlement's boundaries for the rest of the decade.[5]

David, five years younger and far more reserved than Peter, followed in his brother's footsteps as he grew to adulthood. Peter and their mother were concerned about David's education and that of his younger siblings, so for a time a substantial part of the family's income went into sending the children to the Jewell School, which the famous author Pearl S. Buck had attended a quarter of a century earlier. When they could not pay the tuition any longer, the children went to another American school closer to home.[6] After finishing school, David went to work for an American engineering firm whose owner was the father-in-law of Anker Henningsen, Peter's boss.[7] David also joined Peter by enlisting in the American company of the Shanghai Volunteer Corps.[8]

The younger siblings, who ranged in age from four to fourteen years old when their father died, were able to live more carefree lives as children. Their education was the family's highest priority, so their mother and older brothers made sacrifices to send them to private schools for English-speaking children that were run by American or Australian missionaries.[9] Intended for wealthy foreigners, these schools charged tuition that the family could barely afford. In these schools, the children learned the language and customs of the faraway country that the family considered to be theirs. James was also interested in French and made an extra effort to learn the language both in school and from the people around them in the French Concession.[10]

In their free time, they found entertainment in the neighborhood and in the city. They read American comic books and other English-language books, and played badminton, Ping-Pong, and other games with neighborhood friends, most of them Chinese, some of them White Russians. On Sundays, the band of the U.S. 4th Marine Regiment stationed in Shanghai played concerts at the nearby Cathay Theater. Movies at the grand theaters of the International Settlement were major occasions, and the children dressed up to attend them.

The family would occasionally go out to eat at Jimmy's Kitchen, run by American restauranteur Jimmy James; it served hamburgers, french fries, apple pie, and other American classics to Shanghai residents, U.S. Marines, and visiting sailors wanting a taste of home. For sweet treats, the family liked to go to the Chocolate Shop on Bubbling Well Road (later renamed West Nanjing Road), a spot frequented by Americans for its chocolates, ice cream, and ice cream sodas. On special occasions, they went to Sun Ya, a Cantonese restaurant on 719 Nanjing Road East that was popular with the Chinese and Westerners alike and continues to operate as Xinya in the same location today.

The life that Lee Chung Sil and her children had built for themselves as Americans in Shanghai began to fall apart in the fall of 1937. On July 7 Imperial Japanese Army forces in Manchuria invaded northern China and, by the end of the month, had occupied Beijing. The Empire of Japan's attempt to conquer China had begun, starting the Second World War in Asia, more than two years before Nazi Germany plunged Europe into war. On August 13 the war came to Shanghai. Japanese and Chinese forces began a battle for Shanghai that raged for three months and ended in the Japanese occupation of the city outside of the International Settlement and the French Concession. The Kim family members were a few of the millions of people in Shanghai whose lives would never be the same.

The foreign communities of Shanghai faced the most tumultuous and dangerous time in their century-long history. As Japanese and Chinese forces fought for control of the city, a motley assortment of Western military organizations—U.S. Marines of the 4th Marine Regiment, British Army infantry, French Foreign Legionnaires, colonial troops from Indochina, and the multinational units of the Shanghai Volunteer Corps—stood guard around the foreign concessions to keep out the combatants. Among the Americans of the Shanghai Volunteer Corps who were manning the checkpoints and barricades were Peter, a sergeant, and David, a corporal.[11]

Chinese civilians streamed in by the thousands, seeking refuge from the fighting. They came even after a deadly bombing on the second day of the battle, August 14, when Chinese aircraft attacking the Japanese cruiser

Idzumo on the waterfront dropped bombs that descended errantly into the International Settlement. Several bombs hit streets crowded with Chinese and Western civilians, and their blasts killed or wounded more than 3,500 people. The International Settlement's deadly start to the war, which became known as Black Saturday, did not deter hundreds of thousands of Chinese civilians from converging there in search of safety.

Western civilians began to evacuate Shanghai as the fighting thundered around the International Settlement. The U.S. government urged all Americans in China to leave the country immediately, declaring that anyone who stayed did so at their own risk, and sent ships to evacuate U.S. citizens from Shanghai and repatriate them. Within a month, half of the Americans living in Shanghai had boarded the evacuation ships and left. They were joined by American civilians who had fled the fighting in Beijing and northern China and had made their way to Shanghai.

The Kim family faced a terrible dilemma as they contemplated their future in the beleaguered city. Leaving Shanghai on the U.S. evacuation ships was impossible for five of them, since they were officially citizens of China; only James and Betty were Americans from their births in Los Angeles. Peter and his mother made the difficult decision to send sixteen-year-old James and fourteen-year-old Betty to the United States in the belief that they would be safe there, far from the war in China. The rest of the family would have to stay in Shanghai, hoping that the war would not destroy their lives and that one day the family could be reunited.

Peter, wearing his Shanghai Volunteer Corps uniform, took James and Betty to the port town of Wusong, a dozen miles north of their home in the protected foreign communities. There was anchored the passenger liner *President Hoover*, waiting to take on evacuating Americans. The ship had been damaged by a bomb that a Chinese plane had dropped on it accidentally, killing one member of the crew and wounding several sailors and passengers. James and Betty boarded a small boat that took them to the *President Hoover*, separating them from their mother and brothers for the first time in their lives. They were headed to Los Angeles to rejoin their aunt, the wife of the imprisoned Ahn Chang Ho, who would take them in and care for them as long as necessary.

The rest of the family remained where they were as the Japanese forces completed their conquest of Shanghai in October and began their advance from Shanghai to Nanjing that culminated in the fall of the Nationalist Chinese capital in December. With the Japanese invasion driving through the heart of China along the Yangtze River, Shanghai's International Settlement and French Concession became an island isolated in Japanese-occupied territory, with a diminished community of British, American, and other foreign nationals clinging to their lives and businesses there. The fate of Lee Chung Sil and her four sons became inextricably tied to the remaining American community in the final years of the 1930s, as Japan's invasion of China continued and its hostility toward China's ally, the United States, escalated.

Life resumed a degree of normalcy, however, in those years. Peter and David went back to work, and Richard and Arthur went back to school, with Richard attending the exclusive Shanghai American School as a high school freshman starting in 1941. Betty even returned in 1939. Living during her teenage years with relatives whom she barely knew had become intolerable, so she returned to her own family in Shanghai. She helped take care of their mother, whose difficult life had rapidly aged her by her late forties. Eventually four years without hostilities had passed, with Peter and David becoming young adults in their twenties, and Betty, Richard, and Arthur still in their childhoods.

During this time, Peter began a long-term relationship with a woman who, like him, lived between the American and Asian worlds of Shanghai. Ruth Moy, a Chinese American, was about fifteen years older than Peter and already married. She and her husband, Ernest Moy, were both born U.S. citizens and had come to Shanghai to remake themselves in the freewheeling international city. Ernest had started a business, which failed, before becoming an official in the Chinese Maritime Customs Service. Their marriage deteriorated in Shanghai and came apart by the end of the 1930s. Peter and Ruth became a couple after knowing each other for almost a decade and during the decline of her marriage to Ernest. Peter's mother naturally disapproved of his relationship with a married woman much older than he was.

On December 7, 1941, everything changed. On the day that the Imperial Japanese Navy attacked the U.S. Pacific Fleet in Pearl Harbor, starting Japan's war against the United States and the Allied powers, the Imperial Japanese Army marched into Shanghai's International Settlement to seize the commercial center of the new empire that Japan was conquering in Asia. The era of Western domination of Shanghai ended, and the city's Americans, British, and other foreigners were now conquered people. No prospect of liberation existed as Japan's armed forces advanced through Southeast Asia and across the Pacific, seemingly unstoppable.

Defeat and occupation would test the loyalty and resolve of every foreigner in Shanghai, and the ordeal would be especially severe for the sons of Kim Chang Sei and Lee Chung Sil. Americans by upbringing and in identity, they were Asian subjects to the Japanese. The United States did not recognize them as Americans, and whether the war ended in victory or defeat, the Kims could expect nothing from the distant country they considered to be theirs. The Japanese, their lifelong enemies, were now the enemy of the United States as well, but there was no apparent way to fight back while isolated deep within what was now the Empire of Japan. The Kims would have to find a way in the years of war to come.

1. Wedding photo of Kim Chang Sei and Lee Chung Sil. Kim family collection.

2. Dr. Kim Chang Sei. Kim family collection.

3. Lee Chung Sil with her children Arthur, Betty, Richard, David, and Peter, circa 1940. Kim family collection.

4. Lt. James Kim and a fellow officer of the 40th Infantry Division in Hawaii. Courtesy of Richard Kim.

5. Pvt. Peter Kim with an M I carbine during an overland journey by jeep from Chongqing to Kunming, transferring him between JICA offices, December 1944. Courtesy of the George C. Marshall Foundation, Lexington, Virginia.

6. PFC Peter Kim (*middle row, right*) and Pvt. Richard Kim (*middle row, second from the left*) with U.S. Army SOS staff, including Col. Burton Vaughn (*back row, third from the left*) and 2nd Lt. Robert Peaslee (*middle row, third from the right*), in Kunming, January 1945. Courtesy of the George C. Marshall Foundation, Lexington, Virginia.

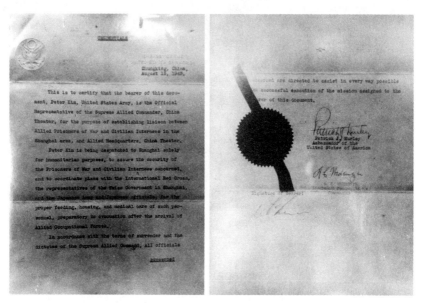

7. The diplomatic credentials issued to Peter Kim, signed by Ambassador Patrick Hurley and Lt. Gen. Albert Wedemeyer. Courtesy of the George C. Marshall Foundation, Lexington, Virginia.

8. Peter Kim with Chinese civilian adviser John Lee during preparations for the final flight to Shanghai at the Liuchow (Liuzhou) air base. Courtesy of the George C. Marshall Foundation, Lexington, Virginia.

9. Peter Kim with one of Operation Sparrow's C-46 transport aircraft at the Dazhang (Dachang) airfield, August 19, 1945. Kim family collection.

10. Peter Kim and officers and aircrewmen of Operation Sparrow with an Imperial Japanese Army officer at the Dazhang airfield, August 19, 1945. Kim family collection.

11. The Operation Sparrow team with Lawrence (*far right, looking away from camera*); his wife, Muriel; and Horace Kadoorie (*sitting*) in front of the Marble Hall. Maj. Preston Schoyer and Peter Kim stand side by side between the leftmost columns. Courtesy of the George C. Marshall Foundation, Lexington, Virginia.

12. Preston Schoyer addressing liberated internees, with Peter Kim standing behind him with his head lowered. Courtesy of Lisa Schoyer.

13. Peter Kim and restauranteur Jimmy James reunited in the liberated Chapei internment camp. Courtesy of Lisa Schoyer.

14. Japanese soldiers doing calisthenics on the roof of the Foreign YMCA building, viewed from Operation Sparrow's headquarters on the thirteenth and fifteenth floors of the Park Hotel. Kim family collection.

15. Peter, Betty, and James (*front row, left to right*) and David, Richard, and Arthur (*back row, left to right*) reunited in Shanghai after the war, October 1945. Kim family collection.

16. Lee Chung Sil (*center*) reunited with her children David, Betty, Arthur, Richard, Peter, and James in Shanghai, October 1945. Kim family collection.

PART 2

1941–45

4

James Kim, American Soldier

WAR WITH JAPAN came as no surprise to James Kim. As a teenager he had witnessed Japan's invasion of China and found himself sent back to the United States to keep him safe. He had been forced to grow up separated from his family as the war continued for four years and gradually drew the United States into the conflict. On December 7, 1941, a few months shy of his twenty-first birthday, he was ready to go to war against Japan.

The four years since James had left Shanghai had been filled with difficulties from the beginning. He and his sister, Betty, had arrived in Los Angeles to live with their mother's elder sister Helen, wife of the imprisoned Ahn Chang Ho. The two teenagers found themselves taken in only reluctantly by their relatives. Their aunt had not seen them or their mother for more than a decade, since they had left the United States in 1926, and she and her own five children lived in a small home that was already overcrowded.[1] While the Ahns' father languished in a distant Japanese prison, the children were going through their own struggles, striving to find their places in America. Eventually they would succeed, but that time was far away in 1937.

Philip Ahn, the eldest son, was a thirty-two-year-old aspiring actor who was just beginning to find some success in Hollywood. In 1937 he got his first major role in *Daughter of Shanghai*, a movie starring Chinese American actress Anna May Wong that was unique at the time in featuring Asian—not Caucasian—actors performing Asian roles. He would serve in the U.S. Army as an entertainer during the war and then have a long career in movies and television that lasted into the 1970s. He received a star on the Hollywood Walk of Fame in 1984.[2]

Ralph, the youngest son at eleven years of age, would serve in the U.S. Navy in 1944–45. After the war he, too, became a successful actor and a prominent Korean American community leader in Los Angeles. He continued to appear in television roles into his nineties in the late 2010s.[3]

Susan, the elder daughter, was a twenty-two-year-old college student who would become a wartime pioneer as an Asian American and a woman in the U.S. Navy. After the attack on Pearl Harbor, she attempted to enlist to join the fight against Japan. Rejected at first, she kept trying and succeeded in getting accepted into the U.S. Navy's Women Accepted for Volunteer Emergency Service (WAVES). In 1943 she became an officer, the first Asian American woman commissioned to lead American sailors. She trained naval aviators to operate machine guns before being assigned to work on signals intelligence from the Pacific theater at the Office of Naval Intelligence, where her heritage became an asset. After the war she became a pioneer again, working as an intelligence analyst in the newly formed National Security Agency.[4]

James had to find his own way, without anyone's guidance. He and Betty were unwelcome visitors in a crowded home, teenagers growing up under an adult who was not their own parent, and they soon found the situation unbearable.[5] By the end of 1937, Betty had moved out, taken in by a dentist's family as a live-in housemaid. James left the Ahn's house a few weeks later in February 1938. He stayed briefly with a friend of Ruth and Ernest Moy's whom he had met shortly after his arrival in Los Angeles. He then moved into a YMCA in Los Angeles, paying for his room with funds from a benefactor whom his older brother Peter, far away in Shanghai, had found for him.[6] The benefactor was J. Frank Holt, another friend of Ernest and Ruth Moy's and the chief financial officer of Arden Farms, a large dairy business in the Los Angeles area.

Living separately, James and Betty went to high school together at Los Angeles's Manual Arts High School until Betty went back to Shanghai in 1939. Betty's departure left James with no family to whom he could turn anywhere in America.

Not wanting to live off of charity from Frank Holt for long, James found a new way to support himself, which led to a new place to live and a new high school. He went to work in Beverly Hills as a houseboy, a live-in servant, cleaning the house and doing the laundry for a family with a spare room for him.[7] Living in Beverly Hills put him into Beverly Hills High School.

Living in one of America's most affluent communities as a servant, James was kept on the fringe of Beverly Hills and its high school. He had no time to go to Friday night football games or any other after-school activities with his classmates. He still made friends and did well academically, particularly in studying French, which he had begun as a child in Shanghai's French Concession.[8]

At the end of the school year, James made his way to Northern California, where he found another houseboy position with a family in Sausalito, a few miles north of San Francisco. There he finished his final two years of high school at Tamalpais Union High School, graduating in January 1941.

After graduation, James got a job at a bottling plant in Sausalito and enrolled in Marin Junior College (now the College of Marin). He completed only one semester before joining several friends in applying for a job as a firefighter with the California Division of Forestry. Accepted into the state's force for preventing and fighting wildfires, he spent the summer of 1941 living in Lake County and battling brush fires in Northern California.[9]

James joined the U.S. Army voluntarily in the autumn of 1941. A peacetime draft had gone into effect a year earlier when Congress passed the Selective Training and Service Act of 1940, and James knew that he would become eligible for the draft on his twenty-first birthday in March 1942. Preferring to volunteer, James enlisted and was inducted on September 11, 1941.

On December 7, 1941, the "date which will live in infamy" in the words of President Franklin Roosevelt, the attack on Pearl Harbor finally made the Empire of Japan the enemy of the United States. Almost half a century had passed since Japan had begun its conquest of Korea and had become the enemy of the Kim family. Now the U.S. Army was going to war with Japan, and James was a soldier in its ranks.

The U.S. Army was all that James had left after the attack on Pearl Harbor. He had no home or next of kin in the United States.[10] He knew nothing about what was happening to his mother, brothers, and sister in Shanghai. With the city under Japanese occupation and the United States and Japan at war, James was completely cut off from them and would be for as long as the war continued. His only hope of seeing them again was for fortune to allow them to survive the war and for the United States to achieve final victory over Japan.

James Kim and the U.S. Army in the war against Japan should have been a perfect match from the beginning, but their relationship almost began with a terrible injustice.

After his enlistment, James had been sent to Camp Roberts, a training center midway between San Francisco and Los Angeles. Assigned to the field artillery after taking army aptitude tests, he began training as a radio operator, but before completing the course, he found himself abruptly transferred out and assigned to a pool of Japanese American soldiers. The army considered them to be potentially disloyal and was separating them from its ranks for discharge, even before the internment of Japanese American civilians began in March 1942. As a Korean American, from a nation under the Empire of Japan, James found himself mistakenly classified as a Japanese American—an injustice on top of an injustice.

James was determined to fight his way back into the mainstream army but had difficulty finding anyone to turn to for help. He went to the commander of his former artillery training battery, but the officer told him that the orders had come from the headquarters of Camp Roberts and had to be followed. If James could not find an officer willing to take his case to any higher army authorities, he would be condemned to be excluded from the war in which he had seemingly been born to serve.

Appealing to a higher power became the way back to where he belonged. He went next to the battery's chaplain, who heard him out and reported his case to the head chaplain of Camp Roberts. The post's spiritual leader turned out to be a clergyman who had served in China as a missionary, and he understood the story of the Kim family's Christian heritage, their flight from Japanese rule in Korea, their struggle to come to America, and their predicament in Japanese-occupied Shanghai. The post chaplain went directly to the commander of Camp Roberts to explain who this obscure Asian private was and why he belonged in the army.

The commanding officer accepted the minister's explanation of the unusual origins of Private Kim, and a few days after the crisis began, James returned to the artillery training program. For the duration of the war James's U.S. Army records would list his race as Chinese, an administrative artifice that made possible treating him as a normal soldier like any other, since China was an allied nation and U.S. citizens of Chinese descent were considered to be loyal to the United States and suitable for military service.[11]

Pvt. James Kim joined the 222nd Field Artillery Battalion, which was part of the 40th Infantry Division, a National Guard outfit made of units from California, Nevada, and Utah. The 222nd Field Artillery was from Utah, and its officers and enlisted personnel were mainly Mormons, with their unit insignia being the Mormon Battalion Monument in Salt Lake City.[12] With a Japanese invasion believed to be imminent, the 40th Infantry Division defended the Southern California coast from Santa Barbara to the border with Mexico, and the 222nd Field Artillery was stationed far to the south at Escondido, near San Diego.[13]

With the 222nd Field Artillery, James began as one of hundreds of buck privates and found himself chosen for a greater role. His combat role was as a radio operator, and as a private he did regular kitchen police and fatigue duty, preparing meals, washing pots and pans, building and cleaning encampments, and doing other chores. Motivated to excel as a soldier, he regularly won the competition to serve as the guard of the battalion commander's tent, an honor given to an especially sharp enlisted man by the officer of the day. The attention that he gained at battalion headquarters changed his life when the battalion's senior officers decided to send him to Officer Candidate School (OCS) to become an infantry officer.[14]

James had stood out among his fellow enlisted men in his several months in the 222nd Field Artillery, and his commanders had identified him as officer material, potentially able to lead men into battle. At the age of twenty-one, the former teenage runaway from Shanghai was starting to find out who he was and what he was capable of.

In April 1942 James departed California bound for Fort Benning, Georgia, for infantry officer OCS. He completed the course despite breaking his tailbone on the obstacle course, an injury that he concealed to ensure that he graduated with his OCS class. His rear end would bother him for the rest of the war and long after it, but he did not let it stop him from finishing OCS on time. He received his commission as a second lieutenant on July 17, 1942. Most of his class went to the 36th Infantry Division of the Texas National Guard, which ended up going to Europe and fighting in Italy, but he returned to the 40th Infantry Division to fight in the Pacific.[15]

James rejoined the division at Fort Lewis, Washington, where since April it had been reorganizing and training in preparation for deploying overseas. His new outfit, the 160th Infantry Regiment, a California National Guard unit with its armory in Los Angeles, was one of the division's three regimental combat teams.[16] Second Lieutenant Kim took over command of the third platoon of Company L of the 160th Infantry Regiment, one of the three infantry companies in the regiment's 3rd Battalion.[17]

James found himself in an unusual situation as an officer of Asian heritage commanding a unit whose soldiers were practically all Caucasian. He was the only Asian American officer in his regiment and the only one that he knew about in the entire division, which had some Chinese American enlisted men and a few Japanese American soldiers serving as interpreters in the division headquarters.

The new platoon leader had little time to acquaint himself with his soldiers and win their respect before the 40th Infantry Division began to ship out for Hawaii starting in early August. The division sailed on board the ss *Lurline*, a prewar passenger liner serving as a troop transport in the Pacific.[18] In Hawaii, the 40th Infantry Division took over the defense of several of the islands from regular army units that were deploying overseas to join the battle for Guadalcanal, which had begun on August 7. The 160th Infantry Regiment defended the Big Island of Hawaii, manning positions on beaches all around the island that were possible sites for Japanese amphibious landings.[19]

Defensive duties in Hawaii continued until October 1943, when the division started training for amphibious operations and jungle combat in preparation for joining the fighting on the islands of the South Pacific. All of the division's units redeployed to the island of Oahu in July 1943, and three months later other outfits relieved them of their remaining coastal defense duties so that they could focus on preparing for combat. They trained to assault beaches from landing craft and simulated infantry attacks in jungle conditions, using live ammunition, to prepare each man and unit for the battles ahead of them.[20]

In December 1943, two years after the 40th Infantry Division had mustered to defend U.S. territory after the attack on Pearl Harbor, the unit's passage to the front lines of the war in the Pacific finally began. Orders to prepare to move out arrived early in the month, giving the fourteen thousand officers and enlisted men of the division a few weeks to ready themselves. James and the thousands of others felt excitement at finally moving forward to fight the war against Japan but also understood the seriousness of what lay ahead for them.

They could have had few illusions regarding the war they were going to fight. To prepare them for the terrible carnage of amphibious assaults, they watched film footage of the bloody battle for Tarawa, fought not long earlier on November 20–23. On Tarawa, the Marine Corps had lost more than a thousand killed and two thousand wounded—a quarter of the twelve thousand marines who landed on the island—in a few days. Officers who had fought on Guadalcanal delivered briefings on their experiences of combat in the jungle against battle-hardened soldiers of the Imperial Japanese Army. That grueling campaign had lasted six months, from August 1942 to February 1943.[21]

Guadalcanal was where the 40th Infantry Division was headed, and on December 20 its units began to board transport ships bound for the island 3,600 miles distant from Hawaii. By the middle of January 1944, the entire division had arrived and was settling into the U.S. base that had been won at great cost a year earlier. There, living with torrential rains, oceans of mud, and swarms of malaria-bearing mosquitoes, the division continued training for its first combat in the jungle. They soon learned what it would be—an offensive to recapture the island of New Britain, 660 miles northwest of Guadalcanal. It was the next leap forward in the "island-hopping" campaign across the Pacific that would eventually lead to the invasion of Japan itself.

The 40th Infantry Division joined an operation that had begun while the men had been transiting to Guadalcanal. The 1st Marine Division, which had led the campaign to capture Guadalcanal, had conducted amphibious landings on New Britain in December 1943 and January 1944 to secure strategic locations on the island. On April 24 the 40th Infantry Division departed Guadalcanal in a convoy of transports to relieve the marines on New Britain. The division's mission was to maintain control of the U.S.-occupied part of the island and contain the Japanese forces isolated in the naval base at Rabaul, which U.S. forces were bypassing on their way north to Japan.[22]

James's 160th Infantry Regiment narrowly avoided fighting a bloody battle as its first experience on the front line. The 40th Infantry Division's initial assignment was to capture a Japanese airfield on the island of New Ireland, north of New Britain, and its plan called for the 160th Infantry Regiment to land first. The division's preparations had escalated to combat-loading their transports and practicing amphibious landings when news arrived that the operation was canceled. Other American troops under Gen. Douglas MacArthur had captured an airfield on the nearby Admiralty Islands, making the airfield on New Ireland unnecessary. The 160th Infantry later learned its landing site was strongly fortified and defended; likely it would have been costly to assault. Fortunately, the 160th Infantry and the rest of the division instead went to New Britain, to an area already cleared of Japanese forces.[23]

On New Britain, the 40th Infantry Division's regimental combat teams manned a string of outposts and patrolled to keep the center of the island clear of enemy forces. They had only a few encounters and skirmishes with Japanese troops, none of which involved the 160th Infantry Regiment. The soldiers mostly struggled against the jungle, whose heat and incessant rains made their lives miserable.

Months of monotony on New Britain finally came to an end in October 1944 when Australian troops relieved the 40th Infantry Division, and preparations began for its next campaign—the return of U.S. forces to the Philippines. It would begin with the largest amphibious assault of the entire war in the Pacific up to then.

Preparations for combat intensified in the months that followed. Replacement soldiers arrived and were assigned to units, new equipment was issued, and infantry and artillery trained and went through test problems to check their effectiveness as individuals and units. Practice amphibious landings honed the men's all-important ability to go from the sea to fighting their way inland.[24]

Three years after the war began for them, James, his fellow soldiers of the 160th Infantry Regiment, and the entire 40th Infantry Division were finally about to face their baptism of fire. They were on the verge of crossing into the world of battle against the Imperial Japanese Army in the jungles and mountains of the Pacific, previously experienced by only the U.S. Marine Corps and a small fraction of the U.S. Army's soldiers. After the war, a few veteran authors such as Eugene Sledge in his memoir *With the Old Breed: At Peleliu and Okinawa* and novelists James Jones in *The Thin Red Line* and Norman Mailer in *The Naked and the Dead* would attempt to convey to the American public what their nation's servicemen had lived through in these campaigns. James Kim was about to enter that world.

5

American Resistance

WHILE JAMES JOINED the millions of Americans who put on the uniforms of their nation's armed forces and went across the Pacific to defeat the Empire of Japan from without, his brothers in Shanghai waged a quiet war to defeat it from within. They became an American underground in the Japanese-occupied Chinese metropolis. Independently, not yet part of any formal military or intelligence organization, they resisted the Japanese occupation and persecution of Americans in Shanghai by any means available to them.

Their actions harked back to those of one of the first American intelligence organizations created during the Revolutionary War. George Washington organized an intelligence network in the New York City area in 1778, after the defeat of his army in New York in 1776–77—"the times that try men's souls," in the words of Thomas Paine. To spy on the British army in New York, Washington had his director of military intelligence recruit civilians living in and around the city among British soldiers and Loyalist collaborators. Washington himself named them the Culper Ring, after the town of Culpeper, Virginia, where he had worked as a surveyor in his first employment at the age of seventeen.

The Culper Ring provided Washington with valuable intelligence until the end of the war in 1783; then it disappeared almost completely from the nation's memory. After living under great secrecy because of the constant threat of discovery and execution, the spies received little postwar recognition, and many of their identities and actions were not discovered until the twentieth century. Their full story would not be told to the American public until the twenty-first century, when new research led to the publication in 2006 of the book *Washington's Spies*, which was then adapted into the television series *Turn: Washington's Spies* in 2014.[1]

In Shanghai, the times that tried men's souls began on December 8, 1941. Soon after the Imperial Japanese Army marched into the International Settlement, the Kempeitai—the Japanese military police that was similar to Nazi Germany's Gestapo—started arresting citizens of Great Britain, the United States, and other Allied countries. The Kempeitai singled out individuals whom they considered to be potential opponents of Japanese rule and took them to an apartment building that they had converted into a dungeon and torture chamber. Called the Bridge House, it became the symbol of the arbitrary cruelty of the Japanese authorities in Shanghai.[2]

Those untouched by the Kempeitai still suffered as they became destitute under Japanese occupation. The new Japanese overlords of the Shanghai International Settlement seized Western-owned businesses that had made some families fabulously wealthy and sustained the city's middle class. The British and Americans found themselves suddenly left with no means of support in the same city where they previously had lived privileged lives. Wartime food shortages further impoverished them as Japanese officials and their Chinese collaborators, who eyed their houses, threatened them with the loss of their homes.

Peter Kim stepped forward to aid his fellow Americans trapped in Shanghai as their world fell apart. Soon after the occupation began, he volunteered to work for the American Association of Shanghai, a social organization that during the war assumed the tasks of trying to protect the rights of Americans and aiding those in need of assistance. His first assignment was to organize food supplies for the needy, establishing a relief center on the grounds of the Shanghai American School. In the summer of 1942, the association moved him to its War Prisoners Committee, which aided U.S. Marines captured at the U.S. Legation in Beijing and on Wake Island who became prisoners of war (POWs) in Shanghai.[3]

When U.S. diplomacy conducted through the neutral nation of Switzerland created an opportunity for some Americans in Shanghai to be repatriated in the summer of 1942 in exchange for Japanese citizens interned in the United States after the attack on Pearl Harbor, the American Association entrusted Peter with organizing the swap. Working with the Swiss Consulate in Shanghai to select several hundred individuals out of the thousands of Americans in the city for repatriation, he gave a few categories of people the highest priority: arrested or interned persons, women and children, U.S. officials, and officers and employees of American organizations and businesses.[4] His diligence and organizational skill made a great impression on the Swiss consul, Emile Fontanel, whose responsibilities included representing the interests of the United States during the wartime absence of U.S. diplomats from Shanghai.

As a result of Peter's work with the Swiss Consulate, the Italian ocean liner SS *Conte Verde* left Shanghai in July 1942 with 639 U.S. citizens on board and headed for a rendezvous off southern Africa with a ship that the U.S. Department of State had chartered for the exchange—the Swedish liner MS *Gripsholm*. The Americans aboard included Judge Milton Helmick, who before the war had been synonymous with U.S. law enforcement in Shanghai as the judge of the U.S. Court for China since 1934.[5]

The Kim family remained as impoverished as any Americans in Shanghai during this time. Peter and David had lost their jobs with American businesses when the Japanese seized them and shut them down, leaving the entire family without any source of income. A lifeline emerged to save them from complete destitution later in 1942, though, as the result of another joint action by U.S. diplomats and the Swiss Consulate.

The U.S. Department of State and the Swiss Foreign Ministry had established a program to aid Americans in Japanese-occupied China by giving them loans from a Swiss diplomatic account funded by the U.S. government. The Swiss Consulate in Shanghai administered the program, which was for U.S. citizens only. The loans, issued in the currency of the Chinese puppet regime controlled by Japan, began in April 1942.[6]

Betty, the Kim family's sole U.S. citizen in Shanghai, became the key to their survival. She began receiving loans from the Swiss Consulate after

October 1942. By the end of 1943, she had received funds with a U.S. dollar value of almost $700, equivalent to $12,000 in 2024. The financial support enabled the family to buy food in Shanghai's markets and remain in their modest house. Moreover, it allowed them to maintain their independence from the Japanese authorities. Supported by U.S. funds channeled through Swiss diplomats protected by international law, the Kims would not be compelled by poverty to collaborate with the Japanese.[7]

Everything changed after June 1942, when the U.S. victory in the Battle of Midway turned the tide of the war in the Pacific. Japanese forces were no longer advancing invincibly toward Hawaii and Australia, and by August, they were fighting to contain the first Allied counteroffensive at Guadalcanal. The white foreigners living in Shanghai now appeared to be a threat, a possible resistance movement in a key center of Japan's overseas empire. Japanese authorities moved to isolate and confine the thousands of American, British, and other Allied country civilians in Shanghai, forcing them into internment camps.

In the morning of November 5, 1942, the Kempeitai rounded up 348 men and herded them into a compound of buildings surrounded by barbed wire. Among them were former members of the Shanghai City Council and police, who were seen as potential leaders of a resistance movement, and retired U.S. Marines and U.S. Navy sailors. Others were ordinary people who had no idea why the Japanese considered them worth detaining. A year earlier, the buildings had been a barracks of the 4th Marine Regiment, which had been withdrawn from Shanghai only a few weeks before the attack on Pearl Harbor. Now the premises were a concentration camp run by the Kempeitai.[8]

All civilians from the Allied countries—men, women, and children—went into internment camps starting in January 1943. On January 23 Japanese orders announced that internments would begin in one week, and on January 31 the first several hundred people reported for their new lives as prisoners. In February, March, and April, group after group assembled for their journeys to the camps, which the Japanese called Civil Assembly Centres.[9]

More than seven thousand men, women, and children lived in the Shanghai internment camps for the remainder of the war. The British, Americans, Australians, New Zealanders, Canadians, Dutch, Belgians, South Africans, and people of many other nationalities lost everything: their homes, their livelihoods, and all but the clothes that they wore and a few suitcases filled with their last possessions. They would spend more than two years crammed together behind barbed wire in more than half a dozen compounds scattered around Shanghai.[10]

When the entire remnant of the American community of Shanghai went into the internment camps, the Kim family was not among them. Part of the reason that they were not interned was that most of them—Peter, his brothers, and their mother—were citizens of China, not the United States, making them subjects of Japan's Chinese puppet state rather than foreign nationals from an enemy country. An even more significant reason was that the Japanese authorities simplistically judged them by their race. The Japanese expected that they would abandon the defeated white foreigners and accept becoming subjects of the Empire of Japan, the new order in Asia.

The foolishness of Japan's race policies extended even to U.S. citizens of Asian descent. One was Betty, born in Los Angeles twenty years earlier. She was allowed to live freely as long as she always appeared in public wearing a red armband with the letter *A* for American; however, she always ignored this Japanese requirement and never faced any punishment. Another U.S. citizen was Peter's paramour, Ruth Moy, who also was still married to an official of the Nationalist Chinese government. Despite her obvious loyalties to the two greatest enemies of their empire, the Japanese allowed her to continue to live freely in Shanghai for the war's duration.

Peter, David, Richard, and Arthur proved the Japanese wrong. They remained steadfastly loyal to their fellow Americans in Shanghai and to the distant United States, even though it had kept them out for more than fifteen years. Soon after the internments began, they found ways to resist the Japanese occupation, establishing the underground that the Japanese had tried to prevent by confining citizens of the Allied powers behind barbed wire.

Peter again led the way by becoming the lifeline to the outside world for the Americans in the internment camps. In March 1943 he went to work for the Swiss Consulate in Shanghai, whose diplomats continued to represent the U.S. government's interest in looking after the safety of its citizens in the city. Emile Fontanel hired him to serve as the consulate's representative in matters relating to the interned Americans.[11]

From the smallest to the largest problems, Peter took charge. He organized the delivery of relief supplies from the Swiss Red Cross to the camps. He learned about issues in the camps and reported them to Fontanel, who passed the reports to the U.S. Department of State in Washington DC. When the United States and Japan conducted another exchange of civilians in the autumn of 1943, again using the *Gripsholm* as a chartered mercy ship, Peter once more organized the release of internees from the camps. Under his direction, almost a thousand people left the internment camps and boarded the Japanese repatriation ship *Teia Maru* on September 19, bound for a rendezvous off Africa with the *Gripsholm* and a safe passage home.[12]

The younger brothers had to wait for their opportunity to do something to resist the Japanese. Richard, fifteen years old when the internments began, would go to a newly built internment camp with a friend named Olof Lindstedt, whose Swedish family had not been subject to internment. The two boys rode their bicycles to the outside of Chapei, a camp located far from the International Settlement in the western outskirts of Shanghai that held mainly Americans. They hoped to see their friends behind the barbed wire, particularly their classmate Ted Hale, who had been close enough to them that the Hales had given their two Irish terriers to the Kims and the Lindstedts to keep during their internment. Richard could only dream of finding their friends and somehow smuggling things to them through the barbed wire.[13]

Unbeknownst to the younger brothers, a way for them to resist the Japanese occupation was developing, and Ruth Moy would be the linchpin of it. Her ties to her estranged husband, however strained they may have been, remained sufficient to connect her to U.S. intelligence. Ernest Moy had become an official in Kunming of the War Area Service Corps, the Nationalist Chinese military organization responsible for supporting the U.S. Fourteenth Air Force. Through him, U.S. Army intelligence became aware of Ruth and her presence in Shanghai. Eventually she would become a key leader of U.S. intelligence operations in Shanghai.

Meanwhile, the entire Kim family resisted attempts to indoctrinate the youngest brothers into becoming loyal subjects of the Empire of Japan. Their mother received a series of letters ordering her to send Richard and Arthur—fifteen and thirteen years of age, respectively—to Japanese language classes. The first two letters she burned in the house's potbelly stove, but she found it impossible to ignore the third, which Korean collaborators delivered in person and forced her to acknowledge. Richard and Arthur reluctantly went to their classes but passively resisted by not paying attention. Another threatening visit failed to push their mother into doing anything about her sons' failure to learn Japanese, and they eventually got away with ceasing to attend and learning nothing.[14]

Surreptitiously, the brothers sought to stay connected to the distant United States and with the Allies' progress in the war, and shortwave radio gave them a slender window to the world beyond Japanese propaganda. The Japanese had long ago attempted to confiscate all shortwave radios, fearing their ability to receive broadcasts from distant radio stations in Allied countries, but a neighbor had succeeded in concealing one. David and Richard would sneak over to the neighbor's house to listen to broadcasts by KGEI, a California-based shortwave station owned by General Electric. It was the only American radio transmission that could be heard across the Pacific.[15]

Radio and its role in the war of information and ideas almost led to Peter's downfall, which in turn could have ended Ruth's work for U.S. intelligence in Shanghai. It began when the Shanghai office of Japan's official news agency envisioned using Peter as a broadcaster of its English-language radio propaganda.

Japanese radio propaganda already had an infamous star—Tokyo Rose, the female announcer broadcasting to U.S. troops in the South Pacific—and around their empire, the Japanese had other voices working for them to spread disinformation and undermine Allied morale. In Shanghai, the Japanese had put a formerly American-owned radio station back on the air, and a white American collaborator had been the station's main announcer since February 1942. He had fallen out of favor by 1943, and Japan's propagandists needed a replacement.[16] Peter drew the attention of Japanese authorities for his skill with the English language during his work for the Swiss consul, including during discussions prior to the voyage of the second repatriation ship in September 1943.

Peter learned about the Japanese plans for him after the Kempeitai arrested him and took him to the Bridge House in early October 1943.[17] His arrest could have also led the Kempeitai to Ruth, endangering her and possibly the rest of the Kim family, but his mother contained the damage with remarkably shrewd thinking in an instant. An unfamiliar knock on the family's door in the darkness of an early morning alerted her to the danger. The "shave and a haircut, two bits" series of seven knocks, familiar to Americans but meaningless to the Japanese, was the family's way of announcing themselves at the door. The pounding on the door meant strangers were there, and through a window Lee Chung Sil could see that they appeared to be Japanese policemen in civilian clothes.

They had to be there for Peter, who was not home, having spent the night at Ruth's house. The peril in the situation was obvious to her. If the Japanese learned that Peter had been staying with Ruth, they would likely question her next, and they might uncover her involvement with U.S. intelligence. The entire Kim family would then come under suspicion, putting all of them in danger. Lee Chung Sil had to do something to obscure Peter's whereabouts that night and quickly.

But first she had to alert everyone in the house that the enemy was at the door and tell them immediately to hide anything that might draw the attention of the Japanese. She awoke David, sleeping in Peter's bed on the mezzanine above the door, and then rushed to the upper floors to wake up Richard, Betty, and Arthur. Richard yanked photographs of American heroes—President Franklin Roosevelt, baseball stars Babe Ruth and Joe DiMaggio—from the upper floor's walls and stuffed them beneath his mattress. Then he lay down on top of them, pretending to sleep. Then she opened the door. Through it surged several agents of the feared Kempeitai.

The Kempeitai demanded to see Peter and stormed through each room of the house, searching for him. Lee Chung Sil told them the most plausible story that she could think of in the moment: Peter had gone to the bakery first thing that morning to buy bread. Her tale was convincing enough that they sat in the living room and waited for Peter to return, despite at first suspecting that he was in the house, possibly in the rumpled bed in which David had slept.

Alerting Peter and setting up his alibi still had to be done, so Lee Chung Sil told David to stay with the Kempeitai in the living room while she went to the kitchen to make coffee. She left the room and sneaked out to a neighbor's house, where she woke up the live-in servant, handed her some money, and told her to go buy a loaf of bread. Then she used the house's telephone to call Ruth's house and tell Peter to hurry home because there was trouble. After she went back to her own kitchen and made coffee, the servant returned with the loaf of bread and change just as Peter arrived on his bicycle. Out of sight of the Kempeitai agents in the living room, Lee Chung Sil took the bread and change, gave them to Peter, and brought him into the living room, where she then told him to hand over the bread and change.[18]

The hastily improvised show succeeded in fooling the Kempeitai into believing her story and not investigating further into where Peter had been, thus protecting Ruth and the Kim family, but it could not save Peter from arrest. The Kempeitai took him to the Bridge House, where they had tortured and broken countless Chinese and Allied civilians since December 1941.

Kempeitai agents interrogated Peter about his past associations with Americans and his activities since December 7, 1941. They clearly had information about him going back more than a decade before the war, and they used it to level a series of accusations against him. They accused him of being an agent of the U.S. Navy, then an agent of the U.S. Army, then an agent of other U.S. government agencies, and finally even an agent of the Nationalist Chinese government in Chongqing. The interrogations and beatings in the dark rooms of the Bridge House continued, day after day, with no end in sight.

After roughing up Peter for days, his tormentors finally began to offer him a way out of the Bridge House. The Kempeitai first demanded to know whether he would be willing to serve as an informant on Americans and other foreign nationals. They eventually offered him an opportunity at a reward—to serve as a radio broadcaster, using his gift of speaking American English, for which others had been paid and given special privileges.

Some had eagerly embraced working for the Japanese and other Axis powers as radio propaganda personalities, and others had accepted it after their detention in the Bridge House, but working for the enemy was unthinkable to Peter and the entire Kim family. He evaded the Kempeitai's offers as long as he could, and his interrogators finally gave up. For ten days, he had endured the Kempeitai's torments in the Bridge House, and he emerged unbroken.[19]

The ordeal had been a traumatic experience, however; he emerged from the Bridge House a changed man for a time. He returned home physically wounded by the ten days of torture and starvation at the hands of the Kempeitai. Mentally he was shaken as well. He had to distance himself from his activities on behalf of Americans in Shanghai that had put him at great risk, which he had to assume would continue. When he informed the Swiss consul of what had happened to him, he also requested to be released from further service to the consulate. Fontanel, concerned with Peter's safety, granted the request.[20]

Life became harder in the winter that followed as the loss of Peter's work for the Swiss Consulate, the inflation slashing the value of Betty's loans, and the growing shortages of food and other necessities in Shanghai drove the family further into poverty. Simply feeding everyone became increasingly difficult, forcing Lee Chung Sil to find food for the family anywhere that she could. Once, after days without having enough for everyone to eat, she surprised them with a plate full of what she declared to be chicken—a great luxury for a family that rarely could afford to eat meat. Richard had noticed earlier that day that the pigeons that he kept in a cage on the roof had disappeared and that the "chickens" were too small, so he knew his pet birds were on the table in front of him. He refused to eat them, but the others did.[21]

As winter gave way to spring in 1944, in the third year of Japanese occupation, Peter's attention turned to escaping from Shanghai. He had considered leaving Shanghai earlier, before his arrest and detention in October, to find U.S. forces in the interior of China and attempt to enlist in the U.S. Army. His ordeal in the Bridge House had broken his will to take that risk, but after taking several months to recover, he was again ready for it. Further emboldening him, the Kempeitai had not bothered him again since releasing him from the Bridge House. They appeared to have lost interest in him, giving him an opportunity to plan and act again.

Escaping Shanghai with at least one of his brothers became urgently necessary in 1944, as the Imperial Japanese Army began to draft Koreans on a large scale. After seven years of war and its massive losses in China and all over Asia, Japan was running out of military manpower, and drafting Koreans was one way to replenish the gaps in its army's ranks. By 1945 the Imperial Japanese Army in China alone had more than one hundred thousand Koreans filling out its units. With Richard now sixteen years old and at risk of being drafted and forced to fight for the enemy, Peter and his mother decided that the time had come for him to leave Shanghai with Richard.[22]

The rest of the family—Lee Chung Sil, David, Betty, and Arthur—would have to stay behind. All six of them leaving at once would be too conspicuous. The risk that the Imperial Japanese Army's draft would take twenty-seven-year-old David was less, and at age fourteen, Arthur would not be vulnerable for a couple of years. Peter hoped that later, after he and Richard had reached safety and joined the U.S. forces in China, he could find a way to extract all of them from Shanghai.[23] But it was a distant hope, which the fortunes of war could destroy at any time. The Kempeitai could take the remaining family to investigate the disappearance of the two brothers. Attempts to contact them in Shanghai could fail. Or poverty could leave them too hungry and destitute to do anything. No one could know what the future would bring in the merciless world war.

Peter prepared for the getaway from Shanghai by joining a group of Chinese civilians that was planning to leave the city in May. Its leader, a friend of Ruth Moy's named Peter Chang, planned the escape route and made all of the arrangements for it. The rest of the group were educated, well-off citizens of Shanghai who after seven years of living under Japanese occupation were finally making a break for free China. They were going to join the millions of refugees who had fled Japanese-occupied China for an uncertain future in the unconquered interior of the country.[24]

The front line between Japanese- and Chinese-controlled territory was almost a thousand miles away, and to reach it, the group would have to move across the country by train, by riverboat, and by land. Along with train tickets, boat passage, and overland transportation to pay for, they would need to buy food and other necessities along the way. Peter had to find the money for all of it, for two, from somewhere.

On May 9 Peter went to the Swiss Consulate to tell Emile Fontanel about his plan to escape Shanghai and to give him advance warning of his imminent disappearance. The consul gathered his staff to give all who had worked with Peter in the past year a chance to bid him farewell. Recognizing that life and death for Peter and his brother were at stake, a Swiss consular official stepped forward and gave Peter money to cover the expenses of the journey.[25]

Fontanel offered as well to aid the man whom he had befriended during their struggles together on behalf of the interned Americans of Shanghai during the past year. The consul said that he would look after Peter's family during his absence and ensure that the consulate's financial assistance would continue. The assurance of support helped to relieve Peter's fears that his family might go hungry and suffer while he was far away and unable to help them in enemy territory.[26]

Another Swiss consular official, Emile Essig, had an idea that he hoped might help Peter at the other end of the journey. He suggested that Peter look for a U.S. official in Chongqing named Walter Fowler, the head of the China office of the Board of Economic Warfare, an organization responsible for economic issues. Fowler was the father-in-law of a friend of Peter's named Robert Biesel, a banker with Chase Bank in Shanghai who had ended up in the Chapei internment camp. Peter had fought to have Biesel added to the repatriation list for the second *Gripsholm* exchange voyage in September 1943. Peter did not know Fowler, but the connection to his son-in-law could only help if Peter succeeded in reaching free China and began looking for friends to help him there.[27]

Peter left the Swiss Consulate rewarded for the good deeds that he had done for the past two and a half years. The generous assistance that his friends at the consulate offered could become the difference between failure and success not only in the journey that he was about to undertake but also in the survival of his family remaining behind in Shanghai. He went home with nothing left to do but to get ready and go.

On May 10, 1944, the day to depart, Peter and Richard had their last meal in Shanghai at Jimmy's Kitchen, the American restaurant that they had been going to since the 1930s. Although its owner, Jimmy James, was in the Chapei internment camp, and the establishment was barely functioning under wartime shortages, it still seemed an appropriate place to bid farewell to the city that had been their home for most of their lives and had done so much to shape who they had become. When they finished, they went home to say goodbye to their mother, brothers, and sister.

The evening was rainy when the entire family gathered for what they all recognized could be the last time that they all would see each other alive. Peter and Richard had dressed themselves in Chinese clothes, disguising themselves as nondescript Chinese civilians in an attempt to blend in during their travels. Lee Chung Sil, who had struggled so long to raise them and to protect them from the dangers of the war, urged them to go forward. She told them, "Don't turn back. Keep going."

Peter and Richard said their final farewells and set off for the railway station.[28]

6

Exodus from Shanghai

THE SHANGHAI SOUTH railway station was where Peter and Richard met the group with whom they would escape from Shanghai. Seven years earlier, the station had been hit by Japanese aerial bombs during the invasion and conquest of the city, and a photograph of a Chinese baby in its ruins became a worldwide sensation and inspired American outrage at Japanese aggression in China.[1] In 1944 the station was still the terminus of the railroad from Shanghai to Hangzhou, the port city a hundred miles to the southwest at the mouth of the Qiantang River that was the objective of the first leg of the journey.

The group, twenty-one people in total, gathered in the station to board the train to Hangzhou with their cover story and papers already arranged. They were pretending to be employees of a Chinese business relocating from Shanghai and Hangzhou to a town farther inland; they were ordinary people only trying to make a living in the Chinese puppet state under the Empire of Japan. To ensure their safe passage on the Japanese-run railway, each man and woman had the *pao chia* certificate that Japan issued to control Chinese citizens and allowed the bearer to travel freely within Japanese-occupied China.[2] The documents would get them past the Japanese and Chinese puppet security personnel patrolling the railway's stations and trains.[3]

Beyond Hangzhou, the group would travel inland out of Japanese-controlled territory along river trade routes and then move overland to the front line of Nationalist Chinese forces to the west. The forward bastion of Chinese resistance since 1939 had been city of Changsha, the capital of Hunan, located 450 miles to the southwest of Hangzhou. Chinese troops had held the line there for five years, defeating Imperial Japanese Army offensives in 1939, 1941, and 1942. The front was far from Hangzhou, but it had hardly moved since before the attack on Pearl Harbor. The journey was likely to be filled with dangers, but if the group made it through them, they could expect to cross into free China within a couple of weeks.

South of Changsha were the forward bases of the U.S. Army Air Forces in China, the ultimate objective for Peter and Richard. From these air bases operated the Fourteenth Air Force under Maj. Gen. Claire Chennault, famed for commanding the American Volunteer Group, better known as the "Flying Tigers." The Fourteenth Air Force was the main U.S. military presence in China in 1944, supporting China's embattled armies with its squadrons of fighters, bombers, and transport aircraft. Peter and Richard hoped that these U.S. forces would accept them as volunteers in any capacity that would help the U.S. war effort in China. But first they had to reach free China.

None of their group's members knew yet that their escape plan was about to collide with a massive change in the course of the war in China—Operation Ichigo (Number One), the Imperial Japanese Army's largest offensive of the entire Second World War. With Japan experiencing devastating defeats at sea since 1942, its still-formidable army in China was planning to change the course of the war by cutting through central China all the way to Southeast Asia. They sought to establish a land bridge to their conquests in Southeast Asia, bypassing the seas controlled by the U.S. Navy. In the process, they hoped to inflict a major defeat on U.S. forces by overrunning and destroying the forward air bases of the Fourteenth Air Force.[4]

Japanese forces had already attacked north of the Yangtze River in April, seizing control of the entire railway from Beijing to Wuhan, and on May 27 an army of more than 350,000 troops advanced toward Changsha. The battle for the city ended with a Japanese victory in mid-June, unraveling the entire defense of central China. Japanese forces then advanced toward the city of Hengyang, threatening the entire chain of U.S. air bases to the south.

These events were still in the future when Peter and Richard boarded the train to Hangzhou in the evening of May 10. The journey by rail went uneventfully, and in Hangzhou, Peter Chang led them from the train station to the office of a trading company located a few buildings away from the Hangzhou Confucius Temple, a historic landmark dating to the twelfth century. There they met a merchant from free China who had come to Japanese-occupied Hangzhou to trade in the black market, exchanging goods between the territories controlled by the two enemy nations. The merchant was preparing to return home with bales of cotton, which he obtained in exchange for tung oil, the Chinese tree oil used for finishing wood. His boats would transport them to Chinese-controlled territory.[5]

Arrangements to move the group past Japanese security were made while the group waited in Hangzhou for the tung oil–cotton exchange to finish. The Chinese trading company had connections to the Imperial Japanese Army's trading organization in Hangzhou, whose cooperation was needed for the inland voyage to proceed. It inspected their baggage—some eighty steamer trunks and bags, all of the remaining worldly possessions of twenty-one people—for contraband; otherwise, it left them undisturbed. Allowing them and their luggage to pass, the trading organization then assigned a uniformed officer of the Chinese puppet army to escort the small fleet of junks out of Japanese-controlled territory. After all business in Hangzhou was completed, Peter, Richard, and their group finally boarded the boats to continue their journey on May 19.[6]

The convoy of river junks took them up the Qiantang River, which flowed past Hangzhou from the southwest. Several miles up the river was the Qiantang River Bridge; at its guard post, Japanese-controlled territory ended. The Chinese puppet army officer went ashore at the guard post to tell the soldiers inside that the boats were allowed to pass. Cleared to sail upriver, the junks with their cargoes and fugitives from Shanghai shoved off and continued the journey on their own.[7]

The junks moved upriver slowly, propelled only by their old-fashioned sails, through territory controlled by no army. After the Qiantang River met the Fuchun River, the convoy passed a last Japanese outpost at Fuyang, about twenty miles upstream of Hangzhou. The junks sailed past it at night, under cover of darkness and completely blacked out to avoid drawing fire from Japanese troops. Beyond Fuyang, the Imperial Japanese Army made no effort to control the countryside, leaving it to the many Chinese guerrilla bands that had emerged in the wake of the Japanese invasion. Some of these groups were loyal to China's struggle for survival, but others were no better than outlaws and thieves.[8]

At one point a force of heavily armed guerrillas stopped the convoy and took away Peter Chang for questioning, keeping everyone else under guard on the river. Peter Kim had never learned to speak Chinese, so he and Richard were concerned that the guerrillas might try to question him as well and find him suspicious. Richard was prepared to use the Chinese that he had learned during his childhood in Shanghai to keep any inquisitive guards occupied, while Peter pretended to be too ill to speak. The planned subterfuge proved to be unnecessary, because the guerrillas returned Peter Chang and sent everyone on their way after warning them to be careful and wishing them a safe journey.[9]

Another guerrilla group proved to be mere bandits. These armed men stopped the convoy and demanded money to allow it to pass. Only after fleecing everyone on board did the thugs allow them to continue their journey up the river.[10]

The junks sailed past more guerrillas and town after town, moving by day and stopping each night. They stopped and disembarked the passengers and their baggage on May 28, ten days after they had departed Hangzhou. Aided by the merchant and his knowledge of the area's trade routes, they found trucks for hire and chartered them for the overland leg of their journey. The trucks were old civilian models with motors converted to run on gas from burning charcoal—a common way to keep vehicles on the road under wartime conditions when gasoline was hard to obtain—so they had to move slowly with their weakened engines. In the afternoon of May 30, Peter, Richard, and the rest of the group boarded them and headed toward Chinese-held territory.[11]

At that very moment, a new peril was threatening their journey: Operation Ichigo had begun its advance to the south three days earlier. A massive Japanese army was moving toward Changsha, ready to overwhelm the Chinese defense of the city and threatening the most direct route to free China. To avoid the advancing battlefront, the trucks headed farther to the south than originally planned. Day after day, they moved slowly along unpaved dirt highways until they were approaching Guangdong, one of China's southernmost provinces.

On June 4 they finally arrived at their destination—the city of Kukong (now Shaoguan). Kukong was the wartime capital of Guangdong; the province's Nationalist administration had moved there when Japanese forces occupied the capital at Canton (now Guangzhou) in 1938. This center of Chinese resistance offered the group's members a temporary refuge and their first opportunity to connect with the world that they were trying to reach.

Peter took an initial step toward establishing the meeting with U.S. officials in the Nationalist capital at Chongqing that his friends at the Swiss Consulate had advised him to seek. He found a telegraph office in Kukong with a line to Chongqing, more than five hundred miles away, and sent a telegram addressed to Walter Fowler at the U.S. government's Board of Economic Warfare office. His brief and cryptic message read, "Please radio Robert Biesel to notify Anker Henningsen that I am now en route to Chungking via Hengyang and Kweilin. Essig sends regards. Peter Kim."[12]

Peter had packed the short telegram with a series of names of people who would establish who he was to Fowler, who had never heard of him before, and could facilitate his entry into the U.S. war effort in China. Mentioning Essig, the Swiss consular official who had referred Peter to Fowler, told Fowler that Peter had come from Shanghai. Biesel, Fowler's son-in-law, owed Peter a debt of gratitude for putting him on the repatriation ship out of Shanghai the year before and would certainly advocate for Peter when Fowler contacted him. Henningsen, who before the war had risked hiring Peter for a job intended for an expatriate white American, would without a doubt do all that he could to help Peter find a place on the U.S. side of the war.

In Kukong, Peter and Richard began to meet individuals who either were from their past in Shanghai or would soon become crucial to their futures. Two such meetings happened in rapid succession on the same day.

First, they saw an unfamiliar small vehicle in the street—a jeep, which they had never seen before—and Peter recognized the man in it. He was Ralph

Morgan, who before the war had been a U.S. Navy chief petty officer serving in Shanghai. Peter approached and introduced himself, and Morgan revealed that he was now an intelligence officer working with Nationalist Chinese forces in southern China. The chance encounter years later in a small city seven hundred miles from Shanghai became an intelligence collection opportunity for Morgan as he debriefed Peter about his journey from Shanghai. When they finished, Morgan said farewell and drove away in his jeep.

Later that day a stranger approached Peter and Richard, tapped Peter on the shoulder, and asked for him by name. Peter was terrified that Japanese intelligence or its Chinese puppet agents had found them. He signaled for Richard to run away, which he did. After the stranger told him that a man wanted to see him and pointed to the door of a house, Peter entered it, expecting the worst.

Inside he found two men in civilian clothes, and he was relieved to find that one of them was Lt. Jack Young, a Chinese American U.S. Army intelligence officer whom he had known as a civilian in Shanghai many years earlier. Young was on his way to Shanghai on a secret mission, and having seen Peter in the streets of Kukong and recognized him, he wanted to learn whatever he could from Peter about the route to Shanghai.

Peter told Young as many details as he could about the underground route that he and Richard had taken from Shanghai. Then he helped him in another way by giving Young his and Richard's *pao chia* certificates, as they no longer needed the identity cards issued by Japan's Chinese puppet regime. Young would need one to travel on the railroads in Japanese-occupied territory. Having done all that he could to help Young, Peter parted ways with him to find Richard and continue their journey.[13]

Outside of Kukong, Peter and Richard had their first encounter with the U.S. Army Air Forces in China, and it was completely out of the ordinary.

It began when they were walking across a field and saw in the distance what they thought was a formation of four single-engine fighters. As the aircraft drew nearer, they saw that the four planes were actually two, each with twin engines and tail booms that from a distance appeared to be two planes flying close together. They had never before seen this type of aircraft, which was the P-38 Lightning, a mainstay of the U.S. Army Air Forces in China and the South Pacific. Without warning, the unfamiliar aircraft approaching them suddenly fired their machine guns. Peter and Richard thought that the planes were strafing them and hit the ground to take cover. They seemed to be under attack from the air, helpless, with nowhere to run and no way to fight back.

Soon they realized that something else was happening. The brief bursts of machine gun fire stopped, and they saw people rush into a nearby rice paddy and place small pennants into the ground. The shots apparently had only been a signal to the people who were now running around, preparing something. The two aircraft descended and landed on the ground marked by the pennants, which now appeared to mark a secret airstrip camouflaged to resemble a rice paddy. Peter and Richard rushed forward to join the crowd around the planes, excitement taking the place of the terror that they had felt moments before.

There they found a U.S. Navy officer, directing a ground crew of Chinese civilians, and two American fighter pilots. Peter and Richard struck up a conversation with the airmen, one of whom was a tall Texan, immediately identifiable by how he talked. The pilots, speaking remarkably openly, explained that they had been on a long-range reconnaissance mission around Hong Kong and needed refueling to return to their base. Peter told them about himself and Richard and their long journey from Shanghai to find an American forward air base.

The pilots then made a surprising offer, as shocking as their machine gun fire a short time earlier: Peter and Richard could come with them, flying in the back of their P-38s. Hearing the pilots make this suggestion, Peter thought that they must be mistaking him for a Chinese airman downed during a long-range mission like theirs, whom they would especially want to rescue out of comradeship. The P-38s each had only one seat, but behind the cockpit was a compartment for the plane's bulky radio that had a small empty space that pilots normally used to carry personal items. The pilots offered to dump their gear so that Peter and Richard could ride in their radio compartments, which a person could barely squeeze into in an emergency.

Their offer was astoundingly generous, but Peter and Richard had to turn it down. Neither had ever been in an airplane before, and cramming themselves into the tiny spaces in the radio compartments of the P-38s looked as if it would be a terrifying way to fly for the first time. They politely declined, saying they had to stay with their group. The pilots wished them well and advised them to look for the U.S. Consulate in Kweilin if they succeeded in reaching the city, promising to alert the consul about the arrival of a Peter Kim. Returning to their refueled planes, the flyers fired up their engines, took off, and flew away toward the west.[14]

The encounter with the fighter pilots brought Peter and Richard no closer to their destination, but if they had needed a sign from above that a successful end to their odyssey was within reach, now they had one. They still had a long way to go, but now they had reason to believe that they were going to make it and that the American forces in China would accept them when they arrived.

A train overflowing with refugees took them on the next stage of their journey. Instead of flying thousands of feet over the countryside in an American airplane, speeding straight toward a U.S. air base at hundreds of miles per hour, Peter and Richard left Kukong on the railroad line that ran inland from Hong Kong and Canton. Chinese civilians were fleeing the city by the thousands, as news of the massive Japanese offensive to the north and rumors of another Japanese force gathering to attack from Canton created fear that Kukong would soon be lost. Peter and Richard had to board a train packed with refugees, who leaned out the windows of the overcrowded cars, rode on top of them, and stood on their steps. Peter and Richard were among the latter, locking their arms around the handrails so that they would not fall off the steps if they fell asleep from exhaustion.[15]

The train was headed to Hengyang, a city less than a hundred miles south of Changsha, where the rail line north from Hong Kong met the line south from Wuhan that was the axis of the Japanese advance. Hengyang had the northernmost U.S. air base in China, but if the Chinese defense of Changsha collapsed, the city and its air base would be the next target of the Japanese offensive. The train arrived with Hengyang under attack by Japanese air raids and its population evacuating the city. Amid mass panic at the mobbed train station, Peter, Richard, and their group found room on another train filled with refugees going south and away from the Japanese onslaught.

The train reached Kweilin the morning of June 8, and immediately upon arrival, Peter and Richard found that the stationmaster was expecting them. A friend of Peter Chang's from school many years earlier, he had been informed of the group's escape from Shanghai and was waiting for them. Finally, after a month on the run, they had found refuge in free China.

The stationmaster also had news for Peter and Richard. He had a telegram from Walter Fowler, who had responded to the telegram that Peter had sent from Kukong. Somehow, Fowler had found a way to reach Peter at one of the cities mentioned in the cryptic telegram from Kukong. Fowler declared that he had radioed his son-in-law Robert Biesel to notify Anker Henningsen, as requested, and that Peter should contact him upon reaching Chongqing. The telegram was the first sign that Peter's plan to join the U.S. forces in China might be successful.[16]

A greater sign came afterward. Peter learned that a U.S. Army intelligence officer in Kweilin knew about his arrival and wanted to see him. So he went to meet the officer at the U.S. air base, a sprawling complex of more than five hundred buildings grouped around the airfield situated below a row of the limestone hills that abounded in the Kweilin area. There Peter found that an incredible coincidence had occurred.

The officer was Capt. Maxwell Becker, the Kweilin-based operator for a top secret U.S. intelligence organization in China called the Air Ground Aid Section. Created in late 1943 to conduct rescue operations for downed American airmen in China, AGAS was interested in escape routes and networks of people who could assist its operations all over the country. Peter's recent experience escaping from Shanghai to Kweilin was of interest to Becker and AGAS. More than that, Becker happened to be uniquely able to understand what had brought Peter to this place. Becker had been born and raised in Korea, and he and Peter had lived improbably parallel lives there.

Becker also had been born in Pyongyang, the son of an American science professor teaching at Union Christian College, Korea's first modern institution of higher education. He and Peter had moved from Pyongyang to Seoul at almost the same time in 1915. Becker's father moved to Seoul to become part of the original faculty of Chosun Christian College when it was founded that year, and Peter's father had moved there to study at Chosun Christian College's medical school.

Three decades later, the war had brought them together in Kweilin to discuss intelligence. Peter had a wealth of information on conditions in Shanghai and how his group had escaped from the city, moved through Japanese-controlled territory, and then made its way through the vast no-man's-land of guerrilla-held countryside and barely governed spaces in eastern China. During the debriefing, Becker realized that Peter's arrival had brought an intelligence windfall and that other military intelligence organizations would want to speak with him as well.[17]

Peter continued his efforts to reach out to old friends from prewar Shanghai and ended up finding exactly the right one in exactly the right place. Through the U.S. Consulate in Kweilin, he succeeded in contacting his closest childhood friend—Roy McNair Jr. They had met eighteen years earlier on the passenger liner that had brought their families to Shanghai in 1926, and when Peter's family had been on the run from Japanese police in 1932, the McNair family had given them shelter. Now Capt. Roy McNair of the U.S. Army was the assistant military attaché in China and stationed in the distant Nationalist capital of Chongqing.[18]

Roy McNair's commander was also the right man in the right place. The military attaché in Chongqing was Col. Morris DePass, one of the U.S. Army's most experienced China hands, whose expertise extended to Korea as well. Years earlier, in the first weeks after Pearl Harbor, Col. William Donovan—soon to become the founder and director of the Office of Strategic Services, the pioneering U.S. intelligence agency—had asked DePass to devise a plan for U.S intelligence operations in China that relied on recruiting Koreans, who had been resisting Japanese imperialism for decades.[19] Now McNair had found DePass a Korean who was eager to join the fight against Japan and had proven his loyalty to the United States. Peter's value to the war effort in China was obvious to DePass, who moved to recruit him right away.

DePass arranged for Peter to fly to Chongqing on a U.S. military transport plane. It was Peter's second offer to fly in an American warplane since he had left Shanghai, and this time there was no mistake about his identity and every reason to accept—except one.

Richard had no place in these plans. Peter would have to leave Richard and their entire group from Shanghai behind in Kweilin. They would have to fend for themselves, with the Imperial Japanese Army moving closer and closer to Kweilin. Fortunately, an old friend from Shanghai was now an American diplomat at the U.S. Consulate in Kweilin and was willing to look after Richard. He was John Service, who later in the war became a controversial figure for his favorable reports on the Chinese Communists and in 1950 was named in Senator Joseph McCarthy's list of Communist Party members in the State Department.[20]

On July 8 Peter boarded a C-47 transport that would take him to meet his future. The plane took off, bound for Chongqing, and soon left Kweilin behind.

Richard remained in Kweilin, working as a laborer at the air base, until the unstoppable advance of Operation Ichigo drew near. Changsha had fallen on June 19, making Hengyang the next target of the offensive, and Japanese forces soon besieged the city's outnumbered and outgunned Chinese defenders. They resisted valiantly for weeks but finally could hold out no longer, surrendering on August 8. The Japanese then continued their onslaught toward the chain of U.S. air bases in central China, with Kweilin next in their sights. U.S. forces had to hastily evacuate the air base and retreat, cratering the runway, burning the buildings, and destroying gasoline, ammunition, and other supplies so that the Japanese could not capture and use them.[21]

Richard left Kweilin during this ignominious retreat. He was fortunate that Peter's friend at the consulate was able to arrange for him to leave Kweilin with a retreating U.S. military unit instead of having to fend for himself, alone among masses of Chinese civilians fleeing by train or on foot. Richard got to ride in the back of a U.S. Army truck, sitting in its cargo bed between barrels of diesel fuel. The truck was part of a convoy headed south, away from the Japanese advance. The convoy reached Liuchow (now Liuzhou), a hundred miles to the south, by the end of the day. The next day it headed west, toward the safety of the U.S. air base at Kunming more than four hundred miles away.

Richard was a sixteen-year-old left on his own in a massive, chaotic war. He had an uncertain future ahead of him but still had ample reason to be optimistic. Caught up in a retreat, a defeat for the U.S. and Allied cause, he was nevertheless finally involved in the Americans' war effort against Japan. It was only a matter of time before American power reversed the Japanese tide sweeping through China, and he now had hope that he would be part of the final victory. But first, he and Peter each had to make that hope into reality.

7

Peter and Richard Kim, American Soldiers

PETER KIM WAS finally at the headquarters of the U.S. forces in China, where his once distant hope of enlisting in the U.S. Army could finally become reality. He had spent a month on the run from Shanghai, then a month in Kweilin trying to make this moment possible. Having flown to Chongqing in a matter of hours on July 8, 1944, he met Colonel DePass, who recognized his unique value to army intelligence and was intent on inducting him as soon as possible. Peter immediately applied for enlistment with DePass's support and assistance.

Then the issue that had done so much to determine the entire course of his life intruded again: Peter was not a U.S. citizen. In the eyes of army bureaucracy, he was a national of China who needed special authorization to join the U.S. Army. Becoming a commissioned officer such as Roy McNair and other friends from Shanghai was out of the question. Even joining the enlisted ranks would take time, since his intended role in the intelligence branch required investigating his background to ensure that he was not an agent of Japanese intelligence. Colonel DePass could do nothing to speed up the administrative process, so a long wait ensued before Peter could enlist.

The rest of July 1944 passed with no answer, then the entire month of August, then most of September. Peter could only wait in Chongqing while Operation Ichigo rampaged across central China almost five hundred miles to the east and advanced toward Kweilin, where he had left Richard. But Peter did not let this time go to waste. He used it to reconnect with his long-lost brother James, whom he had not seen since taking him to the evacuation ship out of Shanghai in 1937 and from whom he had heard nothing since December 7, 1941.

With access to the administrative machinery of the U.S. Army, Peter was able to establish contact with James for the first time since the Japanese occupation of Shanghai had cut them off from each other. While they were together in Kweilin, Peter and Richard had started inquiring about James and asked U.S. authorities for help in sending a message to their brother, who they knew had been serving in the army. In Chongqing, Roy McNair eagerly assisted Peter's efforts to locate James among the army's vast forces scattered all over the world. McNair succeeded in working through the army's globe-spanning bureaucracy to find James and learned not only that James was alive but also that he was serving in the Pacific with the 40th Infantry Division.[1]

The Kim brothers began to reconnect as Peter and Richard, hundreds of miles apart in China, reached out to James on a distant island in the South Pacific. Peter in Chongqing and Richard in Kweilin wrote letters to Pvt. James Kim in California that somehow made their way through the army mail system to New Britain, where Lieutenant Kim was serving with the 40th Infantry Division. James replied using V-mail, or Victory mail, a Second World War military postal system that used microfilm to transport miniaturized photocopies of letters. These small pieces of U.S. military mail, among the millions flying back and forth across the Pacific, started the broth-ers on their long path to reunion.

Peter also used his long wait in Chongqing to reconnect with old friends from Shanghai who were in the city with the U.S. Army or working for U.S. intelligence. Roy McNair was only the first. Another was Maxcy Smith, son of Presbyterian missionary H. Maxcy Smith, who had been interned with his family in Shanghai and released in the repatriation voyage that Peter had organized in 1942. Smith returned to China as a captain in the U.S. Army Air Forces, flying a transport plane for the Air Transport Command.[2] Yet another was Harry Bernard, a graduate of the Shanghai American School who had gone to work for Texaco in French Indochina. Bernard and other

Texaco employees had started the GBT Group (a freelance intelligence organization named after the last initials of its three founders), which worked for AGAS in Southeast Asia. Bernard had relocated to Chongqing, where he was officially a manager for Texaco.[3]

Peter's wait finally came to an end after almost three months had passed. On September 30, 1944, he swore the oath to defend the United States against all enemies and became Private Kim, U.S. Army. At last, he was an American soldier, starting at the bottom of the enlisted ranks.[4]

Assigned to the Military Intelligence Service, Private Kim received orders to go on detached service with a joint intelligence center in Chongqing named the Joint Intelligence Collection Agency (JICA).[5] He immediately became its expert on Japanese-occupied areas of China. His firsthand knowledge of Shanghai and other places that few Americans had seen since Japanese forces had conquered them years earlier soon became widely known and in demand in other intelligence organizations. The OSS, Fourteenth Air Force intelligence, and the intelligence section of the U.S. Forces–China Theater's general staff were among the agencies that obtained the lowly buck private on detail from JICA in the months that followed.[6]

Two months after he enlisted, Peter was reunited with his brother Richard. On December 9, 1944, JICA issued orders transferring Peter to its office in Kunming, the city in the foothills of the Himalayas where the main U.S. air base in China was located.[7] Richard had ended up in Kunming at the end of the long retreat from Kweilin in October.

Again alone in a strange city, Richard had the good fortune to find a place to live with a connection from Shanghai as distant and improbable as could be—Ernest Moy, whose estranged wife, Ruth, had for years been Peter's girlfriend. Richard's only connection to Moy was having been a friend of his son Loring, who had lived with Ruth in Shanghai. Ernest Moy may have had hard feelings toward Peter, but they did not extend to his teenage younger brother at a time of need during the war. Richard had lucked into as good a place to stay as could be found in Kunming—the house of a Nationalist Chinese official holding the honorary rank of general.

Staying there for as long as possible would have tempted many, but Richard was determined to follow in his brothers' footsteps and enlist in the U.S.

Army. For him, though, the problem was that he was too young, being only a few months past his seventeenth birthday. Not until June 1945 would he be eighteen years old and eligible to enlist. But lying about his age was easy when his personal records all were in Japanese-occupied Shanghai, and an officer was willing to help him—Capt. Roy McNair, Peter's best friend from Shanghai. McNair provided a letter attesting that Richard was older than eighteen, and an officer's word was enough evidence for the army.

Richard Kim was sworn in as an enlisted man in the U.S. Army on December 7, 1944, exactly three years after the attack on Pearl Harbor. Like Peter, he was not yet a U.S. citizen, but he was already an American soldier.[8]

Pvt. Richard Kim's first assignment was as a clerk and typist in a Services of Supply (SOS) unit in Kunming. He arrived hardly able to type, so he served under an American civilian working for the SOS as a secretary—a Maryknoll sister named Mary Colombiere. The Catholic nun, from an American organization that had run missions in China since 1921, showed the seventeen-year-old private how to type and handle army administrative tasks.[9]

Richard's SOS unit would cause a dramatic change in Peter's work for army intelligence. In February 1945 its commander, Col. Burton Vaughan, requested Peter for a mission in the distant province of Hunan near the front lines outside of Changsha. Now Private First Class Kim impressed Colonel Vaughan so much that the colonel retained him on an extended detachment from JICA. Vaughan gave him a free hand to survey Shanghai and other coastal cities, and to access any classified information that he needed.

Peter's assignment was to assess the procurement of supplies in Japanese-occupied areas where U.S. and Chinese forces expected to operate later in 1945, but on his own initiative, Peter spent his spare time studying the Shanghai internment camps. Looking ahead to their eventual liberation, Peter assembled information on the locations of the camps, the numbers of people in them, and the materials needed to keep the thousands of internees alive and healthy in a city of millions where food, medicines, and other essentials were already in short supply. His own memories were the most valuable information on Shanghai available. Liberating his friends and compatriots was his personal mission and occupied his thoughts and his efforts night after night. One day, he hoped, his work would help to save American lives in Shanghai.[10]

During this assignment, Peter made a new friend who soon became a key influence on his wartime service in the U.S. Army—Lt. Robert Peaslee. An officer on Colonel Vaughan's staff who was a native of Minnesota and from a family with Republican Party connections, Peaslee took an immediate liking to Peter, as so many Americans had over the years. Peaslee and Vaughan saw that Peter would be a valuable addition to their office, so they sought to have him permanently reassigned to work for them.

They got what they wanted in July 1945, when orders arrived transferring Peter from JICA to the U.S. Forces–China Theater's general staff in Chongqing. Colonel Vaughan and Captain Peaslee had him assigned to the General Staff's Civil Affairs section, the G-5 in army terminology. The G-5 was responsible for a range of key issues relating to the U.S. military alliance with Nationalist China: political and economic affairs, military assistance under the Lend-Lease program, training of Chinese forces, and combined U.S.-Chinese clandestine operations.

After Peter reported for duty at the China theater's headquarters on July 20, 1945, he met two high-ranking officers who would change the course of his life. His official military role as an intelligence analyst remained unchanged, and his rank was almost the same, having been promoted only to technician fifth grade—a Second World War–era rank between private and corporal that was normally used for junior enlisted specialists such as radiomen and interpreters. The reputation that Peter had earned in the nine months since his enlistment preceded him, however, and it soon led to special relationships with two rising-star officers far above him in the chain of command: the G-5 commander, Brig. Gen. George Olmsted, and his deputy, Col. Marshall Carter.

General Olmsted was a 1922 graduate of the U.S. Military Academy at West Point who became a successful businessman in the insurance industry during the 1920s and 1930s. Recalled to active duty in January 1942, he had managed the global Lend-Lease military assistance program. Then he was promoted to brigadier general and sent to China to establish the G-5 general staff section in 1944. After the war, he would build an even larger insurance and banking conglomerate. He used his fortune to endow the George Olmsted Foundation, whose Olmsted Scholar Program became a premier foreign education program for U.S. military officers by sponsoring them to live overseas for graduate study at foreign universities.[11]

Colonel Carter was a 1931 graduate of West Point and would become a key leader of the postwar U.S. intelligence community. Gen. George Catlett Marshall, chief of staff of the U.S. Army during the Second World War, chose Carter as one of his aides while serving as the special envoy to China in 1946 and during his appointments as secretary of state in 1947–49 and secretary of defense in 1950–51. Carter ascended to become a lieutenant general and a leader of two of the main U.S. intelligence agencies. He served as the deputy director of Central Intelligence in 1962–65 and became the fifth director of the National Security Agency in 1965–69.

Olmsted and Carter recognized Peter as both an exceptionally valuable asset to their command and a natural leader. Peter's knowledge of occupied China, especially Shanghai, made him unique among all the officers and enlisted men in the China theater's general staff. His low enlisted rank became meaningless to them. Although Peter had no command authority over anyone, not being an officer or even a noncommissioned officer, Olmsted and Carter entrusted him with independent actions that normally an officer would be selected to perform.

Marshall Carter soon became Peter's close friend. A vast gulf existed between the ranks of the colonel and the junior enlisted man, and their lives up to then could not have been more dissimilar, but these differences mattered little to Carter. Peter became more than a trusted subordinate; Carter came to regard him as a comrade in arms whose life split between Asia and America had brought them together against seemingly impossible odds. They were also near enough in age, with Peter being thirty-three years old and Carter only a couple of years older at thirty-five, that they were more akin to younger and older brothers than a normal enlisted man and a high-ranking officer.

General Olmsted showed his respect for Peter by making him an extraordinary promise. Knowing the depth of Peter's concern for the fate of the Americans living in captivity in Shanghai, Olmsted promised that when the time finally came for U.S. forces to launch a mission to rescue them, Peter would have an opportunity to lead it.[12] A general making this kind of pledge to a junior enlisted man, vanishingly distant in the chain of command, was practically unheard of. Olmsted, a leader and a builder of institutions in the army and in civilian life, saw Peter as worthy of it. But no one could know what would eventually happen if the time finally came for this mission amid the unpredictable events of a world war.

8

American Underground

WHILE PETER AND Richard found their places in the U.S. Army in free China, the rest of the Kim family in Shanghai continued their struggle against the city's Japanese occupiers without Peter there to lead them. The Kims' isolation from the outside world since December 1941 finally opened slightly in late 1944, though, for they had become distantly connected to the U.S. war effort. They became U.S. intelligence assets in Shanghai, brought in by the same American intelligence officer who had met Peter and Richard on their way to free China—Lt. Jack Young.

Jack Young was a Chinese American born in Hawaii who had become a U.S. Army intelligence officer after living a grand life in Shanghai and fighting against the Japanese invasion of China. In 1929 he and his brother Quentin led Theodore Roosevelt Jr. and Kermit Roosevelt on the expedition that caught the first giant panda brought to North America.[1] In 1932 Jack was part of an American mountain climbing team that set a world record by reaching the 24,900-foot summit of Mount Gongga in Sichuan.[2] Married to a niece of Ernest Moy's in 1933, he became an officer in the Nationalist Chinese armed forces after the Japanese invasion began in 1937. After the attack on Pearl Harbor, he faced a mandatory recall to U.S. military service and in December 1943 received a commission as a U.S. Army Reserve officer, becoming First Lieutenant Young.

Lieutenant Young went on to become one of the U.S. Army's leading intelligence officers in Asia. Initially sent to Burma to serve as an aide-de-camp to U.S. Forces–China Theater commander Lt. Gen. Joseph Stilwell, he became a field operative in China in 1944. Fluent in Mandarin Chinese, other Chinese dialects, Japanese, and Korean, and able to blend in anywhere in China, Young was one of only a few officers in any U.S. intelligence organization capable of operating clandestinely in Japanese-occupied China.[3]

Young had by chance run into Peter and Richard in Kukong (Shaoguan) in June 1944 while on his way from Kunming to Shanghai. Young had been moving along the same smuggling trade route that Peter and Richard had followed, but Young went north into Japanese-controlled territory. He had been headed first to the Nationalist capital of Nanjing, which had become the capital of the Empire of Japan's Chinese puppet regime. His ultimate destination was Shanghai. There he would organize an underground network to collect information for U.S. Army intelligence while based in a safe house maintained by a Chinese American who had been living under Japanese occupation since 1941.

Ruth Moy was the owner of the safe house. After Ernest Moy had connected U.S. Army intelligence to her, she was prepared to provide a refuge for American agents operating in Shanghai. A relative by marriage and a friend of Ernest Moy, Young embarked on his journey from Kunming to Shanghai informed about Ruth and her relationship with Peter Kim. Young remembered Peter well enough to recognize him in the street in Kukong.[4]

Young arrived in Shanghai in early July and set about organizing intelligence collection in the city. The Kim family, already known to Young and with proven loyalty to the United States, soon was among his assets.

David and Arthur, the two brothers remaining in Shanghai, acted as a team under Young's direction. Young gave instructions on what information to collect to David, who passed them to Arthur to carry out. Arthur, being only fourteen years old in 1944, was young and harmless-appearing enough to move around the city without arousing the suspicion of Japanese soldiers or police patrolling the streets who might stop and question an adult such as twenty-seven-year-old David.

David never told Arthur who was behind these missions or the purpose of any of them. David kept him in the dark about Jack Young, since he had no need to know, and the less that Arthur knew the less that he could divulge if Japanese soldiers or police captured and questioned him. It was a hard introduction to intelligence tradecraft for the fourteen-year-old, who had no choice but to follow his orders unquestioningly and without any idea of the purpose behind the risks that he was taking.

A series of forays into Hongkew, the quarter of Shanghai inhabited mainly by Japanese civilians, were the riskiest of these missions. Arthur repeatedly received instructions to go to Hongkew to purchase Japanese newspapers and return home with them. These newspapers published reports on Japanese troop movements, economic conditions in Japanese-occupied Shanghai, and other information of military significance, making them valuable open-source intelligence. Obtaining them required traveling several miles across town from the French Concession to Hongkew, north of Suzhou Creek, and then hauling the pile of papers back across town to the French Concession.

Arthur set off from the family house on Route Père Robert on a bicycle, originally purchased by his adult brothers and too large for him, to pedal the several miles to Hongkew. Along the way he had to cross an arched stone bridge over Suzhou Creek. At the center peak of the bridge stood a pillbox with a Japanese soldier who expected anyone crossing the bridge to bow deeply while passing him. The sentry could arbitrarily stop and search—or assault—anyone for no reason. Arthur would then have to pass the guard post again on the return trip from Hongkew.

The bridge crossing was almost Arthur's undoing. During one return trip laden with newspapers, he was struggling to walk his bicycle across the bridge, which was too steeply sloped to pedal, when the Japanese soldier in the middle of the bridge stopped him. Arthur tried to bow, but the adult-size bicycle that he was trying to hold upright had handlebars as high as his chest, making it impossible for him to do more than a partial bow. Enraged by the seeming lack of respect, the Japanese soldier slapped Arthur hard across the face, almost knocking him over. The bayoneted rifle in the soldier's hands could have come next. Arthur dropped the bicycle to bow fully, and the Japanese soldier, finally satisfied, dismissed him.[5]

These missions continued until Jack Young left Shanghai in November 1944. Young returned to Kunming, where he reunited with Ernest Moy and was able to congratulate Richard Kim on his December 7 enlistment in the U.S. Army. Arthur, David, Betty, and their mother remained in Shanghai, where their lives became increasingly precarious as Japan continued to lose the war.

The Kims did not know that James, whom they had not seen for seven years, was at that very moment preparing for his first fight in the long U.S. island-hopping campaign from the South Pacific to Japan's home islands. Soon he would see combat in the battles to liberate the Philippines.

9

Baptism of Fire

A MIGHTY U.S. Navy armada of more than eight hundred ships approached the Philippine island of Luzon on January 6, 1945, ready to start the campaign to liberate the Philippine capital of Manila. A force of more than two hundred thousand U.S. Army soldiers, larger than the Allied armies that had gone ashore in Normandy on D-Day exactly seven months earlier, waited on board the fleet's troop transports. Among them was the 40th Infantry Division, about to experience combat for the first time. Lt. James Kim of the 160th Infantry Regiment was one of the thousands of men about to receive their baptism of fire.

Three days earlier, out at sea, began the harrowing experience of the suicide attacks of Japan's Divine Wind Special Attack Units, the dreaded kamikazes. Dozens of Japanese aircraft appeared and dived from the skies toward the fleet's vessels, their pilots willing to kill themselves for the chance to take an American ship with them. The kamikaze attacks continued, day after day, as the fleet approached Luzon. By the end of the battle, these human-guided missiles had sunk an aircraft carrier and three destroyers, and had damaged forty-three more ships, killing and wounding more than two thousand sailors.

While the kamikazes rained down from the sky, the U.S. fleet opened up a devastating attack of its own on January 6. The big guns of six battleships, cruisers, and destroyers began firing their massive shells at suspected Japanese shore defenses around Lingayen Gulf, about a hundred miles north of Manila and where Japanese forces had landed to begin their conquest of the Philippine capital in December 1941. Carrier aircraft joined the bombardment, flying over the island to bomb targets farther inland. The rain of steel and high explosives continued all day, then the next day, then the next. More than sixteen thousand shells and almost eight hundred air sorties hammered the shore.

As the shells and bombers roared overhead, the hour for the amphibious landings to begin drew closer. Minesweepers carefully cleared Japanese sea mines from the waters approaching the landing beaches. The soldiers waiting to land on those beaches could only wait anxiously and try to sleep at night as the ships' guns blasted away and as the kamikazes appeared to threaten them with death from above.

The moment that they had been waiting for finally came early in the morning of January 9. The order to board the landing craft went out to the troop transports of the infantry divisions in the first wave to hit the beaches. Thousands of soldiers laden with their weapons and gear clambered down rope ladders over the sides of their transport ships to the landing craft waiting in the rough sea below.

Tension was high among the National Guardsmen of the 160th Infantry Regiment as they readied themselves for their first fight against the Japanese. On James's transport, the troops were roused to get ready for action at around 1:00 a.m., and they had hours to kill before the amphibious operation began. An uproar broke out when the ship's loudspeakers announced an order from the captain that all army personnel were to clean their quarters before debarking. The navy's housekeeping instructions enraged men of the 160th who were already anxious about the imminent battle. When the time came to make their way through the ship's corridors to the deck to board their landing craft, many of them let out their anger by pulling their bayonets—sharpened to cut through Japanese guts—out of their scabbards and punching holes in the ship's air-conditioning ducts as they walked past them.[1]

Misery took over as they waited to hit the beach. After boarding their landing craft, they had to wait for hours before heading toward the shore.

The flat-bottomed boats pitched about in the rough sea and made many of them seasick. James became so nauseous that he ceased to care whether the enemy met them on the beach; he just wanted the ordeal to end.

When their landing craft finally headed toward the shore and seemed to hit it, lowering its bow ramp, he and his men rushed over the ramp and plunged into water so deep that many of them had their heads pulled underwater. The craft's hull had grounded on a submerged sandbar, and its ramp had dumped the men into the deeper water beyond it. James's head went under, and he felt that he was drowning, weighted down by his weapon and gear, before he managed to fight his way forward and onto the beach.[2]

On the beach, everything suddenly changed. No machine guns opened fire at them, and not one artillery shell hit the beach. The Japanese were gone. American naval gunfire roaring overhead toward targets farther inland was the only sign that a battle was underway. Unopposed on their landing beach, James and his men collected themselves, got organized, and moved out.

The beach was undefended because the Japanese were now fighting differently than they had on Guadalcanal in 1943 and on Tarawa in 1944. They had retreated inland before the naval bombardment and aerial attacks. They would not fight to the death on the shore or make banzai charges at the beachhead. Instead, they planned to lure U.S. forces into attacking strategically located hills that the Japanese had fortified months in advance, using natural caves and digging tunnels to create underground fortresses that artillery and aerial bombing could not destroy. It would be a preview of what American forces would experience on Iwo Jima a month later and then on Okinawa in April–June 1945.

The 40th Infantry Division had landed on the westernmost invasion beach at the town of Lingayen, with three other divisions landing farther to the east. The 160th Infantry Regiment encountered no opposition as it advanced past Lingayen and moved several miles inland by the evening.[3] The city of Baguio, where James's father had founded a tuberculosis sanitarium two decades earlier, was only a few dozen miles away in the hills beyond the easternmost landing beach. James might have known about it, but in any case, he had no time to be sentimental about a place that was now beyond the Americans' left flank and soon to be left far behind as they marched to Manila.

The advance south toward Manila resumed the next morning, with the 40th Infantry Division continuing to move forward on the right flank and the 160th Infantry Regiment on the division's right. The men encountered little opposition as they advanced down the highway to Manila. Fourteen days later, they had advanced seventy miles and were approaching Clark Field, the airfield forty miles northwest of Manila that had been the main U.S. air base in the Philippines before the Japanese occupied it.

There the troops finally found Japanese forces well prepared and determined to stand their ground. Several thousand infantry with tanks and artillery had dug in at Clark Field and the Bamban Hills that overlooked it, blocking the highway to Manila. In the hills, two ridges were honeycombed with networks of tunnels. Several six-inch naval guns—heavy, long-barreled guns made to be fixed to warships and coastal defenses, with far longer range than army field artillery—were emplaced in caves to threaten the airfield and the route for American troops and supplies moving south past the hills. The naval guns had to be knocked out to clear the way for the advance to Manila to continue.

To take the ridges and destroy the naval guns, the 40th Infantry Division would have to attack Japanese troops occupying formidable fortifications. Japanese machine guns, firing from well-protected positions deep in the caves, could rake approaching Americans with lethal fire while remaining almost invulnerable to the rifles, machine guns, and mortars of the infantry. The tunnels enabled Japanese troops to move unobserved to reinforce positions under attack. Every weapon in the 40th Infantry Division's arsenal would be needed to knock out the Japanese machine gun positions one by one and reduce the underground fortress in the Bamban Hills.[4]

The 160th Infantry Regiment led the assault on the ridges on January 24. M-10 tank destroyers and M-7 self-propelled howitzers, protected by armor and able to fire devastating high-explosive shells from long ranges, fired directly into the caves to knock out the naval guns and machine guns, and to clear the way for the infantry to close in. Infantrymen then had to approach within a few feet of a cave's entrance to finish off its defenders with hand grenades, demolition charges, and flamethrowers.

The attacking infantry had to move forward slowly and carefully, constantly under fire from Japanese machine guns deep in their caves in the ridges above. Machine gun and rifle fire repeatedly pinned the men down, and mortar bombs and hand grenades blasted among them while they took cover. Four days of combat were needed before the 160th Infantry Regiment finally reached the peak of its ridge on January 28. The other ridge, attacked by the division's 108th Infantry Regiment, fell the next day. With the Japanese barrier on the highway to Manila eliminated, the U.S. Army's advance toward the Philippine capital could continue.[5]

The end of the 40th Infantry Division's first major fight of the war was only the beginning of a long, grueling battle in the mountains west of Manila. As most of the U.S. forces that had landed at Lingayen Gulf raced south toward Manila, the 40th Infantry Division continued attacking to the west into the Bamban Hills, pursuing Japanese forces retreating into the rugged terrain of the Zambales Mountains. The hills around Mount Pinatubo—famous half a century later for a 1991 volcanic eruption that killed more than eight hundred people, buried Clark Field in ash, and caused climate change worldwide—became a Japanese redoubt that held out on the long right flank of U.S. forces advancing on Manila. The 40th Infantry Division had to take hill after hill where the Japanese had dug in, determined to resist as long as possible.

A fight for a peak named Storm King Mountain would occupy the 160th Infantry Regiment for more than a week. To reach it, the men first had to take a promontory three hundred yards away from the ridge that they had taken on January 28. The only way to approach the promontory was a narrow neck of high ground, no more than seventy-five yards across at its widest point, that was covered with thick jungle and flanked by steep slopes that would be practically impossible to climb under fire.

In the men's way was a company of Japanese airborne troops from the 2nd Glider-Borne Infantry Regiment. These elite airborne infantrymen were dug into another array of well-prepared defensive positions—150 rifle and machine gun pits that were covered with logs and earth, and concealed by bamboo growing on top of them, or that were made by digging under the roots of large trees—each of which was almost impossible to see and difficult to destroy. Formidable firepower backed them: a 70mm field gun, three

90mm mortars, seventeen light and ten heavy machine guns, and ten small but deadly Japanese grenade launchers that Americans called knee mortars.[6]

James's battalion commander, Maj. John McSevney, was killed at the start of the attack. McSevney was at the front line reconnoitering the Japanese defenses when a burst of machine gun fire suddenly hit and killed him only a few feet away from James. When his men moved forward without him, they had to find the Japanese positions one by one—almost always as the rifles and machine guns inside them opened fire—and destroy the bunkers and the men inside them, all while under fire from other positions in the Japanese defensive system. The fighting went on day after day. The 160th Infantry was able to move forward only a few dozen yards each day, losing men every step of the way. Not until February 6, ten days after it began, would the attack finally succeed in crossing the three hundred yards and reaching the top of Storm King Mountain.[7]

The 160th Infantry advanced again on February 11 to attack another complex of fortified hills. Occupying its caves and tunnels were more elite Japanese troops, elements of the 2nd Glider-Borne Infantry Regiment and a unit of the Special Naval Landing Forces, the Imperial Japanese Navy's marines. The 160th Infantry moved forward supported by artillery emplaced on Storm King Mountain—155mm howitzers from James's old unit, the 222nd Field Artillery Battalion, and a 90mm antiaircraft gun—to blast direct fire at cave machine gun positions. Again, infantrymen endured hails of fire as they moved toward the mouths of the caves to eliminate the Japanese inside them with demolition charges.[8]

James, leading his battalion's demolitions squad, captured the 160th Infantry's first prisoner of war during cave-clearing actions on February 11. Immediately after the explosion of a demolition charge in a cave, he rushed toward the cave's entrance with his Thompson submachine gun raised and saw a Japanese soldier come out, firing his rifle. James killed him with a burst of .45 bullets; then he saw another Japanese soldier stagger out of the cave. Acting on instinct, James moved toward him, ordering his men not to shoot and shouting in Japanese he had learned from the army's Japanese phrase book. When he got close enough, he seized the Japanese soldier, who turned out to be badly wounded by the explosion, with his eyes swollen shut and blood pouring from his ears and nose.

The wounded man gestured that he wanted to be shot, but James instead gave him water and had one of his men give him a cigarette. Inside the cave, they found only the dead bodies of Japanese soldiers killed by the demolition charge. Their captive was alive but could not see or walk, so James had him carried down the hill and taken to the rear for interrogation.[9]

A day later, he led a team crawling along a streambed toward the sound of enemy movement when its point man suddenly was shot dead. James and his men threw hand grenades at the sound of the shot, and as he tried to move forward to get around the enemy sniper, a bullet cut through the hip pocket of his uniform trousers. He dived behind cover and again lobbed grenades, but the unseen enemy escaped.[10]

The entire 40th Infantry Division moved forward to finish off the remaining Japanese forces in the Bamban Hills on February 23. What was left of the enemy occupied yet another prepared defensive system of caves and bunkers in the area's hills. Here their arsenal included another formidable weapon— 20mm automatic cannons. Scavenged from wrecked aircraft and repurposed as infantry weapons, these massive machine guns fired powerful armor-piercing and high-explosive shells made to bring down an airplane. Along with the machine guns, mortars, and rifles of the elite Japanese airborne and marines, the 20mm guns would be a deadly barrier to the approaching soldiers of the 160th Infantry.[11]

The attack of James's battalion stalled only partway up a ridge with the Japanese holding its top. Radio contact with the lead company had been lost, so the new battalion commander sent James forward to figure out what was happening. He had to find its commander, Lt. Chester Robisch, somewhere on the front line and report back to battalion headquarters.

As James climbed the ridge, staying low to avoid presenting a target to Japanese machine gunners and snipers, he found the battalion chaplain lying flat on the ground. The chaplain somehow had been caught in the middle of the fight and was frozen with fear and unable to move. When James pushed him down the hill toward safety, the movement caused the chaplain to suddenly snap out of the fear that had gripped him and start crawling to the rear on his own.

Nearing the front line, James found the lead company pinned down just below the crest of the ridge. A 20mm gun was unleashing bursts of shells at anyone who raised his head or tried to move, intimidating the entire company into staying behind cover. Some were only twenty feet from the nearest enemy position but unable to move forward. Trying to find the lieutenant, James yelled over the 20mm gun's muzzle blasts for Robisch, who shouted back. He told James to wait until the 20mm gun stopped firing and he gave the signal. When the firing stopped and Robisch shouted, "Go!" James leaped from his cover toward the sound of the voice and found himself in Robisch's foxhole.[12]

Robisch explained that neither side had been able to force the other off the ridge and that his company would have to break off the fight soon. His men had enough food and water to last longer, but they were running out of ammunition. Unless resupplied, they would soon have no choice but to withdraw.

To go back and report to battalion headquarters, James first had to run the gauntlet of the 20mm gun again. He waited for a pause in its firing and made his move, jumping behind a rock a few feet back. The 20mm shells followed him, hammering the rock. He signaled the soldiers around him for smoke. When their smoke grenades created a cloud obscuring the enemy's view, he made his next move. The 20mm gun opened up again as he bolted, running wildly and yelling uncontrollably as the powerful shells chased him. As he ran his helmet fell off, and the field glasses around his neck—loaned to him by the battalion commander—flew away and were lost. He escaped the 20mm gun's fire and made his way back to the battalion headquarters.

After James made his report, the battalion commander told him to rest and not go back to the front line until the next day, and he tried to come down from the terror of what he had just been through. He looked for the battalion surgeon to get a sedative so that he could sleep for the rest of the day. He found the doctor in his dugout, got his pills, and turned away to leave when the doctor told him that he had blood all over his pants. James reached back, felt that his backside was wet and warm, and then saw that his hand was covered with blood. He had been shot in the butt at some point during the action and had not even noticed. Suddenly seeing his own blood while his adrenaline was wearing off, he passed out.[13]

James soon recovered from the flesh wound in his rear end and returned to the front line. More fighting from hill to hill followed, with the Japanese still resisting but weakening with each fight. By March 1, the men of the 160th Infantry had been through fifty-three days of combat since their amphibious landing at Lingayen Gulf, thirty-seven of them in the hills west of Clark Field. On March 2 another division relieved the 40th Infantry Division to continue mopping up the Japanese forces in the hills. The tired men of the 40th Infantry withdrew from the front line and back toward Lingayen Gulf for a well-earned rest before their next operation.[14]

The Battle of Manila officially ended the next day. More than two thousand American soldiers had died fighting from the beaches of Lingayen Gulf to the streets of Manila. The battle had almost completely destroyed the city, and more than one hundred thousand Filipino civilians had perished, caught in the crossfire or massacred by Japanese soldiers and marines taking out their anger on the defenseless men, women, and children in their midst. The savagery of Japanese atrocities in Manila provided a grim preview of what Japanese troops would do in the battles to come as they went through defeat after defeat.

After three years of waiting for their turn to fight, the campaign on Luzon from Lingayen Gulf to Manila had been the baptism of fire for James and the entire 40th Infantry Division. Their combat experience had been a long series of inglorious, exhausting, and sometimes terrifying moments, as it has been for millions of soldiers all over the world since time immemorial. Having begun the campaign seasick, James then had pursued and fought a mostly unseen enemy, killed at least one Japanese soldier, and watched his fellow officers and men under his command die. Near the end, he had been shot in the ass. Along the way, he and the 160th Infantry Regiment had taken on and defeated some of the Imperial Japanese Army's best troops, who were dug into the same kinds of fortifications that thousands of American soldiers and marines would die assaulting on Iwo Jima and Okinawa. James would receive a Bronze Star medal for capturing a Japanese soldier at Storm King Mountain and the Purple Heart for his wound.[15]

10

Army Intelligence Officer

A NEW KIND of war began for James and the 40th Infantry Division in mid-March 1945. Their first action had been the massive amphibious assault at Lingayen Gulf and the liberation of Manila. Now their mission became an island-hopping campaign within the Philippine archipelago to secure smaller islands where Japanese forces could threaten crucial sea-lanes. Their operations became largely independent of other U.S. military units. Instead, they fought side by side with Philippine guerrillas, who after years of organizing and waiting were ready to rise to free their homeland. Together these forces would be the liberators of entire Philippine islands.

James took on a new role as well. As the 160th Infantry Regiment took stock of its losses on Luzon and organized for the next campaign, James was withdrawn from the line to become a staff officer. Instead of commanding infantry, James became the intelligence officer (s-2) of the 160th Infantry's 1st Battalion. He had demonstrated an instinctive knack for intelligence when he captured a Japanese soldier to interrogate for information. By the end of the fighting in the Bamban Hills, he was already acting as an intelligence officer, as his battalion commander chose him to report on difficult tactical situations on the front line. James would command the battalion's intelligence section for the rest of the campaign in the Philippines.[1]

The first island of this campaign was Panay. Located two hundred miles south of Luzon, Panay was the sixth-largest Philippine island, whose largest city, Iloilo, had a harbor that was a key to controlling the straits between Luzon and Mindanao, the second-largest Philippine island. On March 15 elements of the 40th Infantry Division boarded amphibious assault ships in Lingayen Gulf for the voyage to Panay.[2] There a guerrilla organization of more than twenty thousand men under Col. Macario Peralta Jr.—a charismatic leader who after the war became a senator and the secretary of national defense in the Philippines—already controlled most of the countryside and was waiting to fight alongside the U.S. Army to complete the liberation of the island.[3]

James's battalion of the 160th Infantry Regiment remained behind on Luzon while the 185th Infantry, one battalion of the 160th Infantry, and the division's reconnaissance troop landed on Panay on March 18. As those units and Peralta's Philippine guerrillas liberated Iloilo and pursued the remaining Japanese forces into the inland mountains, reports of the Imperial Japanese Army's contempt for the lives of its own people came back. In one action, Japanese soldiers cornered by American troops turned their bayonets on those Japanese civilians who had been fleeing with them, killing sixty-two women and children before falling themselves to American fire. In a field hospital about to be overrun, Japanese soldiers killed fifty of their own by injecting them with a sedative and then setting the hospital on fire. The few who escaped surrendered and told their American interrogators about the massacre.[4]

Before the end of March, the 40th Infantry Division was able to turn over pursuit of the remaining Japanese to the guerrillas and begin preparing for the next phase of its island-hopping campaign. The entire division now readied itself for an amphibious landing on the neighboring island of Negros.[5]

The 40th Infantry Division boarded its amphibious assault ships and transports during the night of March 28 and landed on the west coast of Negros the following morning. The 185th Infantry Regiment again led the landing and the drive inland, and the 160th Infantry Regiment followed ashore the next day. The 160th Infantry encountered little opposition until the road upon which it was advancing approached a tall hill commanding the valley. Designated Hill 3155 after its elevation, it soon would be renamed

Dolan Hill, in tribute to 1st Lt. John Dolan, the first officer killed trying to capture it.

Dolan Hill was the anchor of a Japanese fortified area similar to those that the 160th Infantry had fought to overcome on Luzon. Far from the coast, it was beyond the reach of U.S. naval gunfire, and it had avoided notice by aerial reconnaissance. From its peak, the Japanese could observe and fire down on approaching U.S. troops, pounding them with mortars and more of the dreaded 20mm guns. Its slopes and those of the smaller hills around it were studded with bunkers from which Japanese machine guns could rain bullets on anyone trying to advance. The men of the 160th faced a hard fight before they could even reach Dolan Hill and battle their way up it.[6]

Opposing them was a ragtag Japanese force scraped together from what was left in the area: remnants of two infantry battalions and soldiers from transport, airfield, and harbor units with no trucks, airfields, or harbors left to operate.[7] The Japanese were isolated thousands of miles from their homeland with no hope of winning, and all they could do was keep fighting to the death, as ordered by their generals under the authority of their emperor. Delaying the advancing Americans and killing as many of them as possible, in the hope of somehow slowing down the inevitable invasion of their home islands, were all that they had left to fight and die for.

The 160th Infantry would spend almost two months in a seemingly endless struggle to take Dolan Hill. Its advance to the hill took two whole weeks. Japanese troops fought delaying actions by day, and when the Americans went into defensive perimeters at night, the Japanese infiltrated the forests around them and raided under cover of darkness. As the 160th closed in on Dolan Hill, the mortars and 20mm guns opened fire, stalling the advance and killing and wounding men. The 160th Infantry had to fight through rugged terrain cut by ravines and had to take a ring of fortified hills before the men finally reached the bottom of Dolan Hill.

For two days, artillery bombarded the hill in an attempt to weaken its defenders, and on April 17 infantrymen of the regiment's 1st Battalion began the assault. They advanced slowly, needing to cling to tree branches and roots to climb up the hill's steep slopes and eliminate the enemy positions that they found. They moved forward steadily for the entire first day, dug in for the night, and resumed their advance on the second day until they were within a hundred yards of the summit of Dolan Hill. When night fell, they established another defensive perimeter and prepared for the final assault the next morning.

Night attacks sent them retreating down the hill. From their bunkers in the heights above, the Japanese hurled grenades and explosive charges, and fired their mortars into the Americans below them. Unable to fire back at the unseen enemy and too close for their artillery to intervene without risking hitting them if they stayed, they had to fall back. The artillery bombarded the summit to cover their withdrawal and kept hammering it for the remainder of the night.

Day after day, the 160th Infantry resumed its attempts to advance to the top of Dolan Hill, and Japanese resistance stopped them with almost nothing to show for the Americans' effort and sacrifices. They were in a struggle reminiscent of the fighting on the western front in the First World War, being pinned down by Japanese machine guns in a network of bunkers connected by trenches and having any attempt to move forward or even raise a head to look around met by a hail of bullets. The steep sides of the hill prevented their working around the flanks of the defenses.

Even the mundane task of keeping the assault force supplied was a struggle on the steep, trackless hill. The 160th Infantry resorted to hiring hundreds of Filipino civilians to carry food, water, and ammunition to the front line, freeing its own men to fight in the dwindling ranks of the infantry companies on the hill. Engineers began to bulldoze a switchback road up the hill to ease the burden of moving up supplies as the battle went on and on.[8]

While the battle for Dolan Hill raged back and forth, James did all that he could to gather intelligence on its defenses. After James's 1st Battalion was the first unit of the 160th Infantry to try to fight its way up the hill, he regularly visited the infantry companies on the front line and sent the men of his intelligence section to stay with the company commanders full time and send back daily reports. He demanded that the division's Japanese American interpreters, who were normally kept at the divisional and regimental headquarters, be sent to the battalion and its front-line infantry companies to help encourage Japanese soldiers to surrender. Having taken a prisoner of war himself for interrogation using only Japanese words from a phrase book, he hoped that more could be done with the 40th Infantry Division's Japanese-speaking interpreters.[9]

The costly stalemate dragged on for so long that the commander of XIV Corps came all the way to Dolan Hill to confer with the commanders of the 40th Infantry Division and the 160th Infantry Regiment. Sitting nearby and watching the council of war were the officers of the 160th Infantry, including Lt. James Kim and Capt. Walter O'Brien, the regimental chaplain. They listened to Col. Raymund Stanton, the regimental commander, and Maj. Gen. Rapp Brush, the division commander, explain the situation on Dolan Hill to XIV Corps commander Lt. Gen. Oscar Griswold and tell him that the regiment could take the hill if given a few airstrikes to help soften up the enemy.

General Griswold then unexpectedly turned to Father O'Brien and asked for his thoughts on what his regimental and division commanders had just said. "Padre, you've heard all of this. What's your opinion?"

The army chaplain, a Catholic priest of the Capuchin order, had been ministering to the dead and wounded from Dolan Hill. He could not accept his commanders' ongoing optimism about the battle, and now he had an opportunity to speak for himself and the other officers of the regiment whose men had fought and died to take the hill without success. He struggled to find the right words for his thoughts in what appeared to be the only opportunity for anyone to speak freely to the corps commander. For a moment, he looked at the three senior officers before him, not knowing how to tell them what he knew had to be said. He then gave the general the simplest answer that he could: "That's a lot of crap!"

General Griswold smiled at the padre's plainspoken honesty. General Brush and Colonel Stanton did not. Father O'Brien expected to be reprimanded, but no reprimand came. Instead, his opinion ended up prevailing when the commanders made their plan for the next attack on Dolan Hill.[10]

The attack began with all of the infantry withdrawing from the hill, giving up the ground they had fought over and gained at great cost. They were putting a safe distance between themselves and the massive storm of steel and explosives to come. Then the 40th Infantry Division's artillery opened up, commencing a barrage of 105mm and 155mm howitzer shells that began on

May 11 and continued all day. It continued through the next day, then another, and for a fourth day, firing day and night. The artillery concentrated all of its fire on one part of the hill, then moved to others, systematically destroying its entire surface. P-38 Lightning and F 4 U Corsair fighter-bombers and A-20 Havoc twin-engine bombers strafed and bombed the hilltop, flying over a hundred sorties that further destroyed the hill's defenses. In the morning of May 15, the fifth day of the attack, the infantry finally moved forward up the hill again.

They found Dolan Hill and its Japanese defenders totally devastated by the four days of artillery bombardment and air strikes. The trees that once densely covered the slopes had disappeared, reduced to stumps. Pillbox after pillbox was found blasted apart. More than two hundred dead bodies of the enemy were scattered around. The 160th Infantry reached the top of Dolan Hill completely unopposed, not seeing a single Japanese soldier until they found a few dazed survivors on the sides of the hill.[11]

After the capture of Dolan Hill, the 40th Infantry Division continued its operations to clear Japanese forces from Negros for the rest of May 1945 and into the month of June. By early June, they had eliminated most of the Japanese forces on the island, and the last remnants of the enemy were demoralized and falling apart. With their supplies running out, the enemy was barely able to eat enough to stay alive. The 40th Infantry Division's intelligence section set up loudspeakers to broadcast appeals to surrender, which were delivered by the section's Japanese American interpreters and a Japanese prisoner of war who had volunteered to help bring his comrades in alive. Japanese soldiers then began to surrender, with small groups coming in each day to lay down their arms.

Their task of liberating the island of Negros accomplished, the 40th Infantry Division turned over further operations on the island to other U.S. forces and Philippine guerrillas. The 503rd Parachute Infantry Regiment and guerrillas of the Seventh Military District took over the sectors of the division's infantry regiments as June went on, and on July 1, full responsibility for the island passed to the paratroopers. All 40th Infantry Division units on the island returned to Iloilo, Panay, to prepare for their next mission.[12]

11

Victory over Japan

THE NEXT MISSION was the invasion of Japan. Almost four years after the attack on Pearl Harbor, the Allied advance across the Pacific had reached Japan itself. U.S. forces had captured the Japanese island of Iwo Jima after a ferocious battle in February and March 1945, and after landing on Okinawa on April 1 and eighty-two days of fighting, they finally defeated Japanese resistance in late June. Firebombing by B-29 Superfortress bombers had been reducing Tokyo and Japan's other main cities to ashes since March. All that remained was to finish the war by invading and occupying Japan's home islands.

Operation Downfall was the name of the planned invasion of Japan. The enormously powerful U.S. and Allied forces aimed to defeat Japan with two massive amphibious assaults. First, in Operation Olympic, forces would attack the southern island of Kyushu to draw in Japanese forces and to secure staging areas and airfields for the next phase. "X-Day," the date that the U.S. Army and Marine Corps would hit the beaches on Kyushu, was scheduled for November 1, 1945. Months later, in Operation Coronet, U.S. forces would invade the central island of Honshu and surround and conquer Tokyo. "Y-Day," the date for Operation Coronet, would not come until March 1, 1946, at the earliest.

James Kim was preparing to go ashore in the first wave of the invasion. The 40th Infantry Division was one of fourteen army and marine divisions assigned to Operation Olympic, and it would be the first to go into action. Its mission, four days before X-Day, was to attack and secure five islands off the coast of Kyushu that lay astride the sea-lanes to the invasion beaches. With Japanese coastal defenses cleared from the islands, the X-Day landings could proceed. The division would then join Operation Olympic's forces ashore for the long campaign that would follow, likely well into 1946.[1]

The invasion of Japan was to be the largest amphibious operation in the history of warfare, one against a still-formidable enemy fighting to defend their homeland. Three quarters of a million U.S. soldiers and Marines would fight on Kyushu in Operation Olympic and more than a million in the siege of Tokyo in Operation Coronet. Opposing them were Japanese forces that still numbered more than four million men with thousands of tanks and artillery pieces. Millions more Japanese civilians were being hastily trained and armed to fight in the last-ditch defense of their country. Thousands of kamikaze aircraft, suicide attack boats, and other weapons of the Divine Wind Special Attack Units waited to strike at the U.S. fleet as it approached Japanese waters and then floated offshore to support the ground forces.

Massive casualties were expected in the upcoming campaign. An estimate from the Pentagon in June 1945 was that about two hundred thousand U.S. servicemen would be killed or wounded in the invasion of Japan. General MacArthur's staff projected that more than one hundred thousand casualties would occur in Operation Olympic alone.[2] These figures, no more than rough guesses based on U.S. losses in the Battle of Okinawa that was ongoing at the time, would be dwarfed by the scale of Japanese military and civilian deaths, which were likely to number in the millions.

James and his fellow soldiers of the 40th Infantry Division did not need any official estimates to understand the grim task ahead of them. They had experienced how ferociously a few thousand determined Japanese soldiers could resist when isolated thousands of miles from home in a hostile country and with limited weapons, ammunition, and food to eat. Supposedly weak and beaten Japanese units had stopped and bloodied them on Storm King Mountain, then for two months on Dolan Hill. Now the division was going to have to fight millions of Japanese soldiers in the mountains and cities of their own country and backed by the firepower of tanks and artillery on a scale never seen on the islands of the South Pacific. The veteran American soldiers knew that few of them would make it through the invasion alive and unwounded.

They had also seen for themselves the terrible fate that the Imperial Japanese Army was ready to inflict on its own people. On Panay, the 40th Infantry Division's troops had witnessed Japanese women and children killed by their own country's soldiers with sickening cruelty, stabbed to death with bayonets, murdered by men facing them only a few feet away. U.S. forces on other Pacific island battlefields such as Saipan and Okinawa had seen mass suicides by Japanese civilians, forced to kill themselves by the Japanese army. The men of the 40th Infantry knew, as well as anyone, that the Imperial Japanese Army was ready to destroy its own people—every last man, woman, and child—rather than surrender.

For James, the terrible battle to come was going to bring his life in a full circle from where it had started. Living under Japanese imperialism in Korea, his family had left for America in search of a new life. Born in Los Angeles and having moved to Shanghai with his family, James had returned to the States in 1937 as a teenage refugee fleeing the Japanese invasion of China that had started the Second World War in Asia. Now he was about to complete his journey back across the Pacific as a grown man, an officer in the U.S. Army in the first wave of the invasion force that would bring down the Empire of Japan and end the war.

The 40th Infantry Division began preparing for its role in the invasion at the beginning of July. At its base on the island of Panay, its units took in replacements for the soldiers lost in the Philippine campaign, reequipped, and trained for the intense combat expected on the home islands of Japan. Training for the amphibious assaults to be carried out ahead of Operation Olympic on Kyushu occupied the men for weeks in July and August. The army had set up an amphibious training school at Subic Bay, the recaptured U.S. Navy base on Luzon that U.S. forces would continue to use until 1992. Its training exercises sent an entire infantry regiment at a time in transport ships to practice landing on beaches on Panay and Negros.[3]

On August 16 the 160th Infantry Regiment was at sea on its way to a practice amphibious assault when an unexpected announcement blared from the loudspeakers of the transports. The captain of each ship declared that U.S. B-29 Superfortresses had dropped bombs on Japan that each had the power of thousands of tons of explosives, and to stop the destruction of the Japanese people by these new weapons, the emperor of Japan had announced that his nation would surrender and end the war.

All on board James's ship were silent after the announcement. No one could believe that some unknown wonder weapon had suddenly caused the Empire of Japan to give up. Then for several minutes, the soldiers and sailors talked among themselves, all of them certain that there had been some sort of mistake and that the news could not be true.

Everything changed when the captain's voice boomed out of the loud-speakers again. He repeated his announcement, and this time—after the men's lack of reaction during the past several minutes—emphasized that it was no joke.

Suddenly every man on board was shouting in celebration. Fireworks then flew from ships in the convoy into the night sky as antiaircraft gun crews elevated their rapid-fire guns and fired bursts of tracer rounds into the air. The sailors manning the guns threw all discipline and caution to the winds and fired away, expressing the sheer joy that everyone on board felt.

The war was over, and the deadly mission that they had been training for at that very moment would not happen. They were not going to have to invade Japan. They were going to survive the war, and soon they would be going home.[4]

When the 160th Infantry Regiment returned to base, relieved of the burden of preparing to commence the final apocalyptic battle of the war, the unit started a new mission. With the formal surrender of Japan expected in the weeks to come, Japanese forces were still holding out in the hills of Panay, months after American soldiers and Philippine guerrillas had cleared them from the island's cities and coast. Now, 219 days after first going into combat, the men were to bring the war to an end in their sector as bloodlessly as possible.

They accomplished the task in two weeks, in time for the signing of the formal surrender of Japan on September 2. Aircraft dropped leaflets with instructions on where and when to meet U.S. officers to discuss surrender terms, and on August 28 a Japanese advance party of twenty-five men showed up and agreed to terms. On September 1 the Japanese commanding officer and his staff surrendered their sidearms and samurai swords to the commander of the 160th Infantry Regiment. The next day, as Japan's highest military and civilian leaders signed their country's formal instrument of surrender on the deck of the USS *Missouri* in Tokyo Bay, the Japanese lieutenant colonel in command on Panay signed the formal surrender of his forces.

In the days that followed, more than 1,700 Japanese soldiers came down from the hills to lay down their arms and surrender. Along with them came Japanese civilians, some of them women and children, who had followed their army into the hills. All of these men, women, and children would have certainly died—in combat, by suicide, or slain by their countrymen—if their emperor had not accepted the unconditional surrender of Japan after the destruction of Hiroshima and Nagasaki by atomic bombs. Instead of perishing far from home, they went into captivity in the hands of the 160th Infantry Regiment. Soon they would be returned to Japan to rebuild their lives; meanwhile, they were treated humanely by the victorious forces of the United States.[5]

While the soldiers of the 160th Infantry Regiment did their part to bring the war to a peaceful end on their island in the Philippines, decisions in the faraway headquarters of General MacArthur determined where they would go and what they would do when it was all over. In an improbable coincidence, they would be going to Korea, the homeland of James Kim's family.

After the surrender of Japan, MacArthur's staff had decided to send to Korea the army's XXIV Corps, whose three infantry divisions had fought in the Battle of Okinawa and trained for a leading role in Operation Coronet. After determining that these units would not be enough to administer the U.S. occupation zone in Korea, which was south of the thirty-eighth parallel boundary with the Soviet occupation zone to the north, MacArthur's staff looked for reinforcements and decided to use the 40th Infantry Division. On August 22 the division commander received orders to join XXIV Corps in Korea, setting in motion the unit's final mission.[6]

The division had little time to prepare for the completely new mission in an unfamiliar country. Its infantry regiments had to reorganize quickly from their wartime configuration as regimental combat teams into regimental military government teams, which would replace the Japanese colonial administration and govern areas of Korea until new Korean institutions could emerge. Their personnel received briefings on the knowledge of Korea that the U.S. Army possessed. It was minimal, as Korea was a distant part of the Empire of Japan where the army had been unlikely to fight, and only the OSS, the wartime intelligence service under Maj. Gen. William Donovan, was previously interested in the country.[7]

On September 7 the first amphibious transport ship and landing ship tank (LST) convoy carrying units of the 40th Infantry Division departed Panay for Korea. More convoys followed, with one heading out to sea after another every several days. The last convoy did not depart until September 22, nearly completing the sealift of the division's 14,389 soldiers and equipment. Two LSTs that were held back because of storms did not embark until October 5.[8]

Coming from far away in the Philippines, the 40th Infantry was the last division to arrive in Korea, so it was destined for the most distant areas from the initial U.S. landing site at Inchon and the capital city of Seoul. Its main area of responsibility would be Pusan, the port city in the southernmost part of Korea. Delays in clearing Japanese sea mines from Pusan's harbor caused the division's first transport convoys to divert to Inchon. The advance party went ashore at Inchon on September 15 and then moved overland to Pusan by railroad. By October 2, the entire 160th Infantry Regiment and supporting units had arrived in Pusan by land or by sea. The 108th and 185th Infantry Regiments spread out across the rest of the southernmost part of the Korean peninsula from Taegu in the east to Kwangju in the west.[9]

As the U.S. military government in southern Korea, the 40th Infantry Division took part in the many complicated actions that were part of bringing the war to an end and of transitioning Korea from Japanese colonial rule to independence.

The 160th Infantry Regiment's first mission was to process Japanese military personnel and civilians in Pusan and board them onto ships for their repatriation to Japan. The advance party that had arrived overland from Inchon started the task immediately, and only a few days later on September 26, the first evacuation ships departed with 3,675 Japanese soldiers and 5,341 civilians on board. By the end of the first week, 23,843 soldiers and 17,413 civilians had been embarked. All Japanese troops were cleared from the 40th Infantry Division's sector by October 5, but the evacuation of Japanese soldiers from other areas of Korea continued through Pusan until November 1. The repatriation of Japanese civilians went on even longer, going into December.[10]

A total of 394,089 Japanese soldiers and civilians passed through the care of the 160th Infantry Regiment in Pusan by December 19. Going the other way, 482,193 Koreans had returned from Japan to their native land through Pusan.[11] The civilians evacuated each way were all suddenly impoverished, their possessions reduced to only what they could carry in their baggage. They included thousands of women and children and even hospital patients who were sick and requiring medical care in transit. The 160th Infantry Regiment's veteran soldiers and recently arrived replacements handled the task of supervising the evacuations efficiently and humanely, ensuring that the vast movement of people went in an orderly manner and peacefully despite many years of pent-up hostility between the Koreans and the defeated Japanese.

All three of the 40th Infantry Division's regimental military government teams delved into the task of administering their regions of Korea and trying to mediate between the bewildering array of political factions that emerged suddenly in the excitement of liberation from Japanese rule. In the first weeks of the occupation, almost a hundred political parties had emerged. They gradually coalesced into a handful of major factions, two of which would lead the divided halves of Korea in the years to come: the communists, who had begun to organize toward the end of the war, and the nationalists of the Korean Provisional Government, founded in 1919 in Shanghai under the leadership of Ahn Chang Ho, the uncle-in-law of Lt. James Kim of the 160th Infantry Regiment.[12]

No one in the 40th Infantry Division or the entire U.S. military government in Korea likely knew that an officer in a U.S. Army infantry unit in Pusan was a close relative of one of the founders of the Korean independence movement, whose successors would eventually establish the Republic of Korea governing the southern half of the country. James Kim had been with the 40th Infantry Division since it was a National Guard outfit guarding the California coast in the first days after the attack on Pearl Harbor. Aside from his last name, the most common name in Korea, nothing identified him as Korean. He did not even speak the Korean language, which his family had never used during his childhood in Los Angeles and Shanghai.

James had no sense of homecoming in Korea and no special interest in any of his military duties there. Korea felt as foreign to him as it did to any other soldier in the U.S. Army. If participating in the expulsion of Japan's soldiers and colonial occupiers from Korea or the creation of an independent Korea struck him as significant, he did not record those impressions anywhere.[13] Being in Korea at the end of the war would have further reminded him that he was an American.

Every day in Korea was another day that James knew his family was tantalizingly close but still seemingly a world away. Eight years earlier, he had left them in Shanghai. Now, after his four-year journey across the Pacific with the U.S. Army, he was only five hundred miles away from Shanghai. But there was no possibility that his unit would get sent there, and he had no way to contact his family in Shanghai to find out how they were doing or even to learn whether they were still alive.

He also did not know that his older brother Peter was already in Shanghai as one of the first American soldiers sent there on a top secret mission to secure the lives of the remnants of the city's foreign community of which James and Peter had once been a part.

12

Mission to Shanghai— Operation Sparrow

THE SUDDEN END of the war after the atomic bombings had also immediately changed the mission of the U.S. forces in China. In August 1945 they
had been preparing for a long ground war of their own, with the U.S. Army
Air Forces supporting Nationalist China's army, and the OSS and other intelligence organizations conducting sabotage and supporting Chinese guerrillas
behind Japanese lines. On August 16 the mission of these U.S. forces changed
from fighting the war to securing the peace. Their top priority now became
protecting the lives of people from the Allied nations, both military prisoners of war and interned civilians, languishing in prison camps deep within
Japanese-held territory.

The moment Peter Kim had awaited all year had finally arrived. For
months he had been preparing for the day his people in the Shanghai internment camps would be liberated; he had worked long hours on intelligence
reports on both the camps and the city that he hoped would eventually
become useful to a rescue mission. In July General Olmsted had promised
him that he would lead such a mission when the time came for it. Now that
time had suddenly arrived.

Whether Peter Kim would have any role in a mission to Shanghai was unclear, though, since it was one of a vast array of rescue operations that U.S. intelligence organizations—not General Olmsted—were planning.

The OSS had taken the lead in planning U.S. rescue operations. On August 13 OSS headquarters in Chongqing had already laid out numerous missions to fly operators deep into Japanese-controlled territory, with each given a bird code name: Operation Magpie to Beijing; Operation Flamingo to Harbin and Operation Cardinal to Shenyang (then called Mukden); Operation Duck in the Shandong Peninsula, near the city of Weixian (Weihsien); Operation Eagle to Seoul, Korea; Operation Pigeon to Hainan Island; Operation Canary to Formosa; and farther south in French Indochina, Operation Quail to Hanoi and Operation Raven to Vientiane in Laos.[1]

Shanghai was the objective of Operation Sparrow, which faced the largest task of all.[2] More than nine thousand civilian and military prisoners were expected to be in its internment camps. More than seven hundred of them were Americans, with the rest being citizens of Britain, Australia, and other Allied nations.[3]

The commanding general for the U.S. Forces–China Theater, Lt. Gen. Albert Wedemeyer, divided responsibility for executing the missions in two: The OSS would be responsible for the teams north of the Yellow River in Beijing, Harbin, Shenyang, the Shandong Peninsula, and Seoul; and the Air Ground Aid Section would command the teams farther south, including in Shanghai, Hainan Island, and Formosa. The teams would be joint forces, drawn from the OSS, AGAS, and any other organization that could provide needed personnel.[4]

None of the U.S. intelligence agencies operating in China had anyone with firsthand knowledge of the internment camps that Operation Sparrow was supposed to liberate. Nor did any American intelligence officer have experience dealing with the Japanese occupation authorities in Shanghai. Only one man in all of the U.S. military and intelligence organizations in China had both—Peter Kim.

General Olmsted and Colonel Carter knew that they had to find Peter a place on the mission, but they were in a race against time. They had to find a way to secure him a role on the small team of intelligence officers that Operation Sparrow could take on its mission, and do it quickly. The team was hastily assembling at the U.S. air base in Kunming, four hundred miles from the China theater headquarters in Chongqing, and preparing to take off on a one-way flight to Shanghai within a few days.

Peter's military rank as an enlisted man was another crucial problem. He was only a technician fifth grade (Tec 5 or T/5), equivalent to a corporal. His rank had been meaningless to General Olmstead and Colonel Carter, but it would matter on a team of military intelligence officers who had never met Peter before. Without an immediate promotion, he would be a minor and most likely ignored member of the team.

Peter was unaware of General Olmsted and Colonel Carter's intent when he learned about Operation Sparrow. Having returned to Chongqing from a mission out in the field on August 10, he found his intelligence reports removed from his safe, and headquarters was buzzing with talk about the upcoming rescue missions. He waited for days, hearing nothing about any role for him and watching others receive orders to join the Operation Sparrow team and prepare to depart to Kunming. On August 14 he decided to confront General Olmsted and force the issue.[5]

He found General Olmsted in his office and stormed in, interrupting a meeting with a room full of senior officers. Ignoring the generals and colonels in the room, an agitated Tec 5 Kim told Olmsted his story of returning from the field and finding a Shanghai rescue mission being prepared; then he demanded that the general live up to his promise to send him on it.

An enlisted man shouting demands at a general in front of a room full of senior officers normally would end with marching him to the stockade, but instead of calling in the military police, Olmsted and Carter calmly steered the conversation toward the plan that they had already worked out for Peter. Carter coolly told the general and everyone in the room that they had an important matter to discuss with Tec 5 Kim, and Olmsted phoned the head of his staff's clandestine branch and ordered him to have Kim review the Operation Sparrow plan before its final approval. With a smile, Olmsted then told Peter that he was going on the mission and should get going quickly.[6]

Suddenly no longer seemingly forgotten, Peter saluted the general and rushed out of his office to get ready for the mission to Shanghai. First he reviewed the mission plan. His approval memorandum to Colonel Carter recommended that the U.S. government ask Switzerland to advise its consul general in Shanghai to expect the arrival by air of a humanitarian rescue mission so that the neutral diplomat could bear witness to any Japanese mistreatment of the mission and hold them responsible. Knowing that his friend and former boss, Consul General Emile Fontanel, was a stickler for protocol, Peter further advised that the mission carry credentials from the U.S. ambassador to present to him.[7]

Travel orders to Kunming in hand, Peter then hurried to gather his gear and pack for Shanghai. He tried to get some sleep despite the excitement of that day and anticipation of the next.[8]

Early the next morning, Peter found himself ordered to report to the adjutant general section for a highly irregular administrative task: He was to fill out the forms for an application for a direct commission as an officer.

General Wedemeyer's deputy chief of staff, Brig. Gen. Paul Caraway, had not only approved Tec 5 Kim's presence on Operation Sparrow and his recommendations for the mission but also decided that he would have to go as an officer. A formal commissioning was impossible in the few hours that remained before the mission's departure, so General Caraway ordered that Kim should pin on lieutenant's bars immediately and submit the paperwork for a direct commission. They could work out the details later after the mission.

In this highly unusual way, Peter Kim became a first lieutenant for Operation Sparrow as of August 15, 1945. Although he tried to point out that he was not a U.S. citizen and therefore not eligible to be commissioned as an officer, there was no time to waste resisting orders, so he went ahead and filled out the papers. His friends among the officers of the China theater staff then showered him with the uniform and insignia items he needed as a first lieutenant: an officer's cap from one and a first lieutenant's silver bars from the recently promoted Capt. Robert Peaslee.

With the flight to Kunming to join Operation Sparrow taking off soon, the newly promoted Lieutenant Kim hurried to the airfield but found himself again ordered to report to headquarters, this time to Colonel Carter's office. There he found Colonel Carter with Counselor Ellis Briggs from the

U.S. Embassy in Chongqing.[9] Briggs presented him a two-page document with a red ribbon bearing the Seal of the United States. The papers were the diplomatic credentials that he had recommended for the mission, and he was stunned to read that they declared "the bearer of this document, Peter Kim, United States Army, is the Official Representative of the Supreme Allied Commander, China Theater." They bore the signatures of U.S. ambassador to China Patrick Hurley and supreme Allied commander for the China theater General Wedemeyer.[10]

Peter could only stare at Colonel Carter, with no idea of what to say. When the colonel asked him if something was wrong, he tried to explain the unreality of events that morning. In a quavering voice, he explained that he was a lowly enlisted man and not even a U.S. citizen. If anything were to go wrong during the mission, the China theater headquarters would be subjected to severe criticism for selecting an alien common soldier for such a critical duty.

At that point, Counselor Briggs declared that since Kim was not born American, he would take back the credentials and have them changed to name some other member of the mission.

Colonel Carter respectfully but firmly told the diplomat that there would be no change. Carter had gone out on a limb to make extraordinary arrangements to send Peter on the mission. He now knew that Peter's forgotten citizenship status was a major problem, but to him it changed nothing. He said, "I disagree with you, Mr. Minister. Of all the men we have in the entire China theater, this is the only man who by reason of his long residence in Shanghai, an employee of American firms by choice, having served in a voluntary capacity with the American Association of Shanghai, and then at the request of the executive committee of that organization prior to its internment, served on the Swiss minister's staff as a special consultant on American interests, is competent by all his background to perform in this capacity."[11]

When Briggs expressed no objection, Carter said to sign the paper. With a stroke of a pen, Peter Kim became the "Official Representative of the Supreme Allied Commander, China Theater," in the humanitarian mission to Shanghai to ensure the security of prisoners of war and civilian internees. Briggs wished Peter luck, shook his hand, and left the room. Carter walked

Peter out of his office, giving him a few final words of encouragement, after which Peter saluted and took his leave to hurry to the airfield.

Transformed in the morning of August 15 from a junior enlisted man to an officer representing the supreme Allied commander in China, Peter joined a group of OSS and AGAS operators about to depart Chongqing to join their teams in Kunming.

By the time the C-47 transporting the team touched down in Kunming, the emperor of Japan's message announcing the surrender of Japan had been broadcast over Japanese radio. Operation Sparrow was on.

On the C-47 to Kunming and then at the air base, Peter met his teammates for Operation Sparrow, who were drawn from all the U.S. armed services and practically every U.S. intelligence organization in China.

The leader of Operation Sparrow was Maj. Preston Schoyer of AGAS. A 1933 graduate of Yale University, Schoyer had spent much of the 1930s as a teacher with the Yale-in-China program. He had personally experienced the first Battle of Changsha in 1939, when Yale-in-China's campus became an emergency hospital, and he drove an ambulance carrying the wounded there. By 1941 he had become a successful novelist and rising literary figure in New York. Drafted after the attack on Pearl Harbor, he became an intelligence officer in the U.S. Army Air Forces, one of its experts on China. Assigned to AGAS as one of its founders in 1943, he had been organizing rescue operations in China for two years when the call to lead Operation Sparrow came.

The executive officer, Lt. Cdr. Henry Shoemaker, was from the Sino-American Cooperative Organization (SACO), a combined U.S. Navy–Nationalist Chinese intelligence group. Naval intelligence provided another officer, Lt. Sidney Eaton.[12] The OSS sent two officers: Lt. John Cox of the U.S. Marines, who was another former member of the Yale-in-China program, and Capt. Noah Levin of the U.S. Army Medical Corps. Two army enlisted men were assigned to handle administration and communications.[13]

Chinese civilian advisers with expertise crucial to the success of the mission were also going. The team's interpreter was James Wu, a native of Shanghai who could speak English, Mandarin, and Japanese. A banker named John

Lee was going as an economic adviser and would organize buying relief supplies from the local economy for the thousands of civilians in the internment camps.[14]

The plan for Operation Sparrow called for the team to take on risk after risk to reach Shanghai and its internment camps as soon as possible. The emperor of Japan had announced that his nation would surrender, but given that no formal act of surrender had yet occurred, no one knew how the Japanese military commanders in Shanghai would act when Operation Sparrow entered the city that they had ruled for years.

The mission's first risk came even before reaching Shanghai. The 1,200 miles between Kunming and Shanghai—longer than the distance between New York and New Orleans—were too far for a two-way flight by the mission's transport planes. They would have to stage through a forward airfield at Liuchow (Liuzhou), which Japan's Operation Ichigo had overrun a year earlier but had recently been recaptured and put back into service. The mission's planes, approaching Shanghai with no fighter escort, would be defenseless if any Japanese planes challenged them. A lone Japanese fighter pilot eager for a final chance to destroy an American airplane could easily shoot down the lumbering transports and kill everyone on board.

Even if unopposed in the air, Operation Sparrow faced further peril on the ground. The planes would have to try to land at one of Shanghai's Japanese-controlled airfields, whose antiaircraft guns could easily down them as they approached to land. Then they would be at the mercy of the Japanese ground forces. The team could only hope that the first Japanese officers that it encountered, and then the senior Japanese military commanders in Shanghai, would be willing to cooperate with an enemy humanitarian mission when the war had not yet ended.[15]

If the mission survived its first day in Shanghai, then its problems would truly begin. Operation Sparrow's ten men had to liberate a dozen internment camps scattered across miles of city streets. Their sole transportation was a jeep with a cargo trailer, which was the only vehicle that they could fit into their aircraft. Undefeated units of the Imperial Japanese Army would face them as they moved through the city. So would the Kempeitai, whose reign of terror over Shanghai from their headquarters in the Bridge House had not ended yet. Any hostile action by the Japanese would quickly overwhelm any resistance that the Operation Sparrow team could attempt.

On August 17 at 7:30 p.m., with the sun already starting to set, Operation Sparrow took off from Kunming in two Curtiss C-46 Commando transports.[16] One carried the mission's jeep, loaded through the plane's side cargo door; the other the trailer for the jeep. Crates filled with supplies, cans of gasoline, and personal baggage filled the remaining space in each plane. They flew east for less than an hour, landing at a U.S. air base at Luliang for an overnight stop to refuel and try to get some rest. Before dawn the next day, at 4:30, the planes took off again. Four hours later, they reached Liuchow and landed at its airfield.[17]

The team settled into their quarters at the airfield, a tent camp set up in a field, and began unloading the C-46s and preparing for the final stage of their flight to Shanghai. The next day a single C-46 would fly to Shanghai to drop leaflets warning Japanese forces of their arrival. Lieutenant Kim and Lieutenant Eaton volunteered to go on the flight and took on the task of loading the leaflets on the plane. While they worked, a heavy rain began to pour. The rain, part of China's autumn typhoon season, soaked Kim and Eaton, and threatened to make the next day's flight to Shanghai impossible if it did not clear in time.[18]

Major Schoyer dealt with another problem, the air base commander's refusal to refuel their planes. In the hasty planning and organization of the mission, higher headquarters had neglected to send orders to Liuchow to refuel Operation Sparrow, and the air base's officers were not going to give away their gasoline without an argument.[19]

A radio message in the middle of the night changed everything. A transmission from Chongqing informed Schoyer that the Swiss consul in Shanghai had warned Japanese commanders that a U.S. humanitarian mission was arriving soon by air. The brief message did not say whether the Japanese had agreed to cooperate, but it asked for details about the mission, implying that there had been acceptance.[20]

Peter's recommendation a few days earlier that the U.S. government reach out to the Swiss consul in Shanghai had borne fruit. The consul, Peter's friend Emile Fontanel, had already acted decisively to pave the way for Operation

Sparrow. In the morning of August 15, before the noon radio broadcast of Emperor Hirohito's surrender announcement, Fontanel had summoned the Japanese commandants of the internment camps and representatives of the internees to a meeting at his official residence. Fontanel told them that the war was over, Japanese authority over the camps would cease at noon, and a U.S. Army humanitarian mission would arrive soon to establish a liaison between the camps and the U.S. Forces–China Theater headquarters.[21]

Schoyer canceled the leaflet dropping mission and ordered the team to reload the aircraft. They all would fly to Shanghai in the morning if the weather allowed. The entire team went to work to empty the C-46s of leaflets and put back all of their gear and supplies. When they were finished, it was almost 3:00 a.m.

The sky was clear later that morning of August 19. With the rains stopped, Operation Sparrow could fly to Shanghai that day. The C-46s took off from Liuchow just after 11:00 a.m. and headed northeast for Shanghai, 880 miles away.[22]

Under a blue sky, their hours in the air passed uneventfully. Below them the mountains of China's interior gave way to the Yangtze River basin, then to the flatlands and lakes around Shanghai. No Japanese fighters challenged them as they approached Shanghai.

The pilot of the lead plane called Peter into the cockpit. The pilot needed help navigating over the city to find its airfields, and he wanted the mission's expert on Shanghai as his guide. Peter took the copilot's seat next to him. At 4:50 p.m., they were flying over the western outskirts of Shanghai, and for the first time in his life, Peter saw from the air the city where he had lived for almost twenty years. He and the pilot began the search for a place to land.[23]

The first airfield they flew over was Hungjao (Hongqiao), a prewar civilian airport that the Japanese had made into a military air base. Hungjao was located near the Swiss Consulate and the Chapei internment camp, both of which the team was supposed to visit as soon as possible. It would have been an ideal starting point for the mission, and Peter had another reason to prefer it: His family's house was nearby, with his mother and younger siblings whom he had not seen in more than a year.

The pilot flew the big C-46 as low as he dared over the airfield to get the closest view possible, then circled back and did it again. The airstrip turned out to be an unimproved dirt field without a concrete runway, which the heavy C-46s needed to land safely. The dirt field also was more likely to have mines buried in it, increasing the risk that the mission would end in a fiery crash as soon as it landed. The pilot changed course southeast toward the next airfield, Longhua.[24]

Peter was silently pleased that his plane had buzzed his family's house twice during the two passes over the airfield and hoped they would understand the significance of the American airplane flying overhead. Unknown to him, they did. His youngest brother, Arthur, had been outside on the street watching the enormous aircraft that flew past, so low that he could feel the roar of its twin engines and see its details clearly. He recognized that it was an unfamiliar type, unlike the four-engine B-29 Superfortress bombers and P-51 Mustang fighters that had been raiding Shanghai. New to him as well were the U.S. markings on the wings and fuselage—a white star on a blue background, without the red circle in the center that he had seen earlier. The appearance of the plane, which no one had seen before in Shanghai, told him that something significant was about to happen.[25]

The tall pagoda of the Longhua Buddhist temple came in sight a few minutes later, drawing the plane to the airfield near it. Near the Longhua internment camp and even closer to the Swiss Consulate than Hungjao, the airfield would have been another good starting point for the mission. As the airfield drew closer, the team could see Japanese fighter planes lined up in rows and what seemed to be hundreds of soldiers milling about, making it appear too dangerous. The pilot again changed course toward the next airfield, this time to the northeast.

Kiangwan (Jiangwan), in northern Shanghai near the Japanese district of Hongkew, also turned out to be lined with Japanese military aircraft, so the pilot veered away from it and headed west toward the last major airfield in Shanghai—Dazhang (Dachang). As the C-46s flew low over the airfields, everyone looking out the windows could see Chinese flags flying on buildings and firecrackers popping in the streets. It looked as if the people of Shanghai were already celebrating the end of the war and starting to defy the Japanese forces that had occupied their city for the past eight years.[26]

When the Dazhang airfield came into view, it turned out to be different from the others. Another former civilian airport, it had the needed concrete runway, and the Japanese military presence there appeared to be minimal. Only a few small aircraft and military personnel were visible around the airstrip. It was the most distant airfield from the internment camps, in the far northwest of the city, but it would have to do.[27]

The pilot turned the C-46 back to Dazhang and descended to land. After almost half an hour of flying over Shanghai, Operation Sparrow's lead plane touched down on the runway and made a routine landing at 5:15 p.m. The trailing C-46 followed a few minutes later. The team was finally safely on the ground in Shanghai.[28]

Looking out the windows of their aircraft, they could see Japanese soldiers with rifles in their hands approaching. Schoyer opened the door and led Peter and the rest of the team down the ladder onto the tarmac to face them.

A Japanese lieutenant first met the team, and then a lieutenant colonel arrived. Schoyer, speaking through Wu, explained the humanitarian mission that had brought them to Shanghai and asked for permission to move from the airfield to the Swiss Consulate. He also requested that the Japanese army assist them by providing vehicles to transport them and their gear. The lieutenant colonel was not hostile, but he was uncertain about what to do. He had heard nothing from his chain of command about the civilian internment camps, which were completely outside of his responsibility at the airfield.

Schoyer and Wu succeeded in persuading the lieutenant colonel to go as far as he could to cooperate. He ordered his troops to bring trucks and load the mission's gear and supplies onto them. He also sent a request to his superiors for permission to take the team to the Swiss Consulate.[29]

The Americans and Japanese were cooperating, unloading the aircraft and preparing to move out, until a car drove onto the airfield and out of it stepped a colonel. He was obviously drunk, having spent an afternoon drinking away the shame of defeat. Regardless of his condition, he was the commanding officer of the airfield, and all the Japanese soldiers stopped what they were doing and stood at attention. When Schoyer attempted to speak with him through Wu, he berated and threatened the interpreter, reaching for his sword. After looking at Schoyer, the colonel stopped himself. He shouted to his men that they were to take the Americans to the Bridge House. He wanted them delivered to the Kempeitai, who would figure out what to do with them.[30]

At the mere mention of the Bridge House, Peter felt his skin crawl, remembering his ten-day ordeal of beatings and torture there two years earlier. Schoyer knew about the Bridge House from Peter's intelligence reports, but he was powerless to stop the colonel from taking them there and sabotaging Operation Sparrow's first day on the ground.

The movement to the Bridge House finally started more than an hour later, at 7:30 p.m., after the sun had already set. With only twilight remaining, the colonel's car led a convoy of vehicles away from the airfield. The American jeep and Japanese army trucks carried the Operation Sparrow team, the aircrews of the C-46s, and the Japanese soldiers guarding them. They headed southeast toward the Bridge House, six miles away.[31]

The convoy drove slowly through the darkness for several miles until it crossed paths with another column of Japanese army vehicles and halted. The other column carried staff officers from the army headquarters in Shanghai who took over for the colonel and ordered the column of vehicles to follow them to their command post. Who these Americans were and what to do with them could be sorted out properly there.[32]

They turned left to head east toward Hongkew, where the army and navy headquarters were located. The column was most of the way there, near Hongkew Park, when another group of Japanese officials stopped it. They were consular officials accompanied by officers from the Japanese army, Special Naval Landing Forces, and police. The Japanese consuls had been informed about the U.S. mission and the Swiss consul's instructions to cooperate with it. They took over responsibility for the convoy and redirected it toward the Swiss Consulate.[33]

The column drove south and merged onto North Sichuan Road, crossing Suzhou Creek on the historic Sichuan Road Bridge and heading almost another mile through downtown Shanghai to the French Concession. They turned right onto Avenue Joffre, a broad street then named after the commander in chief of the French Army in the First World War and now called Huaihai Road, and three and a half miles down the avenue finally reached their destination. At 9:00 p.m. the convoy made a final turn onto Route Doumer (now Dong Hu Street) to arrive at the Swiss Consulate.[34]

Emile Fontanel and his staff were waiting at the front door of the consulate's official residence, having been informed by the Japanese that the U.S. mission was on its way. Fontanel and his deputy, Wilhelm Schilling, received each man as he entered. Peter waited in the darkness at the end of the line, knowing that his appearance would be a surprise to Fontanel and all of his friends at the consulate. After the last man in front of him had been received, Peter finally emerged from the darkness and strode into the residence.

Fontanel and Schilling widened their eyes in disbelief when they saw their old associate and friend walk through the door wearing a U.S. Army uniform and introducing himself as Lieutenant Kim. When the shock passed, they both grasped his hand and greeted him enthusiastically but briefly, knowing that they had important business to start immediately.

They went to the residence's dining room, now serving as a conference room, with the Americans and Japanese seated on opposite sides of its long table. Fontanel and Schilling sat at the head of the table; Schoyer, Shoemaker, Levin, Eaton, Cox, and Kim to their right; and the Japanese diplomats and military officers to their left.[35]

The time had come for Peter to officially introduce himself, so he rose from his seat, said, "Sir, I have the honor to present my credentials," and handed the document to Fontanel. Fontanel read it and instantly understood what it meant: his friend had returned to Shanghai as no ordinary U.S. Army officer but rather as the official representative of the supreme Allied commander in China. He declared his acceptance and passed the document to the Japanese for their review.[36]

The Japanese officials, already shocked at the sight of an Asian as a U.S. military officer, did not understand. They and their empire had long viewed their enemies crudely and simply by race, and to them, Americans were white. Their ignorance was why Peter was there as a free man and not languishing in one of their internment camps himself. Now even the uniform and insignia of a U.S. Army officer and the credentials signed by the U.S. ambassador and the commanding general in China could not suddenly enlighten them.

An English-speaking Japanese diplomat seated across from Peter asked a question that everyone on his side of the table must have been thinking: "Are you the interpreter?"

The disrespect from a Japanese official provoked Peter's immediate reaction. "You have the document in your hands. It states that I am the Official Representative of the Supreme Allied Commander, China Theater. I am NOT the interpreter!"[37]

When that exchange ended, as the senior officer and commander of the mission, Major Schoyer took over the meeting. It soon became apparent, however, that the Japanese diplomats and military officers across the table were little more than errand boys, with an army lieutenant in charge and none of them having authority to speak for their superiors. When Schoyer attempted to present the mission's objectives, the lieutenant interrupted him to declare that Japan had not surrendered and that the Americans were fortunate to be unharmed, repeatedly saying that they were lucky there had been no "regrettable incident" upon their arrival in Shanghai. He ended the meeting by saying that more senior officers would come to talk the next day.[38]

As soon as the Japanese left the consulate, the Swiss did their best to make the exhausted Americans comfortable for the night after their long journey. Fontanel had a buffet laid out for them with beer, Scotch whiskey, and bottles of champagne to celebrate their safe arrival. Along with the food and drink, Fontanel had cots set up all over the residence—in the dining room where the meeting had just occurred, the living room, the hallways—so that everyone could sleep in comfort. It would be the first decent night's sleep that most of them had in four days.

Fontanel made special accommodations for Peter, his long-lost friend. Fontanel assigned him the residence's guest suite, which had a proper bed, a private bathroom, and an overhead fan—luxuries that most U.S. military personnel in China had not seen in years. Giving the entire guest suite to one man was bound to create resentment among the others, so Fontanel tried to explain to Schoyer and Shoemaker the close relationship that Peter had with him and others in the Swiss Consulate earlier in the war. The explanation probably did little to satisfy Schoyer and Shoemaker, who had to sleep on cots.[39]

Peter spent little time in the guest suite. As the rest of the team converged on the guest suite's bathroom, the first one that they had seen all day, Peter and Fontanel walked to the veranda to talk privately. They had much to discuss. Fontanel had not known whether Peter was dead or alive after his escape from Shanghai a year earlier, and Peter did not know anything about what had happened to his family since then. They sat on the veranda all night, talking until dawn about everything that had happened in the past year.[40]

In this way ended the first day of Peter's return to Shanghai with Operation Sparrow. The next day, after their night of rest in the civilized confines of the Swiss Consulate, the team would begin the liberation of the internment camps.

13

Victory in Shanghai

IN THE MORNING of August 20, the Americans and Japanese again faced each other across the dining table in the Swiss Consulate. This time the Japanese delegation was prepared to talk about the mission, and their terms were strict. They were willing to give access to the internment camps and to the American POWs in Shanghai, but they demanded that the Americans move through the city only with permission and with a Japanese military escort. All movements would occur in enclosed vehicles with their identities as U.S. military personnel hidden: caps off, military insignia removed, and civilian clothes over their uniforms. Their weapons, radios, and other equipment would be impounded, and they would be allowed only one radio transmission to their headquarters to announce their safe arrival in Shanghai.[1]

Major Schoyer listened to the demands and shrewdly saw an opportunity. He could see that the Japanese were afraid of them. The day before, crowds of Chinese civilians celebrating the defeat of Japan had been visible from the air over Shanghai. The Japanese negotiators appeared to be fearful of what would happen if the sight of American soldiers caused civilians to start an uproar in the streets and emboldened mobs to defy Japan's soldiers and police. In a metropolis of four million people, the consequences for Japanese troops and civilians could have been catastrophic.

The result of the negotiations was in part a compromise and in part a calculated risk. Schoyer consented to his team moving through the city only with Japanese permission and with Japanese military escorts but insisted on keeping all of their weapons, radios, and other equipment, and on having their communications be unrestricted. Schoyer agreed that his men would remove their caps and military insignia, and put civilian clothes over their uniforms, but he was counting on the Japanese being too preoccupied with their other problems to start an argument over uniforms when the team made its first movement to an internment camp.[2]

The team did not visit an internment camp that day. Instead, Schoyer made a request through Fontanel for permission to move from the crowded Swiss Consulate to a larger building that could better accommodate the Operation Sparrow team and serve as its long-term base. The Japanese granted the request, so in the evening of August 20 the entire team and their accompanying aircrews boarded their jeep and another convoy of Japanese vehicles to take them to their new headquarters.[3]

Their new base was the Marble Hall, a mansion on Bubbling Well Road (now West Yan'an Road) that is still a Shanghai landmark in the twenty-first century.[4] The Marble Hall had been the residence of the Kadoorie family, one of the wealthiest in prewar Shanghai. The Kadoories were Baghdadi Jews who had migrated to Mumbai and then to Hong Kong and Shanghai, building a vast business network across the British Empire in Asia. Sir Eleazar "Elly" Kadoorie, made an honorary knight commander of the Order of the British Empire in 1926, had been detained in Hong Kong in December 1941 and had been allowed to return to Shanghai in 1942 and live above the stables of the Marble Hall with the mansion's servants while Japanese officials occupied the house. Elly Kadoorie died in those stables in August 1944. In 1945 his sons, Horace and Lawrence, were living there with Lawrence's wife, Muriel, and their two children after being released from house arrest and the Chapei internment camp.[5]

Named for the white Italian marble of its walls, columns, and staircases, the Marble Hall had more than twenty rooms, and its ballroom had been one of the social centers for Shanghai's wealthy merchant families.[6] None of the men of Operation Sparrow were likely to have been welcome there before the war. In the changed world of Shanghai at the end of the Second World War, the remnants of one of the foreign community's leading families greeted them there as liberators.

When the Operation Sparrow team arrived at the Marble Hall after a mile-long drive, the men found the mansion emptied of its Japanese occupiers. Horace, Lawrence, and Muriel were waiting to take them into the Kadoories' reclaimed home and help them to settle in.[7]

The liberation of Shanghai commenced on August 21.

As the day began, the airmen who had flown Operation Sparrow into Shanghai departed. With the mission's presence in Shanghai established, the Japanese ordered the American aircraft and their crews to leave the city immediately. Japanese army vehicles took the crews from the Marble Hall back to Dazhang, and soon afterward, the two C-46s flew low over the Marble Hall in a roaring farewell salute.

The Operation Sparrow team spent the morning preparing to liberate the first internment camp. The men were going as American soldiers, sailors, and marines, with their insignia remaining pinned or sewn onto their uniforms, their caps on their heads, and their sidearms riding in their belt or shoulder holsters. Bringing pajama tops to put over their uniforms, in case the Japanese insisted, was their only precaution.[8]

They were also going that day under a new name—the American Military Relief Mission to Shanghai. Intended to make clear that they were there for the relief of Allied civilians and POWs, not to take over authority from the Japanese, the name was another precaution against provoking the Japanese.[9]

The men of the American Military Relief Mission emerged from the Marble Hall at around 11:30 a.m. to meet the Japanese soldiers who would escort them to the internment camps. As the Americans approached the Japanese soldiers and their vehicles, they paused and waited to see whether the soldiers would challenge them for appearing in their U.S. military uniforms. No challenge came.[10]

Maybe higher Japanese commanders, occupied with other problems, had failed to inform the soldiers sent to the Marble Hall that the Americans had agreed not to wear their uniforms in public. Maybe the officer on the spot decided that starting a confrontation with the Americans was not worth the trouble. Why did not matter at that moment. What mattered was that they were going to enter the internment camps as American soldiers, sailors, and marines, openly, for all to see.

Their vehicle convoy left the Marble Hall and headed west toward Chung Shan (Zhongshan) Road, which wrapped around Shanghai like a ring road. The Chapei and Lincoln Avenue internment camps were located along the road in the western outskirts of the city. The convoy drove down Bubbling Well Road about two and a half miles and turned right onto Chung Shan Road, and a few blocks later, it turned off Chung Shan Road and drove up to the front gate of the first internment camp.[11]

Chapei occupied nineteen acres that had once been a university campus. Damaged by Japanese aerial bombing and artillery fire in 1937, the campus had two surviving buildings that housed more than a thousand interned civilians. The majority of them were Americans, with the remainder being mostly British, Canadians, and New Zealanders.[12] For the past several days, they had been in limbo. The Japanese guards had abandoned the camp, leaving their former captives not only to step freely outside the barbed wire fence for the first time in years but also to fend for themselves. With food supplies low in Shanghai, finding enough for everyone in the camp to eat had been difficult. Relief from outside was needed as soon as possible.

A jubilant crowd greeted the men of the American Military Relief Mission. They were the first friendly troops that anyone in the camp had seen since the U.S. Marines had left Shanghai in November 1941, and their arrival meant that the long ordeal of internment was over. Schoyer, Peter, and the entire team received a heroes' welcome, cheered with the roar of hundreds of voices and swarmed by grateful men, women, and children. They shook the countless hands held out to them.

The Americans in the crowd soon realized that the U.S. Army lieutenant with an Asian face among their rescuers was one of their own. Peter Kim had been part of their community in Shanghai for almost two decades, and he had been their lifeline to the world outside of Chapei until his escape from Shanghai a year earlier. Now he had returned as one of the liberators sent by the U.S. armed forces.

The team went to a small platform to stand before the assembled people of the camp. Schoyer addressed them to explain the end of the war, the situation in Shanghai, and what to expect in the upcoming days. When he finished, the crowd began to chant a demand for Peter Kim to speak. Schoyer stepped aside, and Peter came forward, with no idea what to say after the unexpected call for a speech. He said the first words about their situation that came to mind, words that applied more than a little to himself: "Any fool can be taught to fire a gun, fly a plane or drive a tank. The real heroes of this war are you and many like you who, though defenseless, remained steadfast and loyal in the face of a brutal enemy. To the extent we can, we shall restore you to your homes and property. God bless each of you for bearing your hardships for so long. Thank you!"[13]

When the speeches concluded and the cheers subsided, the entire team went to work figuring out the condition and needs of the people in the camp. Captain Levin, the team's medical officer, delved into the health of the population with the camp's physicians. Schoyer met with representatives of the camp's leadership and inspected the compound. Peter and the other officers spoke with one person after another about their lives in the camp and how they were doing. They saw that everyone looked thin from the food shortages toward the end of the war, but no one appeared emaciated from starvation. Everyone was excited by the end of the war and eager to get out of the camp and rebuild their lives.[14]

As the team wrapped up its work, the men had to stop again and again to pose for photographs with men, women, and children who were thrilled to immortalize the day of their liberation. For Peter, these encounters were reunions with old friends. One was Jimmy James, the restauranteur behind Jimmy's Kitchen, the Shanghai fixture where Peter and his brother Richard had eaten their last meal before their escape from the city. In captivity, Jimmy had run Chapei's kitchen. He was one of many who greeted Peter as their liberator and looked forward to his assistance in trying to resume the lives that the war had interrupted.[15]

The Lincoln Avenue internment camp was only a mile away from Chapei, but it was a world apart. A walled compound filled with fourteen houses, it had been built before the war as housing for employees of the Bank of China. After the Japanese invasion in 1937, the compound had been looted and then used as a barracks and stables for a Japanese horse cavalry unit. In June 1944 it became a camp for the last Western civilians not yet interned: the elderly, the disabled, and the sick who previously had been allowed to stay in their homes with caregivers. In the end, the Japanese would not allow even these weakest and most vulnerable to escape captivity.

More than three hundred people, most of them British, ended up in Lincoln Avenue. Many of them had arrived in ambulances or on stretchers, too old or ill to walk to their internment. Living with them were a few dozen young and able-bodied men and women, transferred from other camps to serve as caregivers. Equipment and facilities for their care were nonexistent.[16]

The people of Lincoln Avenue were as happy to be liberated as those of Chapei but were in a pitiable state. Thirty-three had died in just over a year. Dozens were so ill that the Japanese had moved them out of the camp and into hospitals.[17] As the team inspected the camp and discussed the condition of its people with camp representatives, Dr. Levin faced a far more difficult task figuring out their medical needs than he had for those confined in Chapei.

An American POW turned out to be among them. The Japanese had captured PFC John Jesse on the first day of the war while he was serving in the U.S. Marine detachment guarding the U.S. Embassy in Japanese-occupied Beijing.[18] After years in POW camps with his fellow marines, Private Jesse had become chronically ill, and the Japanese had transferred him to the Lincoln Avenue camp in June 1945. The American Military Relief Mission ended Private Jesse's three years, eight months, and thirteen days of captivity and brought him back into the U.S. armed forces, taking him with them when they boarded their vehicles and returned to the Marble Hall at the end of the day.[19]

During the days that followed, the relief mission's journeys around Shanghai continued to all of the remaining internment camps and then to the hospitals where civilian internees and POWs were receiving treatment. On August 22 the team entered the Yangtzepoo (Yangpu) and Pootung (Pudong) camps, which together held more than 2,000 people. The next day the men visited Longhua, which held almost 1,800 internees, and the Ash camp, which had more than 400. On August 24 Dr. Levin, Lieutenant Eaton, and Lieutenant Cox visited St. Luke's Hospital and Shanghai General Hospital, where they found almost two hundred patients from the internment camps. In St. Luke's, they also found four American POWs, tuberculosis patients who had been captured on Wake Island in December 1941.[20]

In the afternoon of August 24, the entire American Military Relief Mission to Shanghai reassembled in the Marble Hall for a meeting to organize their work on the vast array of tasks that lay ahead of them. The commander, Schoyer, and the deputy commander, Shoemaker, laid out the responsibilities of each of the eleven men of the team, which now included the recently liberated Private Jesse. Peter's task was to take care of the countless problems of the people in the liberated internment camps, fulfilling the crucial mission that Colonel Carter and the generals of the China theater had chosen him to perform. Ten days after he had stormed into General Olmsted's office demanding to go on the operation to Shanghai, the hard work was about to begin.[21]

14

The Caretaker of Shanghai

AT THE END of the day on August 24, Peter Kim faced a daunting task as he looked ahead. He was back doing the work he had undertaken years earlier, looking after the well-being of his compatriots in the internment camps in Shanghai, but this time his responsibilities were vastly expanded. Along with hundreds of Americans, thousands of British, Canadians, Australians, New Zealanders, and citizens of other Allied nations now relied on him. None of them had the good fortune of his hosts in the Marble Hall, who were already in possession of their majestic prewar family home. Most had nothing but the clothes on their backs and a claim to a residence or business that the Japanese had confiscated years earlier.

All that Peter had been able to bring with him to solve their problems were the sheets of paper containing his credentials as the representative of the supreme Allied commander in the China theater. The resources and manpower of the U.S. armed forces would eventually arrive in Shanghai to help, but they were still hundreds of miles away in free China and the Pacific.

The food supply in the camps soon ceased to be a problem, thanks to the long reach of U.S. airpower. The relief mission reached out to headquarters in Chongqing, using the radios that Schoyer had argued with the Japanese to keep, and sent requests for airdrops of food and medical supplies.[1] The U.S. Army Air Forces in the Pacific answered the call with B-29 Superfortress bombers based on the island of Saipan. Left idle by the end of hostilities,

B-29s that had rained bombs on Japan's cities only a few weeks earlier now flew to Shanghai with canisters filled with relief supplies in their bomb bays. The canisters descended by parachute toward the camps starting on August 27 and kept coming every day.

American canned food from the vast U.S. military supply chain across the Pacific soon gave everyone more to eat than they could handle. Cans of Spam, powdered milk, peaches, jam, and other foods that had been unimaginable luxuries only a few days earlier soon were abundant, along with Hershey's chocolate bars and Lucky Strike cigarettes. The sudden rain of meat, milk, and fruit from the skies soon overfed men, women, and children who for months had subsisted on little more than a bowl of rice or a potato or a beetroot a day.

Returning people from the camps to the homes that the Japanese had taken from them years earlier was another problem entirely. While U.S. air forces ruled the skies over Shanghai, the Japanese still ruled the city itself, and its millions of Chinese civilians were increasingly beyond anyone's control.

At the end of the war was a moment when the defeated and soon-to-depart Japanese could take away the remaining riches of the International Settlement, and the Chinese who had lived on its fringes could loot it as well. Japanese military and civilian officials were already hauling away truckloads of furniture and other plundered items from the houses that they were abandoning. Mobs of Chinese were descending on abandoned properties to take away anything that remained.[2] A race against time had begun, and three days had already passed since Peter had promised the liberated people in the Chapei internment camp that the relief mission would do its best to restore them to their homes and property.

Before any action could commence, Peter had to negotiate with a commission of Japanese civilian officials set up to manage the disposal of confiscated properties. An array of issues had to be addressed concerning how to determine the lawful owners of properties confiscated years earlier, the rights of persons who had rented rather than owned their residences, the rights of Japanese occupants facing eviction, and many others. Negotiations with the commission over the details went on for days until a final agreement was concluded on August 27.[3]

The agreement required Peter and the Japanese commissioners to work together. Japanese authorities would require the Japanese occupants of confiscated homes to guard them against looting by remaining in possession of them until their former residents were ready to reoccupy them. Peter would provide the commission with information on the rightful owners and occupants of properties, and the commission would authorize them to return to their former residences by issuing certificates allowing them to inspect and reoccupy their homes, and to guard them against looting.[4]

The immense task of sorting out the claims of thousands of people and restoring them to their former homes began the next day. An August 28 meeting in the Marble Hall to discuss the arrangements with representatives from each camp kicked off the effort. Peter then immediately went to work, gathering information from people in the camps so they could obtain from the Japanese commission the official authorizations to reclaim their homes.

Relief mission tasks elsewhere in Shanghai drew Peter in as well. One was helping to gather intelligence on the last American POWs in Shanghai, whom the Imperial Japanese Army refused to release before the formal arrival of U.S. forces in the city. The POWs were being held in the Foreign YMCA, a majestic ten-story, Italian Renaissance–style building on Bubbling Well Road.[5]

The POWs were eight army airmen and naval aviators who had been captured late in the war and imprisoned in the Bridge House for interrogation by the Kempeitai. When the relief mission learned about the men's detention in the Bridge House and demanded their release, the Kempeitai released them into the custody of the Japanese army, which moved them to the Foreign YMCA on August 25.[6]

The ongoing confinement of American POWs in the Foreign YMCA building became even more awkward when the relief mission moved right next door on August 28. Major Schoyer obtained permission from the Japanese to move his headquarters from the Marble Hall to the Park Hotel, which was located next to the YMCA. The Park Hotel was another Shanghai landmark that had opened as a luxury hotel in 1934 and, at twenty-two stories, was the tallest building in Shanghai—or anywhere in Asia—into the

1960s. The relief mission secured its entire thirteenth and fifteenth floors to use as a second base in Shanghai, with the hotel rooms of the thirteenth floor serving as the team's living quarters and the VIP apartment suites on the fifteenth floor becoming their office space.[7]

The POWs were stuck in a strange holding pattern, still confined by the Japanese but with liberation tantalizingly close. The relief mission's officers visited them daily to check on their welfare, but with Japanese soldiers watching them at all times, they had to be careful about what they said to avoid provoking their captors. They had stories to tell about the abuse that the Kempeitai had inflicted on them in the Bridge House but had no way to convey them without risking being overheard by the English-speaking Japanese soldiers guarding them.

Peter Kim found a way to get the information the POWs wanted to say right in front of the Japanese. He did it using a code that he knew no Japanese soldiers would be able to decipher. Peter had learned it during his teenage years in America and knew it as well as or better than the Ivy League–educated intelligence officers of the relief mission. It was pig latin.

When Peter began speaking to the POWs in that child's code talk, familiar to generations of American children, they understood exactly what the unfamiliar lieutenant with an Asian face was doing and responded in the pig latin that they had learned many years earlier. In this way began the U.S. investigation of Japanese war crimes against American POWs in Shanghai.[8]

The American Military Relief Mission soon ceased to be alone in Shanghai as the OSS, U.S. Army units, and ships of the U.S. Navy began to arrive in the city. In the afternoon of August 31, a flight of five C-46s appeared unannounced over Longhua and landed, delivering an OSS group and an army POW team that assumed care of the POWs in Shanghai.[9] In the morning of September 2, just before the surrender of Japan, a group from the Air Transport Command landed at Dazhang to take over the airfield and prepare it to handle the air traffic of incoming U.S. forces. The next day, the entire Park Hotel came under U.S. military control to serve as a headquarters for the U.S. Seventh Fleet, which was on its way to Shanghai.[10]

On September 11 Operation Sparrow's relief mission came to an end when an OSS party arrived under the name Operation Sparrow II. The OSS took over intelligence operations in Shanghai from the original Operation Sparrow under Major Schoyer.[11] The next day, Schoyer announced the end of the American Military Relief Mission in Shanghai.[12]

Peter's work looking after the remnant of the foreign community of Shanghai continued but now with his original comrades in the China theater's G-5 staff. General Olmsted personally flew into Shanghai to assess the situation in the city in early September. To ensure that essential services continued uninterrupted as Japanese authority came to an end, he sent officers from his staff in Chongqing to take charge of the administration of electric power, the telephone network, water, sewage, and other services that a city of millions of people could not live without. The officers arrived on September 8. Their leader was Peter's friend Capt. Robert Peaslee, whose old lieutenant's bars Peter was wearing on his uniform.[13]

Captain Peaslee and Lieutenant Kim took over practically the entire civilian administration of Shanghai. Peaslee oversaw the dismantling of Japanese control over the Shanghai Waterworks, the Shanghai Power Company, and the Shanghai Telephone Company, supervising their immediate return to their prewar British and American owners. After restoring these utilities to their former owners, he ensured the supply of coal for the power plants, water purification chemicals for the waterworks, and other materials essential to their operations.[14] Peter continued supervising the supply of food and other life support to the people in the liberated internment camps and the restoration of their property.[15]

Among the thousands whom Peter returned to their homes was the British family of a boy named James Ballard. Four decades later, as the author J. G. Ballard, he would publish the most famous account of Shanghai's internment camps, the novel *Empire of the Sun*, which became the basis of the 1987 motion picture of the same name.[16] When Operation Sparrow liberated the camps, James Ballard was not yet fifteen years old and had endured two and a half years confined with his parents in the Longhua camp. Thanks to Peter's work, in early September they were able to reoccupy the house that the Japanese had taken from them in 1943 and start to rebuild their lives.[17]

Nationalist Chinese troops soon arrived in the city to complete the liberation of Shanghai from Japanese occupation. The high commands of the United States and Nationalist China had chosen these troops to accept the surrender of Japanese forces in the city and to liberate it in the name of China, establishing clearly that Shanghai was to be a Chinese city from then onward. They arrived in the tens of thousands, having been flown into the city by the U.S. Army Air Forces and transported by sea by the U.S. Navy. As Japanese troops laid down their arms and their commanders turned over control of the city, the Allied victory over Japan was finally realized in China. By late September, the liberation of the city was complete.

15

Reunion in Shanghai

PETER'S ARRIVAL IN Shanghai with Operation Sparrow had brought freedom for the long-suffering foreign communities of the city, and victory for the United States and the Allies became his family's victory as well. Soon he would be reunited with the family that he had left behind in Shanghai more than a year earlier. If the fates allowed, all of his brothers scattered around Asia by the tides of war would also return.

Peter would have gone to see his family during his first day in Shanghai if the situation had allowed. In the Swiss Consulate that night, the urge to see them had been overwhelming, and he even had asked Emile Fontanel if he could borrow a bicycle and civilian clothes so that he could sneak out the gate of the consulate to go to their house. Fontanel had rejected the idea as too dangerous, with Japanese soldiers watching the consulate and the Americans inside it. Peter instead stayed with the mission, and Fontanel assured him that he would send one of his deputies to tell Peter's mother about his return.[1]

Soon afterward one of Fontanel's deputies walked up to the Kim family's house on 198 Route Père Robert and knocked on the door. Arthur, playing kickball in the street with Chinese neighbors, watched the well-dressed European walk down the lane of ten houses to his house at the end. His mother answered the door and was joined by his brother David once it was clear that the visitor was not Japanese. The Swiss diplomat told them the momentous news that Peter had returned to Shanghai and was staying at the Swiss Consulate. With the extreme caution that she had learned to survive during years of living under Japanese occupation, Lee Chung Sil said she did not know anyone named Peter in the hope that the stranger would go away.

Prepared for the moment, Fontanel's envoy showed her a signal from Peter. He pulled from his pocket a pack of Lucky Strike cigarettes from America, Peter's favorite brand, which had been unavailable in Japanese-occupied Shanghai for years. Lee Chung Sil immediately understood the meaning behind the pack of cigarettes and invited the stranger into the house to hear him out.

What he had to say was the first that she learned about any of the three sons that the war had torn away from her. She learned that Peter was not only in Shanghai but also in the service of the U.S. Army as an officer leading an important mission. And he had already sent a message home. The large airplane that had twice buzzed the house on August 19 had been carrying him and had been following his directions.

The news was beyond anything that she or any of her children who remained with her could have imagined, and it changed the world for them. They knew that the war was coming to an end, but now there was a sign that one of their missing men was returning and returning as an American officer. Arthur now knew the meaning of the mysterious plane that he had seen roaring past him. Now they had to wait for Peter to come to them, whenever it might happen.

Days later a strange small vehicle appeared on Route Père Robert. It was a U.S. Army jeep, which no one in the neighborhood had ever seen before. Eyes followed it as it drove past, and excited chatter began as people began to notice that the driver was an Asian man in the uniform of a U.S. Army lieutenant. It was Peter, returning home. His mother, David, Betty, and Arthur welcomed him back joyfully but still in disbelief. Not long before, they had not known whether he was dead or alive. Now he was back as an officer in the U.S. Army and with powers beyond anything that they could have imagined.[2]

Richard was the next to return. He arrived on September 8 with the first wave of U.S. Army personnel sent from Kunming to set up the Shanghai Base Command, which would operate Shanghai's port as a supply base for U.S.

and Chinese forces. Barely older than eighteen years of age, he already held the rank of sergeant only nine months after enlisting. His promotion from a private assigned to work behind a typewriter to a noncommissioned officer had been almost as rapid as Peter's elevation to lieutenant. The three stripes on Richard's sleeve attested to his new importance as a native of Shanghai in the ranks of the U.S. Army in China, which suddenly considered him valuable to the administration that it was setting up in the city.

He arrived by air in a C-54 transport, flying in an airplane for the first time in his life more than a year after he and Peter had turned down rides in P-38 Lightning fighters while on the run deep in China's interior. Landing at Longhua airfield, Richard saw the strange sight of armed Japanese soldiers surrounding his airplane on the tarmac. The Imperial Japanese Army in Shanghai had not yet surrendered and continued to control the airfield. Its units were still marching through the streets, asserting their authority as if Japan had not lost the war, even as the Shanghai Base Command's advance party rode in trucks from the airfield to downtown Shanghai. There they arrived at a hotel that was to serve as their living quarters.

Contacting home became as simple as picking up a hotel telephone. On arrival, Richard immediately got on a telephone and had the Shanghai Telephone Company's operator connect him to his family's house.[3] Eventually Peter picked him up in a jeep and drove him home for his reunion with the family.

There his mother greeted him with questions that she would not have asked him a year earlier: Did he want a cigarette? Did he want a beer? He had not done any smoking or drinking before he left home. To her, he was now different. He had left as a boy and had returned as a man, and a few adult habits were to be expected. He still did not smoke or drink, so he turned down the offers and went straight to reuniting with everyone.

The family shed tears of joy over seeing each other again after so much time and so much that each of them had been through, and they shared laughter over the things that had somehow gone well for them. Most of all they had countless questions—questions about how Richard and Peter had escaped from Shanghai to free China, what they had seen along the way, how he had joined the U.S. Army, and why it had so rapidly made him a sergeant.

When the family had last seen him, he had been a seventeen-year-old in danger of being drafted into Japan's army, his life likely to be thrown away in the service of the enemy. Now he was an American soldier, one given authority over others.[4]

Sgt. Richard Kim's position with the Shanghai Base Command made a difference on a day in late October that would feature one of the pivotal moments of their lives. On October 27 he showed up at the house with a jeep and told everyone that they were going to an official celebration of Navy Day, an event commemorating the sailors of the U.S. Navy that he had arranged for them to attend.[5] David, Betty, and Arthur crammed into the jeep for the ride through the city to the distant Shanghai Bund waterfront. There they boarded the cruiser USS *Nashville*, the flagship of Task Force 73 of the U.S. Seventh Fleet in Shanghai.[6]

The U.S. Navy's major surface combatants were known to have the best food in the U.S. armed services, and the flagship's crew lived up to that reputation for their guests on that special day. The galley served a seemingly limitless supply of steaks from the ship's meat lockers. Ice cream, nonexistent in Shanghai since before the war, came out of the freezers for dessert. All of the Kim siblings ate in a way that they could not remember having done in years, with Arthur enjoying it most of all. Acting as the teenager he was, he ate more ice cream and rich food than his body could handle. Before the day was over, he would twice have to rush from the festivities to the railing and throw up over the side of ship.

After they ate, there was entertainment that they had not experienced since before the war—a newly released motion picture from Hollywood. The movie was *State Fair*, a Rodgers and Hammerstein musical in Technicolor starring Jeanne Crain and Dana Andrews. Viewed on a ten-thousand-ton cruiser, a floating island of the United States, the color film set in the Iowa State Fair was a brief glimpse of the faraway country that David and Betty had not seen for years and where Richard and Arthur had never been.

After the party, Richard drove everyone back to their house in the jeep. Entering the house, they saw unfamiliar U.S. Army gear strewn all over the living room: a helmet, a pistol belt, a musette bag, and other army luggage. Someone unexpected was visiting, and Richard thought that he knew who it must be. He rushed upstairs, followed by David, Betty, and Arthur. Together they saw their mother sitting with a man in uniform. The man was their brother James, who had last been in their house eight years earlier as a sixteen-year-old boy.

Lt. James Kim had been in Korea trying to find a way to go to Shanghai and return to his childhood home and family. His division had been returning veteran soldiers to the United States to be discharged and sent home, and with almost four years of service and Bronze Star and Purple Heart medals earned in battle in the Philippines, James qualified for discharge under the points system that the U.S. Army used to determine eligibility for demobilization.[7] James had nowhere to go and no family to rejoin in the United States, though. He had to find another way to return home.

James once again created his own way forward, remarkably similarly to how he had fought his way out of second-class citizen status and potential discharge from the army almost four years earlier. Just as he had done as a private when he argued that he was not a Japanese American, James spoke with a chaplain about his situation and got the spiritual leader's support for an extraordinary request—an application for an emergency leave of absence to look for his family in Shanghai. It would allow him to leave the unit that had been his home for almost four years but stay in Asia as an officer in the U.S. Army. His demand, backed by a clergyman, once again proved to be persuasive, and the division staff approved the request.

In late October James boarded an LST in Pusan that was part of the U.S. Navy's fleet of transport ships providing a shuttle service between Korea and port cities in China. The five-hundred-mile voyage from Pusan to Shanghai passed sluggishly in the slow-moving amphibious assault ship, capable of steaming at no more than twelve knots. At the Shanghai waterfront, he hired a pedicab to take him to his family's house in the French Concession. With childhood memories of rampant crime in the streets of Shanghai, he did not trust the bicycle rickshaw driver and kept his .45 pistol out of its holster and in his hand, ready to use as soon as necessary, all the way from the waterfront to Route Père Robert.[8]

Standing outside of a house that he believed was his childhood home, James thought that everything looked different. He knocked on the door, and when it opened, an unfamiliar-looking woman came out and told him that no one was home. Confused by the baffling reception at a house that he barely recognized, he began to back away. Uncertain about whom he was facing, he asked hesitantly, "Mom?"

The unfamiliar woman, who had been talking cautiously as if to a stranger, suddenly changed. "Jimmie! Jimmie!" she cried out, now recognizing the son whom she had not seen in eight years. Standing in front of her was not her teenage boy but a grown man, wearing the uniform of an officer in the U.S. Army like his older brother. James now saw his mother, who had grown older and cautious after so many years of protecting her family in a city under enemy occupation. Both deliriously happy, they went into the empty house and began the long process of trying to talk through some of the things that had happened to each of them in the intervening years.[9]

David, Betty, Richard, and Arthur walked in later that day after the Navy Day festivities. When Richard led everyone into the upstairs living room where James and their mother were talking, James briefly did not recognize the U.S. Army sergeant moving toward him, arms outstretched to give him a hug. He needed a moment to realize that the sergeant was his brother Richard, whom he had last seen as a ten-year-old boy and a year earlier had communicated with from afar by telegram. Overcome by emotion, they all embraced for the first time in years—all but Arthur.[10]

"Where is Art?" James asked, with his youngest brother standing right in front of him.

At that moment, it was painfully clear to Arthur what had happened. His own brother had no idea who he was. He had been only seven years old when James left, and with the passage of time, he had grown into a teenager whom James did not recognize.

Arthur had faced Japanese soldiers with fixed bayonets in the streets of Shanghai without flinching, but the pain of this moment was more than he could take. Tears came to his eyes as he reminded James who he was. It was not the homecoming of his brother the war hero that he or anyone else would have expected.

It was only one moment in the life of a family whose members had all survived a war that had taken the lives of millions, but it said much about how long and how deeply the war had separated them. For years they had all lived through events and done things almost incommunicable to anyone who had not experienced them firsthand. They were all now different from whom they had been before, changed by the years and by what they had seen and done. The end of the war had reunited them, but they had a long way to go to understand each other again.

PART 3

Return to America

16

Americans at Last

THE KIM FAMILY was completely reunited for the first time since the Second World War in Asia began eight years earlier, but they inhabited an obviously dying world that would soon cease to exist. Shanghai was going to be a Chinese city, without the foreign empires, concessions, and communities that had defined it for a century. The handwriting was on the wall for foreigners in Shanghai, and they were leaving the city to return to their countries of origin. Amid the exodus, all but a few of the Kims faced being left behind, even after all they had done for the U.S. war effort in China.

In a cruel irony, Peter was assigned to serve as a military assistant to the U.S. consul general in Shanghai, to aid the repatriation of Americans to the United States, but neither he nor most of his family was eligible to go with them. Only James and Betty were U.S. citizens; the rest, having been born in Korea and Shanghai, were not. Peter and Richard's service as volunteers in the U.S. Army, and the risks that David and Arthur had taken for U.S. intelligence in Shanghai, counted for nothing under the U.S. immigration laws in 1945.

Peter's commanding officers, led by Col. Marshall Carter, stepped forward to try to right the wrong that their country's national policies had created. Having put his own reputation on the line by trusting Peter—a foreign national enlisted man in the guise of a U.S. Army officer—to represent the U.S. commanding general in Shanghai, Carter understood that Peter and his family were Americans exiled in Shanghai who had amply proven their loyalty to the United States during the war. Knowing the situation that they faced, Carter was determined to find a way to bring all of them back to the United States. He came up with a daring, long-shot plan: to lobby Congress to enact a special law granting citizenship to Peter Kim and then to pass more for the rest of the family.

Congress has the power to pass a private law, an act providing benefits to a specific individual. A private law can address any of a wide range of issues within the powers of Congress, including granting citizenship or permanent residence. Colonel Carter and his staff decided to attempt to persuade a member of Congress to introduce a bill for a private law granting citizenship to Peter Kim and commit to the months-long effort necessary to gain the votes required for the bill to pass. If that campaign succeeded, then they would try to secure additional acts of Congress to grant citizenship or permanent residence to the rest of his family, bringing them to safety in the United States as well.

Support for U.S. citizenship for Peter Kim went all the way to the top of the U.S. Forces–China Theater's chain of command. The generals who had led the U.S. Army in China officially endorsed Colonel Carter's campaign, lending it the influence that their names might have on anyone in the Capitol who might listen.

General Olmsted gave his "complete and unreserved endorsement" of citizenship for Peter Kim. Writing as Peter's commanding officer in a letter addressed to the Department of State, Olmsted described at length Peter's obviously American identity from his childhood in the United States to his adult life in Asia and then Peter's outstanding wartime actions in Shanghai, in his journey to free China to enlist in the U.S. Army, and in the relief mission to Shanghai. "Such demonstrations of patriotism and loyalty can only be regarded as inherent, and I feel it would be a great injustice to allow such devotion to our ideals to go unrewarded," he pleaded.[1]

General Wedemeyer, the supreme Allied commander in China, in whose name Peter had been sent on the relief mission to Shanghai, also provided a letter of support. He wrote, "I wish to take this opportunity to express my whole-hearted approval of the work done by Peter Kim, U.S. Army, on behalf of the United States Forces, China Theater, and to give my unqualified endorsement to any steps which may be taken on his behalf in his request for United States citizenship."[2]

All of this support from military commanders in China would have amounted to nothing in Washington if Colonel Carter could not send the right envoy, one who fully understood the gravity of the situation and somehow could get an audience with a member of Congress who might take an interest in the cause of one faraway and obscure American soldier. Fortunately, exactly the right man for the task was in Shanghai preparing to return to the United States. He was Capt. Robert Peaslee, Peter's friend and comrade in arms in Kunming, Chongqing, and Shanghai.

Peaslee, scheduled to depart Shanghai for demobilization in late October, was from a Minnesota family that was prominent in the state's Republican Party. They were connected to Senator Joseph Ball, a Republican from Minnesota, who happened to have become especially interested in causes similar to that of Peter Kim and his family.

Senator Ball had not been afraid to act against his own party when necessary to address crucial wartime problems. As a newly elected senator in 1940, he had broken with the party's isolationists to support the foreign policies of President Franklin Roosevelt. Ball also had crossed party lines to endorse Roosevelt's reelection in 1944. After the war, he had become concerned with addressing the problems of the millions of displaced persons in war-torn Europe. He was as likely as anyone in Congress to take an interest in the plight of a war hero in Asia who had remained loyal to the United States in the face of Japanese persecution and now needed refuge.

After three days of flying across the Pacific, in short hops from one island base to another, Peaslee finally landed in San Francisco and then took further military flights across the country to Washington. In the nation's capital, he first met officials at the Department of State and the Department of Justice to discuss Peter Kim's case. The Department of State's Passport Division and a Department of Justice immigration expert gave him the same answer: The country's immigration laws tied their hands. The laws did not allow even the president to intervene, ruling out any action by the entire executive branch of the U.S. government. Only Congress could act to help Peter and his family.[3]

Having confirmed the assessment of Colonel Carter and the military staff in Shanghai, Peaslee went to Capitol Hill for the meeting with Senator Ball that his family's connections had made possible. Ball turned out to be as receptive to what he had to say and as sympathetic toward the cause of Peter Kim and his family as everyone concerned in China had hoped. Peaslee showed the senator the letters of recommendation that he had brought with him from China, a letter from Peter telling his life story, and a report that Peter had written on his efforts to protect American property in Shanghai. Peter's story made a powerful impression on the senator, who immediately agreed to submit a bill for the naturalization of Peter Kim to the Senate Committee on Immigration.[4]

His mission in Washington accomplished, Peaslee moved on. The next day, he boarded a train to New York to visit the big city before returning to Minnesota to visit his family and then heading home to Los Angeles.[5]

True to his word, Ball prepared and submitted the promised legislation within a few weeks. On November 19, 1945, Ball introduced Senate Bill 1607, "A Bill to Provide for the Naturalization of Peter Kim."[6]

The bill was only the start of a long process, however, one that everyone knew would take months. The legislative process required the Senate Committee on Immigration to approve the bill before it could reach the floor of the Senate for a vote. The House of Representatives would also have to approve the legislation, and getting it through the House would be a separate lengthy process. To secure passage of the bill, Ball would have to educate other senators and representatives—who had little time and attention to give to a private law for an obscure foreign national—on who Peter Kim was and why he should be let into the country. All of this effort would take a long time, and it was as likely as not to produce nothing in the end.

During the long wait for action in Washington, Peter had to make his way through the problems of his military duties and everyday life in Shanghai. Serving without pay was one of them. At the time of his rushed and irregular elevation to lieutenant, no one had considered that U.S. Army regulations would make it impossible for him to receive his regular salary. Peter was still officially in the enlisted ranks, not a commissioned officer, and regulations barred him from receiving an enlisted man's salary while acting as an officer.

The problem had begun as soon as he had pinned lieutenant's bars on his uniform and embarked on Operation Sparrow, and it continued in postwar Shanghai. He ended up stuck in a strange limbo, invaluable to the army and the Department of State but ineligible to be paid even a cent for his service.[7]

Peter was unable to provide any support to his family at a time when they needed it urgently. With the war and Japanese occupation over, the Swiss-administered loan program for U.S. citizens in Shanghai came to an end. Betty received a final loan on September 30, 1945, after which the family lost its wartime means of support.[8] Until businesses in Shanghai reopened and created jobs, the family would have to rely on the military pay of its sons to get by.

For months Peter's superiors on General Wedemeyer's staff engaged in discussions with the Pentagon to try to clear away the bureaucratic snafu, but ultimately they had to give up and have him revert to the enlisted ranks.[9] Coming in January 1946, the apparent demotion was embarrassing to Peter in his dealings with Western and Chinese civilians for the U.S. consul general, as it created the impression that he had fallen into some sort of disgrace.[10] But it brought to an end a difficult five months in which he had been unable to help provide for his family despite his stature in the U.S. military in Shanghai.

Fortunately, his brother James was there to help. He had been living with the family and using his military pay—now at the salary level of a captain—to help support them. He was there on emergency leave from his infantry unit at first, but in December 1945 he was formally transferred to the U.S. Forces–China Theater's staff, with the official authorization of his living arrangements arriving in March 1946.[11] He had applied for the transfer a year earlier, when letters from Peter and Richard had reached him on New Britain and he had tried to join them in China. The transfer request had been approved but was lost in someone's files until James reported his arrival in Shanghai.[12]

Peter's reputation with the U.S. military in China was undiminished by the dispute over his rank, and his superiors again took his case all the way to Washington to seek justice for him. General Wedemeyer's staff sent a demand to the Pentagon that despite Peter Kim's lack of U.S. citizenship, the War Department should authorize making him an officer in the U.S. Army by granting a waiver of the citizenship requirement—a rare action during the Second World War or any other era. Reversing its earlier stubbornness on the salary issue, the War Department granted the waiver. On February 25, 1946, Peter Kim was sworn in and properly commissioned as a second lieutenant in the U.S. Army.[13]

Peter's cause gained an invaluable advocate in the Pentagon and on Capitol Hill when Colonel Carter rotated out of China and went to Washington for his postwar assignment. In his new position as a staff officer at the War Department, he was able to work the system to guide the China theater's requests for action on Peter Kim through the Pentagon's bureaucracy. Carter's influence helped to secure the War Department's approval of the citizenship requirement waiver for Peter. Even more importantly, he met with Senator Ball regularly to remind him of the urgency of pushing the months-old bill for Peter Kim through the legislative process.[14]

More months passed before news from Washington finally arrived. In June Senator Ball's bill finally made it out of the Senate Committee on Immigration to face a vote on the floor of the Senate. Ball also found a member of the House of Representatives willing to introduce the legislation in the House—Walter Judd, a Republican also from Minnesota's congressional delegation. Judd, a staunch anti-Communist who had served as a medical missionary in China in the 1930s before going into politics, introduced the House bill for Peter's naturalization as a U.S. citizen in mid-July.[15] The Senate voted on the bill on July 17, and it passed as Private Law 808, "An Act to Provide for the Naturalization of Peter Kim."[16]

President Truman signed the act into law on August 2, 1946.[17] Finally, more than nine months after Robert Peaslee had gone to Washington to advocate on behalf of his friend Peter Kim, the American people's elected representatives had officially declared him to be worthy of U.S. citizenship.

Marshall Carter, Robert Peaslee, Joseph Ball, and all the others who had struggled to move the act through Congress had made history. The U.S. government had taken the first step toward righting a great injustice. The eldest son of Kim Chang Sei, who had dreamed of himself and his family becoming Americans, was at last welcome to become an American by citizenship as well as in spirit. Two decades had passed, and years of wartime sacrifices with no expectation of anything in return had been necessary to make it possible.

Peter Kim finally became a U.S. citizen when he swore the oath of allegiance to the United States on December 4, 1946. It happened in Shanghai, where his family's American journey had been diverted for two decades.[18]

Peter remained in China after becoming a U.S. citizen, as China's civil war between the Nationalists and the Communists escalated in 1947. Halfway through the year, he finally left Shanghai as the U.S. Army closed down its entire presence in the city and all of China, never to return.

On June 30, 1947, the now thirty-five-year-old Peter Kim boarded a military transport plane for the long series of flights across the Pacific to the United States. More than twenty years had passed since the last time that he had last set foot in the country, when he and his family had left the United States against their will in 1926. Now he was returning as an American citizen and an officer in the U.S. Army, a respected—perhaps even legendary—figure among those who had led the U.S. armed forces in China during the Second World War.[19]

The rest of the family remained in limbo, though, waiting for their turn at gaining U.S. citizenship that might never come. Senator Ball had promised Robert Peaslee that he would continue introducing further legislation for Peter's brothers, sister, and mother, but there was no certainty that he would be able to follow through on that pledge or that he would again succeed in moving the bills through Congress.

James now took up the struggle for the family's future. The army had scheduled his return to the United States in August 1946, and he intended to fight for his family there.[20] He had volunteered for the army in September 1941 as a largely aimless young man, not certain of where he belonged. Five years later, on the other side of the test of combat, he was a proven leader whose service in the nation's defense anyone would respect. He would go to Washington and advocate for the next legislation to bring his family members to the United States.[21]

Soon after the enactment of the law granting U.S. citizenship to Peter, James left Shanghai and arrived in San Francisco. He went on leave for sixty days and kept going all the way to Washington. Upon his arrival in early September, he began to search for a member of Congress to sponsor a bill for a private law granting U.S. citizenship to Richard.

First, acting on Peter's recommendation, James looked up the journalist Philip Potter at the Washington bureau of the *Baltimore Sun*. A war correspondent who had covered the end of the Second World War in China and the resumption of the country's civil war, Potter had taken an interest in Peter's case and was willing to use his network of connections to help the family's cause. When James told him about the need for legislation to admit Richard into the United States, Potter encouraged James to write to Senator Ball at his home in Minnesota.[22]

James sent a letter to Senator Ball on September 12 that led to a meeting in Washington on October 1. James explained Richard's story and the need for another private law for him, presenting the senator with an array of letters of recommendation from the same China theater commanders who had supported Peter: General Olmsted, now returned to his prewar position as chairman of an insurance company; Colonel Carter; and others.[23]

Before his meeting with Senator Ball, James left Washington and took a train to Massachusetts for another meeting that was crucially important for Richard's future. On September 25 James received a cable from Peter, sent though Philip Potter, informing him that Richard was leaving Shanghai on a troopship bound for the United States. He would arrive in Seattle and then continue overland to Camp Beale, an army base outside of Sacramento. Peter advised James to meet Richard at Camp Beale, but first James needed to work out an arrangement that had been devised in Shanghai for Richard to continue his schooling in America.

The McNairs, their friends in Shanghai for two decades, had a family history of attending the Mount Hermon School, a private boarding school in Northfield, Massachusetts. The McNairs urged Peter and James to try to enroll Richard in Mount Hermon. There Richard could stay in the United States as a student and complete the high school education that the war had interrupted, financed by the GI Bill benefits that he was eligible to receive even though he was not a U.S. citizen. The McNairs informed the school about Richard and their support for his application and set up a meeting with the school for James.

James contacted Mount Hermon and pleaded Richard's case with the headmaster; then he took a train to Northfield to meet the school's admissions committee. The recommendation from the McNairs and James's persuasion were successful. Mount Hermon admitted Richard even though he was overage at nineteen years old and lacked any previous school records, and the school had never before admitted a student entering under the GI Bill.[24]

Meanwhile, the U.S. Army in China had set in motion its own action to send Richard to the United States. Its commanders, not wanting to leave Peter Kim's brother behind, had not waited for Congress to act and quietly arranged to send him across the Pacific. When the Shanghai Base Command disbanded and returned its personnel stateside for demobilization, Sgt. Richard Kim went with them instead of being discharged in Shanghai. On September 25 he boarded the troop transport *Fred C. Ainsworth* and departed Shanghai. He stepped onto American soil for the first time in his life when the ship arrived in Seattle on October 8.[25]

A train took Richard from Seattle to Camp Beale in Northern California. Now Beale Air Force Base, Camp Beale was then an army base that had become a demobilization center for soldiers returning from Asia, including those of the Shanghai Base Command. There Richard found James waiting for him with news about his future at a New England boarding school and the ongoing campaign to get him U.S. citizenship. On October 24 Richard went on terminal leave from the army and left with James to start his life as a civilian and student in America.[26]

Richard would need all of the time that his status as a student could buy, because the legislative process on Capitol Hill worked even more slowly for him than it had for Peter. Months passed before Senator Ball was able to introduce the bill to grant Richard citizenship through naturalization. On January 8, 1947, the bill was introduced and referred to the Senate Committee on the Judiciary.[27] Twice it went to the Senate for a vote but went back to the committee for amendments. The slow, back-and-forth process continued for the entire year and into the next. The Senate finally voted on the bill and passed it on June 10, 1948, but the House never voted on it before the end of the legislative session.[28] The bill ultimately died when Senator Ball lost his campaign for reelection in 1948, removing its sponsor from Congress.

During the long wait, Richard thrived as a student at his New England boarding school. Years older than his classmates and far more mature after all that he had experienced, he did exceptionally well at the Mount Hermon School. Its headmaster, Howard Rubendall, a graduate of Dickinson College in Carlisle, Pennsylvania, supported Richard's application to his alma mater. After graduating high school in 1948, Richard enrolled in Dickinson, again relying on the GI Bill to pay the tuition.[29]

Richard graduated from Mount Hermon with more than his high school education. The daughter of a Mount Hermon faculty member, Catharine Rikert, had become his high school girlfriend. They married in April 1949 while he was a freshman at Dickinson. The wedding took place at St. Thomas' Episcopal Church in Washington DC, where Franklin and Eleanor Roosevelt, Harry Truman, and Woodrow Wilson's widow, Ellen, had worshipped.[30] Richard's father, whose life's work had been to bring his family to America, would have been proud to witness his son's marriage in the nation's capital in a church of presidents.

James had arranged the wedding ceremony in Washington DC for his younger brother. By then he had been living in the nation's capital for almost two years, starting his own postwar life.

After his brief time in Washington getting Richard's bill started, James had ended his military service at the Presidio in San Francisco.[31] At the Presidio from October 1946 to June 1947. he spent most of his time performing routine peacetime administrative duties, such as serving as a billeting officer and managing the officer's club.[32] Like millions of GIs returned from the war but not yet demobilized, he was looking forward to leaving the armed services and trying to figure out what to do with the rest of his life.

A career in foreign affairs began to interest James as a way to put to good use what he had experienced and learned during the war years. Some of the inspiration for this idea may have come from his duties in support of a high-level diplomatic event at the Presidio—a visit by Crown Prince Amir Saud of Saudi Arabia.[33] As the manager of the officer's club, James organized the luncheon at the Presidio during the crown prince's official visit to San Francisco on February 7, 1947.[34]

To pursue a career in foreign affairs, he would have to resume the college education that he had abandoned when he dropped out of a junior college in California in 1941. He applied to enroll in Georgetown University's School of Foreign Service. When he was admitted, he resigned his commission and returned to Washington to enroll in the 1947 summer session and start working on his bachelor's degree.[35]

A crisis arose in November 1948 when Richard received a letter from the Immigration and Naturalization Service (INS) claiming that he was living in the United States illegally and would be subject to deportation. Ordered to report to the INS office in Philadelphia, Richard was told there that there would be a hearing to determine his status and whether he would be deported. This development, coming within a few days of Senator Ball losing his election, forced James into action again.[36]

James secured a second chance for Richard's bill by getting Ball's assurance that he would ask another member of the Senate—Homer Ferguson, a Republican from Michigan—to reintroduce it.[37] Ball also wrote to the commissioner of the INS to ask that the agency postpone the deportation proceedings while Senator Ferguson's bill was pending. James regularly followed up with the INS to confirm that the commissioner acceded to Senator Ball's request and to ensure that the INS staff in Philadelphia followed the commissioner's decision.[38]

Senator Ferguson pushed the legislation forward rapidly as soon as the new year began. On January 5, 1949, he introduced a bill that would grant Richard permanent resident status, which was less than the naturalization as a U.S. citizen of Senator Ball's original bill in 1947 but was enough to keep Richard safe from deportation.[39] The Senate passed it on February 8.[40] The House passed it as well on March 16, and President Truman signed the act into law on March 29 as Private Law 11.[41] Incredibly, in less than three months, Ferguson had accomplished what Ball had been unable to do for two years.[42]

By an act of Congress, Richard was now safe to stay permanently in the United States. After his marriage to Catharine a few weeks later in April, U.S. citizenship soon followed as well. Finally, almost two years after leaving Shanghai and arriving in the United States for the first time, he was indisputably an American.

All of the Kim brothers who had served in the U.S. Army during the war were now U.S. citizens, along with their sister, Betty. Two acts of Congress and three years had been needed for the family to get this far. David, Arthur, and their mother still lacked the protection of U.S. citizenship as the 1940s drew to a close. The brothers would need to take more action to secure their family's safety as the specter of another war spread over Asia in the year 1950.

17

Reunited by the Korean War

THE OUTBREAK OF the Korean War in June 1950 brought about the final stage in the return of the Kim family to the United States. The North Korean invasion of South Korea resulted in a U.S. military response that recalled the brothers who had served in the Second World War to the armed services, further cementing their commitment to defending the United States against its foreign enemies. At the same time, U.S. concern over the hostility of the recently created People's Republic of China helped open the door for the last members of the Kim family in Shanghai to come to the United States.

Peter went to Korea first, having never left the army. He had made it his career after Col. Marshall Carter and the generals in China had done so much to make him an officer and a U.S. citizen. Although a decade older than the normal age for a lieutenant, he had settled into a steady career in the peacetime army, protected by the senior officers who had held him in such high esteem during the war. He became an intelligence officer, one of a select few whose backgrounds in Asia made them uniquely valuable. In June 1950 he was at the Army Language School in Monterey, California, preparing for a tour of duty in Japan.

The start of the Korean War made Lt. Peter Kim suddenly urgently needed in the country where he had been born. He had not been there since 1928, when he had been only sixteen years old, but few officers in the U.S. armed services were familiar with Korea at all. He went to serve as an intelligence officer with the Eighth Army, which was the main U.S. ground force in Korea.[1]

Peter arrived in Korea in November 1950, when Communist Chinese forces were beginning their intervention in the conflict that would turn an expected United Nations (UN) victory by Christmas into an ignominious retreat. He arrived too late to help prevent the intelligence failures that contributed to the underestimation of the massive Chinese army sent to defeat U.S. and UN forces as they approached the Yalu River. Instead, he helped the Eighth Army weather months of crises that saw a withdrawal from North Korea, the loss and recapture of Seoul, and the establishment of a bloody stalemate by the summer of 1951. He continued to serve in Korea until June 1952.

James would be the next to go, but only after completing the return of the Kim family from Shanghai to America.

In June 1950 James was a captain in the U.S. Army Reserve, which he had joined to earn extra money while he finished his degree at Georgetown University. Called to active duty for the Korean War, he got permission to stay in school in Washington while he fought to take care of a matter of life and death for his family: His mother and his brother David were still stuck in China, now ruled by the victorious Communists, who would soon become the enemy of the United States in a war in Korea between the free world and the Communist bloc.[2]

David had remained in Shanghai as his brothers left for the United States after the Second World War. He had both a job with an American company to support him and the family house on Route Père Robert to live in, and with no apparent prospect of an act of Congress to let him into the United States, he had had no reason to leave the city that had been his home for more than two decades. He stayed there alone after Betty left to move to Hawaii and Arthur, accompanied by their mother, joined her there to attend high school as a foreign student in 1947. Lee Chung Sil and Betty returned to Shanghai in 1948 and, with David, tried to live a semblance of normal lives as Nationalist China fell apart in the civil war and Communist forces advanced toward Shanghai.[3]

Everything changed when Shanghai fell to the Communists in 1949. Their next-door neighbor on Route Père Robert since the 1930s, a Chinese man named Chang who had worked as a telegraph operator for the French police, suddenly revealed that he had been a Communist agent all along. He immediately asserted Communist authority over the neighborhood, with himself as the boss. Chang did nothing against David, Betty, and their mother even though he knew of their ties to America and had seen Peter, James, and Richard in U.S. Army uniforms a few years earlier. David, Betty, and their mother knew that Chang's personal sympathy toward them would not protect them for long, though, so they soon began planning to escape from the newly declared People's Republic of China.[4]

In April 1950 they finally made their move to leave Shanghai. Betty, an American citizen, went to the waterfront and used her U.S. passport to board a boat headed for the British colony of Hong Kong. David and their mother joined the thousands of people who fled on foot from Shanghai to Hong Kong, more than 750 miles away.

Before abandoning the house that had been the family's home through a world war and a civil war, they first had to plant a cover story with the neighborhood Communist Party leader next door. As they prepared their escape, they mentioned to Chang from time to time that they were going to visit Suzhou, a city only about sixty miles away. Chang apparently understood what they were doing and played along. The day before their planned departure, Chang visited their house and told Mrs. Kim to have a good time in Suzhou, reassuring her that he would look out for their house while they were away. She believed that he knew what they were doing and was hinting that he would cover for them as long as he could.[5]

David and his mother walked out of Shanghai with a Chinese friend who had been the office manager of the American company where David worked. They arrived in Hong Kong on April 29, luckily only two days before the British closed the border to refugees on May 1. There they met Betty, who had arrived earlier by sea. They then sent telegrams to Peter and James in the United States, reporting their situation and asking for help.[6]

James immediately went into action to try to get David and their mother out of China. He was already occupied with preparing for his final exams so that he could graduate from Georgetown University in June and, on top of that, with serving an active duty assignment at the Pentagon as a reserve officer. These responsibilities suddenly became insignificant as he focused all of his time and attention on his distant family in their moment of crisis. He reached out to every person and institution in Washington that he thought might be able to help but with little idea of whether any of them could.[7]

First, James contacted the International Refugee Organization, a multi-national body the UN created to aid the massive numbers of people displaced by the Second World War that was later succeeded by the United Nations High Commissioner for Refugees. The organization told him that its charter covered only European refugees and excluded Asians. With no help coming from the only international organization seemingly set up for his family's situation, he had nowhere to turn but the U.S. government.[8]

Next, through some of his professors at Georgetown University, he sought help from the U.S. Department of State. Assistant Secretary of State for International Organizations John D. Hickerson, a lecturer at George-town, put James in contact with the chief of the State Department's Visa Division.[9] Dr. Jules Davids—a professor of diplomatic history whose students later included Jacqueline Kennedy and Bill Clinton and who became a contributor to Senator John F. Kennedy's Pulitzer Prize–winning book *Profiles in Courage*—introduced James to the State Department's Office of Protective Services.[10]

The State Department officials advised James that they could do nothing to help, and neither could anyone else in the entire executive branch of the U.S. government. Their hands were tied by the same U.S. immigration laws that had sent his family out of the United States a quarter of a century earlier. Only Congress could make an exception to the laws, so James would again have to go to Congress to find a solution to his family's crisis.[11]

Fortunately, James already had connections in the Capitol that the Kims had made over the past several years. While Senator Ball was no longer in office, Senator Ferguson still was, and his staff knew James from their work on Richard's bill in 1949. James also knew a staff member of the House majority leader, Representative John W. McCormack from Massachusetts, who had gone to work on Capitol Hill earlier in 1950 after serving as the proctor for another of James's professors at Georgetown. Dr. Davids persuaded the staffer to help secure the majority leader's support for legislation to help James's family.[12]

Peter, far away in California, also reached out to figures from his past for support. He wrote to Representative Walter Judd, the Republican from Minnesota who had introduced the House bill for his naturalization as a U.S. citizen in July 1946.[13] Peter had later met Judd on a congressional delegation to Shanghai in 1947. He believed that Judd might again sympathize with the family's situation and be willing to act on the Kims' behalf.[14]

Peter also contacted Judge Milton Helmick of the U.S. Court for China in Shanghai, whose release from Japanese internment and repatriation to the United States Peter had supervised in 1942. Now retired in his home state of New Mexico, the judge drew on the contacts from his many years in the legal profession to help the family of the man who had done so much for him and all of the captive Americans of Shanghai years earlier. Helmick referred Peter to one of his former judicial clerks, who had become a lobbyist for a liquor industry organization in Washington.[15]

James met the lobbyist W. H. McMains in his office in the National Press Building—two blocks from the White House—in early July. As just another obscure college student on the GI Bill trying to earn money for school, James had worked at the National Press Building as a switchboard operator and gofer for the Washington bureau of the *Baltimore Sun* in the previous year. Now he needed expert advice from a Washington insider. He got what he needed from the man whom Judge Helmick had recommended.

McMains advised James to take the family's case all the way to the top of the U.S. government and offered to take the message himself to his connections on Capitol Hill. He instructed James to write two letters: one to President Truman and the other to Senator John Chandler "Chan" Gurney, a Republican from South Dakota who had been chairman of the Senate Armed Services Committee from 1947 to 1949. McMains knew Gurney well and believed that he would view the Kim family's cause favorably. McMains would take the letter and deliver it to the senator in person to make sure that it received the attention that it needed.[16]

James acted immediately after receiving this advice. He carefully wrote lengthy letters to Senator Gurney and President Truman that told the family's story in its entirety: their struggle to come to America and stay there in the 1920s, their father's suicide, their years in Shanghai, the brothers' loyalty to the United States and their military service in the Second World War, and the desperate plight of David and their mother stranded in China. He finished them by July 10.[17]

The letters that Peter and James wrote to members of Congress bore fruit almost immediately. On July 11 Judd introduced a House bill, H.R. 9082, to admit David and his mother into the United States as permanent residents.[18] On July 13 Gurney introduced his own Senate bill, S. 3914, to do the same for David, his mother, and the youngest child, Arthur, as well.[19]

Senator Gurney soon went far beyond introducing legislation. As McMains had hoped would happen, Gurney embraced the cause of the Kim family and made it his personal project for the 1950 legislative session. He soon had James visit him in his Senate office regularly to discuss how to move the bill—the "Kim Bill," as he called it—forward through Congress.[20]

In one of their meetings, Senator Gurney took James to meet the entire Senate Judiciary Committee and its powerful chairman, Senator Pat McCarran. The committee was the gatekeeper that would make or break the fate of any bill on an immigration matter, and McCarran, a Democrat who had represented Nevada since 1933, was well known as being hostile to immigration from Asia. Gurney knew that he would have to make a strong impression on the committee—especially McCarran—for his bill to have any hope of moving forward. On a day when James showed up wearing his military uniform with his captain's bars and Bronze Star and Purple Heart ribbons from the Second World War, Gurney saw an opportunity to impress McCarran and the committee that was too good to pass up.

Gurney called McCarran to tell him that the young man whose mother and brother had escaped from Shanghai was in his office, and he would like McCarran to meet him. McCarran, about to go to the Judiciary Committee's hearing room to start a meeting, suggested that Gurney bring him to the committee's cloakroom, where he could spare a few minutes before the meeting. Gurney agreed, but instead of going to the cloakroom, he walked James through the corridors of the Senate office building and straight into the hearing room to present him to the assembled committee members, who were waiting for the chairman to arrive.

By the time that McCarran appeared, Gurney had introduced each member of the committee to the uniformed and decorated Asian American veteran of the Second World War. James's presence changed minds as he shook hands and talked with the committee members. Among them was Estes Kefauver, a recently elected senator from Tennessee who was about to become famous for his investigation of organized crime, with nationally televised hearings that would expose millions of Americans for the first time to the existence and workings of the Mafia.

Another was Warren Magnuson from Washington State. During the Second World War, Magnuson had championed a 1943 act bearing his name that allowed Chinese immigration into the United States for the first time since 1882. He asked James about rumors of corruption at the U.S. Consulate in Hong Kong, where consular officials were said to be demanding bribes before issuing visas. James responded that David had mentioned these rumors but that there was not any definitive proof. Magnuson talked about initiating an investigation of these allegations, but James said nothing about this idea.

When McCarran entered, no doubt nonplussed by his wait in the cloakroom, James had already won over the room. McCarran's peers had seen for themselves that Gurney's bill was about the family of a real American who was ready to go to war for the United States for a second time. Gurney introduced McCarran to James, and the senator understood the tone among his peers and acted accordingly. Motioning for the committee clerk to approach, McCarran put his arm around James's shoulder and instructed the clerk to work with Gurney to move forward the bill for James's family. The chairman then gently pushed James and Gurney toward the door to clear the room so that he could begin his committee meeting.[21]

Gurney's adept manipulation of his colleagues had opened the way for the Senate's approval of a private law admitting the last of the Kim family remaining in Asia into the United States, but the House side of Congress remained a problem. Walter Judd was less active in trying to move his bill forward, and even if he had tried, he had little influence on the House Judiciary Committee. As a result, his bill remained stuck in the committee with little hope of reaching the full House for a vote. So Gurney reached out across the houses of Congress and across the aisle to work on the committee's Democratic Party leaders.

During another meeting in Gurney's office, not long after crashing the Senate Judiciary Committee meeting, James watched Gurney call Representative Ed Gossett, a Democrat from Texas on the House Judiciary Committee. Gurney told Gossett about what had happened on the Senate side and suggested that Gossett receive James in his office to learn more. After hanging up, he told James to hurry over to the House office building to meet the congressman.

James ran across Capitol Hill to Gossett's office, where he found a waiting room full of people with appointments and an admiral at the head of the line. He worried that he would have to wait a long time before getting an audience with Gossett and then not have enough time to say everything that he wanted. But when the office door opened, Gossett shook hands with the admiral, apologized, and told him that he would have to wait but not for long. James would come first.

Gossett brought James into his office and had him take a seat. James thought Gossett would give him only a few token minutes, say a few nice words, and send him away with nothing more than a vague promise to look into the matter. One member of Congress after another had done exactly so in the preceding days when James had visited them in their offices and tried to plead his family's case. James watched as Gossett sat in his chair, leaned forward to pick up a cigar from his desk, and put his feet up on the desktop. He then said plainly, "I understand you have a problem. Tell me about it!"

The congressman's casual attitude might have appeared unserious or even disrespectful to some, but to James, it was inspiring. Gossett clearly had no intention of hustling him out of the office as soon as possible. He was ready to hear the full story and had made himself comfortable in anticipation of a long discussion.

James proceeded to tell Gossett all about his family's sacrifices in the Second World War and the crisis that threatened them now. He reminded Gossett of the urgent need to pass the bill before it was too late to help. As he finished, he passed on Gurney's recommendation to amend the House bill to include Arthur, as the Senate bill did.

Gossett waited until James had finished before saying anything. He put his feet down, sat up, and talked as plainly as he had at the start of their meeting. "Son, I can't speak for the Senate, but I can tell you that this House will pass the bill you want!"

James was overcome with emotion, shedding tears of joy in front of the congressman. Finally, he had found a member of the House of Representatives who was willing to go out on a limb and unequivocally promise that he would do anything necessary to get the bill passed. He would even amend Judd's bill to conform it to Gurney's Senate bill by adding Arthur to the family members to be admitted for permanent residence. James left feeling hopeful that Gossett would follow through on his promise and do whatever was necessary to pass the bill.[22]

Gurney clearly had chosen Gossett as carefully as McMains had chosen him. Nothing in the history or constituency of the congressman from Texas suggested that he would take any interest in the case of an obscure family from Asia. But Gurney knew him well enough to see that he would get involved and that he was the right member of the House Judiciary Committee to move the Kim bill forward.

Gossett did not disappoint James in the weeks that followed. In a Judiciary Committee meeting to consider private bills, Gossett introduced an amendment to Judd's H.R. 9082 that added Arthur to the Kim family members—David and their mother—granted relief from the immigration laws. Gossett brought up his amendment out of order, before H.R. 9082 was scheduled to be considered by the committee, accelerating the committee's review of the bill and the release of it for a vote by the full House of Representatives. On August 16 the House voted on H.R. 9082 and passed it, sending it to the Senate for the upper chamber's approval.[23]

The Senate was ready for the House bill after Gurney's work to sway its Judiciary Committee. Already acquainted with James and the family, the Judiciary Committee approved H.R. 9082, which was practically identical to Gurney's bill. The Senate passed the House bill without amendment on September 14.[24]

In this way, Congress passed "An Act for the Relief of Mrs. Chang-Sei Kim, David Kim, and Arthur Kim" as Private Law 1028, which President Truman then signed into law on September 27, 1950.[25] Only seventy-eight days had passed since the introduction of the original House bill on July 11, setting an incredibly rapid pace for the passage of a private bill or any kind of law. Peter's bill had taken almost nine months to pass; Richard's, more than two years.

With these three acts of Congress admitting members of the Kim family into the United States, the elected representatives of the American people had righted a historic wrong a quarter of a century old and acknowledged unequivocally that each of the Kims was more than worthy of being an American. It was a moment for them to be optimistic, especially coming at a time when the war in their former homeland of Korea appeared to be developing into a victory for the free world. A few days earlier, U.S. and South Korean forces had recaptured Seoul from the North Korean army, and the allied forces under the United Nations were preparing to cross the thirty-eighth parallel to bring the war in Korea to an end.

Passing a law in Congress was only the first step toward bringing the last members of the Kim family into the United States, however, as it became the responsibility of the executive branch to carry out the will of Congress. Bureaucrats in Washington and overseas inevitably were going to act—or not act—as obstructions. No one could know on September 27 when David, Betty, and their mother would be permitted to board a ship in Asia and return to the United States.

James immediately sent a telegram to David telling him that the bill had passed and that he should inform the U.S. Consulate in Hong Kong of it. To ensure that the consulate would soon receive the news from its own formal channels as well, James called one of his State Department contacts, an assistant to the chief of the Visa Division, and requested that he send a cable to Hong Kong with the news. The assistant said that he would do so but that sending the cable would be at James's expense. James was happy to pay to send the message overseas as soon as possible, but it soon became apparent that his money and effort had been wasted. The consulate in Hong Kong was not interested.[26]

As the month of October passed, David's letters told James that nothing had happened after so much effort had gone into passing the act in Congress. David and their mother were still stuck in Hong Kong with no prospect of leaving, and Betty was staying with them. The U.S. Consulate continued to insist that they would have to wait for their turn to be allowed to go to the United States, and it would say nothing about when that turn might come.[27]

The language that Congress had used may have given the State Department's consular officials in Hong Kong too much leeway. The law stated, "Mrs. Chang-Sei Kim and David Kim may be eligible for admission into the United States for permanent residence provided they are otherwise admissible under the immigration laws."[28] By permitting their entry into the United States rather than mandating that it happen, the law left ample space for bureaucrats far away in Asia to do nothing for as long as they pleased.

Discouraged by the lack of progress, which continued almost to the end of October, James did what he had done so many times during the campaign to get the bill passed: He went to Senator Gurney's office to speak with the senator in person.

When James reported what he had learned from David and expressed dismay at how little the act of Congress had affected the U.S. Consulate in Hong Kong, Gurney was also surprised and acted immediately to fix the situation. He picked up his office telephone, asked for the overseas operator, and requested that the operator connect him to the U.S. consul general in Hong Kong. When the operator pointed out the time difference—it was midafternoon in Washington and about 4:00 a.m. in Hong Kong—the senator exclaimed, "I don't care what time it is over there!" He demanded to be connected immediately.[29]

About five minutes later, the operator called back with a most likely barely awake consul general on the line. Gurney greeted the consul and pretended to apologize about calling at that time of day in Hong Kong. He then politely expressed surprise that nothing had been done about Mrs. Chang Sei Kim's case and said that he would appreciate a report back on the matter as soon as possible. The senator winked at James. He had just gotten the consul general's attention, no doubt about it, and they could expect action from the consulate in Hong Kong soon.[30]

The next day, Gurney called James to inform him of what the consul general had reported. The consul had immediately contacted James's mother, making sure that everything was on track for her to leave Hong Kong soon. Instantly, all of the necessary arrangements were in place to allow her to start her new life in the United States. In just over a week, she would be able to board the passenger liner ss *President Wilson* and leave behind China forever.[31]

Lee Chung Sil, accompanied by her daughter, Betty, boarded the *President Wilson* on the Hong Kong waterfront on November 4, 1950. Exactly thirty years earlier in November 1920, as a young woman embarking with her husband, Kim Chang Sei, on their journey to the new world, she had made another voyage across the Pacific Ocean while pregnant with the child who would become James. This time, she and Betty were bound for Hawaii to start their lives in America all over again. It may never have happened without the intervention of Senator John Chandler Gurney, a Republican from South Dakota, who had embraced the Kim family's cause and gone to extraordinary lengths to support their return to America.[32]

David did not board the ship with them, though. The consulate had left him out of the arrangements made for his mother in response to Senator Gurney's late-night demands. It may have been an act of passive bureaucratic resistance, doing no more than the letter of what the senator in distant Washington had demanded. Perhaps it was out of spite, an act of retaliation against David for bringing pressure from Congress that had inconvenienced them. Regardless of why it happened, not including David in his mother's immigration and travel arrangements had left him stranded by himself as a refugee in Hong Kong.

Soon after his mother and Betty had departed, his chances of ever reaching the United States seemed to disappear entirely when the consulate dropped a bombshell on him. The consulate declared David to be medically unfit to be admitted into the United States, claiming that his X-rays showed that he had a case of tuberculosis. The infectious disease—the same disease that his father's career in medicine and public health had been dedicated to fighting—disqualified David from entering the United States.[33]

The consulate's declaration came as a complete surprise. David had submitted his medical records, not expecting any problems with them. He had received a clean bill of health from a doctor, who had seen no signs of tuberculosis in his X-rays. The consulate's seemingly arbitrary diagnosis put his hopes of immigrating to the United States on hold, possibly forever.

David had previously told James about rumors circulating around Hong Kong that some U.S. consular officials were demanding money under the table before they would issue U.S. entry visas. Refugees were ideal targets, as they were willing to do anything to escape and had no one to defend their rights. The consulate's seemingly inexplicable finding of tuberculosis in David's X-rays may have been one of many attempts to shake down visa applicants for bribes.

Months earlier, when Senator Gurney had introduced him to the Senate Judiciary Committee, James had been given an opportunity to raise the issue in Congress. Senator Magnuson had asked him about rumors of corruption at the consulate in Hong Kong, but James could say only that the rumors existed. When Magnuson offered to initiate an investigation, he had said nothing.[34] The opportunity passed, and now it was long gone.

Instead of turning to Senator Gurney or anyone else in Congress, James worked with his main contact at the State Department, the assistant to the chief of the Visa Division. Together they reviewed the relevant statutes and concluded that the law allowed some leeway in tuberculosis cases that could be interpreted in David's favor. A cable to the consulate in Hong Kong followed, but as the State Department deferred to its overseas posts on visa matters, a long process of trying to persuade the consulate to change its decision followed.[35]

A month later, the consul in Hong Kong reversed the earlier decision and granted David the visa that he needed to go to the United States. But even then, a new problem emerged to keep him in Hong Kong: Finding passage out of Hong Kong had become impossible.

By December 1950, Chinese Communist forces massed in the mountains of North Korea had attacked U.S. and UN forces and sent them retreating in disarray. The Korean War was escalating from a small conflict between the United Nations and North Korea into a war with Communist China, backed by the Soviet Union. The small British colony of Hong Kong had ample reason to fear that the massive People's Liberation Army would soon attack the city. With panic spreading, people were jamming the offices of steamship companies and airlines, desperate to escape. Soon every berth on a passenger liner was taken, and even seats on transpacific airliners—exorbitantly expensive and normally used only by the wealthy—were sold out.

In despair, David wrote to James that he was considering giving up and going back to Shanghai. There at least he would have a place to live in a familiar city, and he could stop living in constant uncertainty as a refugee.[36] Eight months in Hong Kong, especially the past month, had drained his spirit. The U.S. Consulate's obstruction of his departure for the United States, followed by the mass run on shipping out of Hong Kong, had finally crushed his will to continue.

James, after seeing David's message, was again desperate for help. After all that the family had been through over the years and all of his efforts during the preceding months, the last member of his family marooned in China was in real danger of being lost. There seemed to be no way out for David and nothing that anyone in Washington could do about it, since the problem was no longer caused by any barriers put up by the U.S. government. With no idea what could be done or who could possibly help, James went to see W. H. McMains, the lobbyist who back in July had figured out how to bring the Kim family's cause to the Capitol. Maybe he could think of something, James thought.[37]

Meeting again in McMains's office in the National Press Building and close to breaking down in tears the entire time, James explained what had been happening to David for the past several months. McMains heard James out, thought about the problem, and calmly suggested that James go to a nearby movie theater and spend some time watching a motion picture while he made a few telephone calls that might help.

James did as McMains asked, with no idea what the lobbyist had in mind. He went to the theater and sat down to watch a movie but was too preoccupied to pay any attention. He gave up, returning to McMains's office within an hour. McMains was smiling when James walked in, and he had good news to tell.

The veteran of Washington politics had called a friend who was a lobbyist like himself, a vice president in charge of congressional relations for Pan American World Airways, or "Pan Am." America's leading international airline, Pan Am had been synonymous with transpacific flight since the 1930s, when its famous Clipper flying boats had pioneered passenger service between the U.S. mainland, Hawaii, and Hong Kong. McMains told James that David was going to fly out of Hong Kong on Pan Am, and all that James had to do to make it happen was go to the Pan Am office a few blocks away on Sixteenth Street, identify himself, and buy David a ticket.

James was stunned. Every flight out of Hong Kong in the near future was known to be full, with not a single ticket remaining. He asked McMains what he had done.

McMains explained that his friend at Pan Am had secured a seat for David. Pan Am's booking policies always set aside one or two seats on each flight for any Pan Am executives who might need to fly on company business. At McMains's request, the airline's Washington lobbyist had used his influence in the company to reserve one of those seats for David on any flight out of Hong Kong.

Pan Am's airfare from Hong Kong to Honolulu was expensive—$615, or about $8,000 in 2024—so McMains advanced part of it to James to help him raise the funds as soon as possible. On December 6 James went to the Pan Am office with the full $615 and bought David a ticket for Pan Am Flight 828 from Hong Kong to Honolulu. James sent a telegram to tell David of the sudden change in his fortunes and about the flight arrangements, and in an instant, David was finally all set to leave China and join the rest of the family in the United States.

On December 11, 1950, David boarded his flight at Hong Kong's Kai Tak Airport, the city's main airport until its replacement, Hong Kong International Airport, opened nearly half a century later. He had never flown in an airplane before, just as his brothers had not before they joined the U.S. Army, and now he was leaving China by flying first class on America's premier airline. After multiple stops on its way across the Pacific, the flight landed in Honolulu on December 13. David was finally safe on U.S. territory.[38]

Now all the Kim family members were in the United States and would never again have to leave the country that they had always considered to be theirs. James's mission to bring home the last of the family remaining in China was finished, and their father's dream, when he had brought his family across the Pacific to the United States thirty years earlier, had finally been fulfilled.[39]

18

American Intelligence Officers

BRINGING THE LAST members of the Kim family to the United States and finally ending its quarter-century-long exile in Asia would have been the accomplishment of a lifetime for most. For James, now twenty-nine years old, this act was only the beginning of his becoming the person that he would eventually be, and it would be followed by more life-changing events before the year was over.

Georgetown University granted him his bachelor's degree after excusing him from classes and final exams so that he could focus his attention fully on his family's struggle. James became the first college graduate in the family since their father had earned his medical degree in Korea in 1916.

The U.S. Army had plans for James now that he had cleared up his family obligations. There was a war to fight, and the war was going badly. With U.S. forces in Korea retreating, President Truman declared a national state of emergency on December 16, and in early January 1951, Communist forces captured Seoul again. Capt. James Kim, one of only a few Korean American officers in the entire U.S. armed forces, was urgently needed. Soon after his college graduation ceremony, his reserve duty at the Pentagon ended, and he found himself sent on his way across the Pacific.

James had been an infantry officer leading men into battle in the Second World War, but he found himself assigned to an entirely different kind of duty in Korea. The army assigned him to the Central Intelligence Agency.

The CIA in 1950 was a fledgling organization that bore little resemblance to the global intelligence agency that it would later become. Founded only three years earlier, it had barely begun to gather the people and expertise that it needed for the challenges of the emerging Cold War. In Korea, the agency had already been part of major failures of intelligence, having been taken by surprise by the North Korean invasion of South Korea in June 1950 and then by the Chinese military intervention in the fall.

In October 1950 a new CIA director had taken charge—Gen. Walter Bedell Smith, a distinguished officer who had served as Supreme Allied Commander Dwight Eisenhower's chief of staff during the Second World War and as the U.S. ambassador to the Soviet Union in 1946–48. Recognizing the agency's deficiencies, Smith immediately began to act to remedy the weaknesses in its organization and personnel. For the war in Korea, the CIA needed people with knowledge of the country that the agency did not have yet.

Capt. James Kim, one of the few officers of Korean heritage in the U.S. armed services, was exactly whom the CIA needed. Serving as the intelligence officer of an infantry battalion in 1945 had already introduced him to intelligence work, and his postwar studies at the Georgetown University School of Foreign Service had educated him about the broader context of U.S. actions overseas. Although his only experience living in Korea during his adult life had been his brief stint there with the U.S. Army in 1945, and he barely knew the country's language, he was still more knowledgeable than anyone else who could be found. Moreover, his loyalty to the United States was beyond question given his years of military service and the medals that he had earned in combat in the Second World War.

The CIA sent James to its forward detachment in Pusan, the port city on Korea's southern coast. Five years earlier he had participated in the repatriation of hundreds of thousands of Japanese and Koreans through Pusan, and U.S. and South Korean forces had held out there against the North Korean invasion in August and September 1950.[1] He became the CIA's chief of base in Pusan and would serve in Korea for the duration of the war.[2]

Without knowing it, James was blazing a trail that his younger brothers would soon follow as they, too, became involved in the war in Korea.

Richard soon followed James into serving in the U.S. military during the Korean War, following yet another path that was distinctly his.

When the Korean War began, Richard had just completed his sophomore year at Dickinson College in Carlisle, Pennsylvania. He was also a master sergeant in the Pennsylvania National Guard, enlisted into its ranks by a providential coincidence. He attended an Episcopalian church in Carlisle whose rector happened to be the head chaplain of the Pennsylvania National Guard's 28th Infantry Division. The rector encouraged Richard to enlist, telling him that he could regain his Second World War rank as a sergeant and earn extra income to supplement the GI Bill benefits that he was relying on to attend college. With school expenses to pay and a wife to support, he reluctantly agreed to do it, more for the extra money than anything else.[3]

The massive U.S. military buildup needed to fight the Korean War and contain the Communist bloc worldwide soon included Richard's National Guard unit. In September 1950 the Department of Defense federalized four National Guard divisions for service overseas. Two would fight in Korea, and two would go to Europe to bolster the defense of the recently created North Atlantic Treaty Organization (NATO) against possible aggression by the Soviet Union. One of the units ordered to deploy to Europe was the 28th Infantry Division.[4]

Richard could have applied for deferment from active service. He was a college student and a married man, so he had two justifications for relief from the obligation to serve overseas. Avoiding the call-up was unacceptable to him, though, when his older brothers were going to war. Peter was already in Korea, and James was expecting to go after the campaign in Washington for David and their mother was completed. Richard was eager to follow his brothers into the wartime army again.

The U.S. Army had other plans for him though.

MSG Richard Kim was the chief noncommissioned officer in the 28th Infantry Division's intelligence section in September 1950. When the division went to Camp Atterbury, Indiana, to train for its overseas deployment, Richard did not go with it. Instead, he found himself commissioned as a second lieutenant and sent to Fort Bragg, North Carolina. There he joined the

525th Military Intelligence Group, which was preparing military intelligence teams for the war in Korea.[5]

The newly commissioned military intelligence officer trained for the war in Korea until the group returned to Fort Bragg from a field exercise in Texas. An unmarked brown envelope was waiting for him. When he opened the mysterious package, he found orders to report to Washington for a new assignment. The army had detailed him to the CIA.

Lieutenant Kim might have expected to follow James to the CIA's post in Korea, but like the army, the CIA had its own plans for him. Richard found himself assigned to the CIA field office in the U.S. Navy base complex at Yokosuka. Later the CIA reassigned him to the field office in Tokyo. He would serve in Japan for the duration of the Korean War and beyond.[6]

Arthur also followed his older brothers into the Korean War. Not yet a U.S. citizen or in the U.S. armed forces, he faced the longest path to the war of any of them.

He had left Shanghai in August 1947, sailing aboard a U.S. Army troop transport bound for Hawaii. Still only seventeen years old, he traveled with his mother on a U.S. military vessel as Peter's dependents. They went to live with Betty in Honolulu, where she was making a living working for Ming's, a prominent Hawaiian jewelry store. There Arthur finished his last year of high school at President Theodore Roosevelt High and stayed to continue his education at the University of Hawaii.

A struggle to stay in school followed. Arthur's problems began soon after his high school graduation in 1948, when Betty and their mother left Hawaii to return to Shanghai. Separated from his family for the first time, Arthur found it hard to concentrate on his studies. David sent money to pay for tuition, but Arthur was otherwise alone and without support. To have a place to live, he boarded with the family of a Korean Methodist minister and did chores for the church as a jack-of-all-trades helper. Financial hardship created a distraction that led to failing grades. If he did not improve enough to stay in school, then he would lose the student visa that allowed him to stay in the United States.

Peter tried to extend a lifeline to his youngest brother. He and Ruth had married in early 1948—freed to do so after she and her long-estranged husband, Ernest Moy, finally formally divorced after the war—and they were living in California while Peter was stationed at the Army Language School in Monterey. Concerned about Arthur's future and wanting to find a way to eliminate the distractions that were holding him back, Peter invited Arthur to live with him and Ruth and to attend nearby Monterey Peninsula College.

Arthur moved into Peter and Ruth's house, but the arrangement did not work out. Ruth did not share Peter's concern for Arthur's future, even though he had risked his life in the streets of Shanghai following her orders a few years earlier. She did not get along with him and refused to let him live in the same house. She made him leave, forcing him to find somewhere else to live.

To stay in school, Arthur resorted to moving ninety miles away to the inland city of Modesto. There, with the assistance of the Korean Methodist minister who had housed him in Hawaii, he found a Methodist church secretary willing to rent him a room in her family's house. He worked as a houseboy in exchange for the room and his daily meals, and attended Modesto Junior College. To earn some income, he went to work outside the house after school and during weekends. In what was then and still is primarily an agricultural area, the work was on a farm. He was milking cows by hand at a dairy farm when the Korean War began in June 1950.

Far away in Washington, his older brother James was fighting for the legislation to admit him, David, and their mother into the United States. In Korea, the battlefront seesawed back and forth until a massive Communist Chinese military intervention sent U.S. and UN forces reeling south in defeat during the winter of 1950. With his older brothers going to war, Arthur decided to act on his own to change the course of his life. Now nineteen years old, he, too, could enlist, and he figured that his Chinese language skills, which he had picked up during his childhood in Shanghai, would be useful to the U.S. armed forces in their fight against Chinese forces in Korea.

Volunteering for military service proved more difficult for Arthur in California than it had been for Peter and Richard in China during the world war a handful of years earlier. Arthur first approached an army recruiter, who turned him away, telling him that the regular army could accept only U.S. citizens for enlistment. Arthur then asked the draft board in Modesto about entering through the draft, but the board told him that it was not taking noncitizens on student visas.

Arthur did not let the rejections stop him, and the Modesto draft board's denial gave him an idea. He no longer needed a student visa to stay in the country after being made a U.S. permanent resident by an act of Congress. He quit school and borrowed ninety-nine dollars—more money than he had at the time—from the owner of the dairy farm where he had been working to buy a one-way ticket on a ship to Hawaii. Entirely voluntarily, he had registered for the draft in Honolulu while living there a year earlier, foreseeing that a wartime draft could become his path to citizenship. Now he hoped that a draft board in heavily Asian American Hawaii would view him more favorably than the one in largely white, rural California.

Upon arriving in Honolulu in April 1951, Arthur contacted the draft board to say that he was again in Hawaii under its jurisdiction and that he had quit school, so it should draft him. Then he waited for a response.[7] Three months later, on July 9, 1951, his draft notice arrived.[8]

In the army, Pvt. Arthur Kim found a new world where he was needed, as his older brothers had in the Second World War. The army's intelligence branch eagerly snapped up the newly inducted private, whose Chinese language skills were urgently required since Communist Chinese forces had intervened in the Korean War. He became a specialist in prisoner of war interrogation and was sent to serve in one of the main intelligence units of the U.S. Eighth Army in Korea, the 302nd Military Intelligence Company. He became only the second Asian American in the company, which needed any knowledge of the people and languages of Korea and China that the army could find for it.

For its base in Seoul, the company in 1952 received a large house that from 1945 to 1949 had been the headquarters of the Korean Provisional Government and the residence of its leader, Kim Ku. Cpl. Arthur Kim's quarters were the room where Kim Ku had been assassinated in June 1949, which the company headquarters had allocated to him without knowing its significance. This coincidence connected Arthur to a key figure in the history of Korea and a perilous moment for his own family. Twenty years earlier, Kim Ku had planned and organized the April 1932 bombing of the Japanese military command in Shanghai that had led to the arrest and death of Arthur's uncle Ahn Chang Ho and had forced his own family to go into hiding.[9]

From this base in Seoul, Arthur participated in actions all over Korea, including the interrogation of prisoners of war in the massive POW camp on Geoje Island. By 1952 it held more than 150,000 North Korean and Chinese POWs who had been relocated from camps on the mainland of Korea. The enormous population had grown beyond the ability of U.S. and South Korean guards to control, and diehard Communist POWs had seized control of much of the camp. Communist groups armed with improvised weapons staged uprisings and murdered former comrades who had turned against the North Korean and Chinese Communist regimes. In May 1952 a North Korean plot succeeded in capturing the U.S. general commanding the camp, and he was held hostage for several days.

While violence raged inside the camps and North Korean and Chinese generals at the peace negotiations in Panmunjom demanded the return of all of their captured soldiers, U.S. Army intelligence linguists carried out the difficult task of screening the many thousands of POWs for those who did not want to go back. Arthur, who had himself left Shanghai just ahead of the Chinese Communist victory a few years earlier, participated in the interrogations of Chinese POWs. In interrogation sessions on Geoje and then on the island of Cheju after Chinese POWs were relocated there by the end of 1952, he identified many who refused to return to the People's Republic of China and demanded to be sent to Taiwan.

Unexpected dangers sometimes arose during these POW interrogation missions, including the terrifying experience of being mistaken for the enemy. North Korean and Chinese POWs were issued U.S. Army fatigues to wear, and as an Asian junior enlisted man wearing minimal insignia on his uniform, Arthur was easy to mistake for a prisoner. His commanding officer once confused him for a POW and pushed him into a truck full of prisoners who were about to be sent back to their prison camp after an interrogation session. In a panic, Arthur shouted the captain's name and a stream of American curses, demanding to be let out. Fortunately, the officer recognized his mistake and let Arthur out of the truck.[10]

Lesser instances of being mistaken for a Korean bothered Arthur during his wartime service. While driving a jeep across a bridge over the Han River, he stopped at a checkpoint and had to deal with a military policeman who questioned him in simple broken English, assuming that he was Korean. Even responding in perfect American English and showing his U.S. Army dog tags did not dispel the disbelief of the military policeman, who still thought that Arthur had to be Korean because of his last name. After these incidents, Arthur painted the largest rank chevrons on his helmet that he could after his promotion to corporal, thinking that the extra-large stripes might help make him appear more obviously American.[11]

By the end of the war in July 1953, Arthur had been promoted to sergeant and, as a noncommissioned officer, was in charge of operations for his military intelligence company. Moreover, he had become well known at the CIA's office in U.S. Eighth Army headquarters in Seoul, located only two blocks from his company's headquarters.[12] His brother Capt. James Kim, the CIA's chief of base in Pusan, was a regular visitor at the CIA base in Seoul, whose cover name was the Joint Advisory Commission, Korea (JACK).[13] The staff at the JACK became familiar with the nearby younger brother of their chief of base in Pusan and identified the Chinese-speaking army sergeant as an ideal recruit for the CIA.

Two years after struggling to find a way to volunteer for the U.S. Army when he was not yet a U.S. citizen, Arthur was on his way to a career as an American intelligence officer.

[CHAPTER 749]

AN ACT

To provide for the naturalization of Peter Kim.

Be it enacted by the Senate and House of Representatives of the United States of America in Congress assembled, That upon compliance with all other provisions of section 701 or 702 of the Nationality Act of 1940, as amended (56 Stat. 182–183; 8 U. S. C. 1001–1009), Peter Kim, Army of the United States, Army serial number 10500015, may be naturalized pursuant to either of said sections as may be applicable, notwithstanding the fact that at the time of his enlistment or induction into the armed forces of the United States, he had not been lawfully admitted to the United States and was not a resident thereof.

Approved August 2, 1946.

[CHAPTER 40]

AN ACT

To provide for permanent residence status of Richard Kim.

Be it enacted by the Senate and House of Representatives of the United States of America in Congress assembled, That in the administration of the immigration and naturalization laws Richard Kim, who served as a member of the armed forces of the United States, shall be considered to have been lawfully admitted for permanent residence as of the date of his last entry into the United States, upon the payment of the visa fee of $10 and the head tax of $8. The Secretary of State is directed to instruct the proper quota-control officer to deduct one number from the appropriate quota for the first year that said quota is available.

Approved March 29, 1949.

[CHAPTER 1068]

AN ACT

For the relief of Mrs. Chang-Sei Kim, David Kim, and Arthur Kim.

Be it enacted by the Senate and House of Representatives of the United States of America in Congress assembled, That, notwithstanding the provisions of section 13 (c) of the Immigration Act of 1924, as amended, Mrs. Chang-Sei Kim and David Kim may be eligible for admission into the United States for permanent residence provided they are otherwise admissible under the immigration laws.

SEC. 2. The Attorney General is authorized and directed to record the lawful admission for permanent residence in the United States of Arthur Kim as of the date of his last entry into the United States upon payment of the required visa fee and head tax. The Secretary of State shall, upon the enactment of this Act, instruct the proper quota-control officer to deduct one number from the appropriate quota for the first year that such quota is available.

Approved September 27, 1950.

17. The published texts of Private Law 808, An act to provide for the naturalization of Peter Kim; Private Law 11, An act to provide for permanent residence status of Richard Kim; and Private Law 1028, An act for the relief of Mrs. Chang-Sei Kim, David Kim, and Arthur Kim. U.S. Government Printing Office.

18. James Kim at his Georgetown University commencement ceremony. Kim family collection.

19. Pvt. Arthur Kim in 1951. Army Signal Corps photo; courtesy of Arthur Kim.

20. Capt. James Kim and Cpl. Arthur Kim at the headquarters of the 302nd Military Intelligence Company in Seoul, 1953. Courtesy of Arthur Kim.

21. Mrs. Ruth Kim receiving the Presidential Medal of Freedom at Fort Ord, California, September 15, 1951. Presenting her with the medal is Maj. Gen. Robert A. McClure, a founder of U.S. military psychological operations who had nominated her for the award in 1945. Courtesy of the George C. Marshall Foundation, Lexington, Virginia.

22. Marshall Carter and Peter Kim around 1970, after their retirements from military service. Courtesy of the George C. Marshall Foundation, Lexington, Virginia.

23. (*above*) North Korean defector No Kum-Sok shaking hands with Vice President Richard Nixon, flanked by James Kim and Representative Joseph Holt, the son of J. Frank Holt, James Kim's benefactor in 1938–39. Kim family collection.

24. (*left*) James and Jane Kim on their wedding day in Seoul, April 19, 1954. Kim family collection.

25. Lt. Col. James Kim's headstone in Arlington National Cemetery, declaring his service in World War II and the Korean War and his Bronze Star and Purple Heart medals. Author photo.

26. Maj. Richard Kim with the Special Forces in Vietnam. Courtesy of Richard Kim.

27. Maj. Richard Kim receiving his second Air Medal from Brig. Gen. William Ray Peers, 1964. Courtesy of Richard Kim.

28. (*above*) Lt. Col. Richard Kim receiving congratulations for his promotion in 1969 from Lt. Gen. Alfred D. Starbird, commander of the Defense Communications Planning Group and Operation Igloo White, and Rear Adm. James R. Reedy. Courtesy of Richard Kim.

29. (*left*) Rev. Richard Kim, 1980s. Courtesy of Richard Kim.

30. The retired reverend Richard Kim with his grandson Schuyler Shigemura at a Yonsei University exhibit on the life of Dr. Kim Chang Sei. Courtesy of Richard Kim.

PART 4

Four Careers in Intelligence and Special Operations

19

Maj. Peter Kim,
U.S. Army Intelligence

AFTER THE KOREAN War, Peter's service as an intelligence officer in the U.S. Army continued for more than a decade. His career continued to be inextricably tied to that of Gen. Marshall Carter, who had befriended him in China, had chosen him for the Operation Sparrow mission to Shanghai that changed the course of his life and the lives of his entire family, and then had led the campaign to reward him with U.S. citizenship.

Peter again served under Marshall Carter's command in 1960, when the then–major general became chief of staff of the Eighth Army, the U.S. Army's forces in Korea. Carter chose him to serve as his aide-de-camp, a choice assignment that normally went to a young officer considered to be a rising star on his way to higher ranks and senior leadership positions. Carter faced criticism from his peers for selecting an overage captain whose career had already reached its peak, but he ignored them, responding that the army's foremost Korean American intelligence officer was a most appropriate aide for the second in command of U.S. forces in Korea. Serving as Carter's aide-de-camp was Peter's second and final assignment in the country.[1]

In the early 1960s, Peter again served at the Army Language School in Monterey, California. A decade after training there and taking in his younger brother Arthur as a struggling student, Peter became the director of the school's Special Projects and Analysis Division. In this assignment he reached his final rank of major.

Peter and Marshall Carter continued to be the closest of friends as Carter rose to leading positions in the intelligence community. Promoted to lieutenant general, Carter became the deputy director of the Central Intelligence Agency in 1962. In 1965 Carter became the director of the National Security Agency, a position that he held until his retirement in 1969.

In 1964, twenty years after volunteering to enlist in the U.S. Army in China as a fugitive from Shanghai, Maj. Peter Kim retired from military service. A civilian for the first time since returning to America, he went to work for the Ampex Corporation, a leading manufacturer of audiotape recorders that had developed the first commercially successful video tape in the 1950s. He became a member of the marketing team of Ampex, which sold equipment to the armed services and the intelligence community.

Ruth Moy, now Mrs. Ruth Kim, had in the meantime received exceptionally high honors for her actions during the Second World War. In 1951 she received the Presidential Medal of Freedom, the nation's highest civilian honor. The award cited her operation of a safe house for U.S. Army intelligence in Shanghai and her crucial contributions to U.S. intelligence collection in 1944. The medal was the only award granted to any member of the Kim family for their actions resisting the Japanese occupation in Shanghai during the Second World War.[2]

Peter and Ruth settled down near his last post in Monterey, in the picturesque seaside town of Carmel-by-the-Sea. Long home to writers and artists such as Jack London, John Steinbeck, and Ansel Adams, Carmel was becoming a favorite residence of numerous Hollywood celebrities, from Bing Crosby to Clint Eastwood. For Peter and Ruth, it was a world away from the strife that they had lived through in Shanghai for so many years. In Carmel, they finally found a peaceful place to call home after spending the prime years of their adult lives in a city under enemy occupation and then in two decades of military service.

Ruth, fourteen years older than Peter, passed away first. She died of natural causes in 1977 at the age of seventy-nine. Her passing took away perhaps the only person, aside from his brothers, capable of fully understanding what

Peter had lived through in the preceding half century of his life. He remarried a few years later, but the connection to his new bride could never have been the same.[3]

Another pillar of Peter's life disappeared in 1993 when Marshall Carter passed away at the age of eighty-three in Colorado Springs, Colorado. Remaining as close as brothers despite time and distance, the two men and their wives had gathered regularly over the years to reminisce about the old days and maintain their friendship. With Carter's death, Peter lost his closest friend and one of the last connections to his past.[4]

Peter was almost alone as he reached eighty years of age, with no children of his own and his family scattered all over the United States. His brothers' careers in intelligence had sent them all over the world and eventually to the Washington DC area on the other side of the country. David, Betty, and their mother had all settled down in Hawaii in 1950. The last time that the entire family had been together was after he, James, and Richard had returned to Shanghai in 1945 as victorious American soldiers, before taking their separate journeys to the United States beginning in 1946. With no family or wartime friends within thousands of miles, he became increasingly isolated in his old age.

On February 25, 1995, Peter committed suicide. He took his own life at the age of eighty-two, more than sixty years after his father had done so at half his age. Peter's passing ended a great American life that had begun in Pyongyang, grown to adulthood in the United States and Shanghai, and blazed a trail back to America for himself and his family through extraordinary wartime actions.

Tragically, Peter gave up on life early in the year when the fiftieth anniversary of victory in the Second World War inspired new interest in long-ignored actions of the generation that fought the war. Within a few years, the nation began to call it the Greatest Generation, and stories of wartime actions that had been hidden by ongoing secrecy or simply overlooked for half a century began to be told to the public. If Peter had held on longer, his story of overcoming seemingly insurmountable obstacles to liberate thousands of Allied civilians in Operation Sparrow and to win his American citizenship might have found an appreciative audience. The premature end of his life in 1995 meant that he was not around to tell his tale when the world was ready to listen.

From a cliff near Carmel where Peter's journey had come to an end, his ashes were scattered in the Pacific Ocean that he had crossed so many times in his life. No cenotaph or other memorial to him exists anywhere.

One place, however, has preserved the memory of Peter Kim and his extraordinary life into the twenty-first century, a place that no one would expect. The George C. Marshall Foundation, an institution dedicated to perpetuating the legacy of General of the Army George Catlett Marshall—chief of staff of the U.S. Army during the Second World War, secretary of state and then secretary of defense under President Truman, and architect of the Marshall Plan—preserves the papers documenting the life and military service of Peter Kim, along with his final army uniform and officer's sword.[5]

Lt. Gen. Marshall Carter, a protégé of George C. Marshall, served after his retirement from the military as the president of the foundation for its first fifteen years. Carter made sure that the life of his best friend would be permanently memorialized in his own personal papers in the George C. Marshall Foundation's archives. Housed at the Virginia Military Institute in Lexington, the archive maintains this testament to the life and significance of Peter Kim. It should endure as long as Americans care to preserve the memory of the generation that fought the Second World War and look to it for example and inspiration.

20

James Kim, CIA Pioneer

JAMES'S ASSIGNMENT TO the CIA during the Korean War set him up for what would become his life's work. After the negotiation of an armistice brought hostilities to a close in July 1953, he resigned his commission as a regular officer in the U.S. Army and joined the CIA full time as a civilian. He would stay with the agency for more than two decades, and as the organization grew, he quietly rose in its leadership ranks, higher than anyone could have imagined for an Asian American in his era.

When James left Korea, he returned to the United States on an assignment for the CIA. In April 1954 he was chosen to escort a prized North Korean defector to the United States. No Kum-Sok, a Soviet-trained fighter pilot who had flown numerous combat missions during the Korean War, had escaped from North Korea in September 1953 by flying his MiG-15 fighter south to Kimpo Air Base outside of Seoul. No received a reward of $100,000 for defecting with an operational MiG-15, followed by a far greater prize: permission to emigrate to the United States. James received the task of taking No to his new home in America.[1]

James escorted No on flights to Manila, then to San Francisco, and ultimately to Washington DC. James took the star defector to the Capitol, where only a few years earlier he had lobbied for the legislation that let his mother and younger brothers into the country. There to show them around was Representative Joseph Holt, a Republican from California who was the son of J.

Frank Holt, James's benefactor when he was alone and living in a Los Angeles YMCA in 1938. No met Vice President Richard Nixon in his Senate office, and Holt then introduced him to Congress on the floor of the House of Representatives.[2]

James then took No to New York, where No appeared on the NBC television morning news program *Today*, which featured him in an interview. James served as No's translator on the *Today* show, a media appearance that would be considered unthinkable for a CIA operations officer.[3]

No's ultimate destination was Wilmington, Delaware, where the CIA arranged for him to attend the University of Delaware to help him adjust to life in the United States. James drove him there and set him up for his new life as a college student before introducing him to his new handlers, opening a bank account, teaching him how to handle his finances for the first time, and helping him to understand his new country.[4]

James returned from Korea with more than just a prized intelligence asset. He also returned with a bride, whom he met at his CIA post in Pusan.

Jane Yang was a native of Seoul who had escaped with her family ahead of the North Korean occupation of the city in June 1950 and fled to Pusan. In Pusan, she was hired by the personnel officer of the CIA forward detachment that James commanded. James, still unmarried at the age of thirty, could not help noticing the pretty but shy and modest young woman working in his office. After hours she and some of her co-workers would play the piano in the house that served as the detachment's headquarters, and he would listen silently, unnoticed by her.

Eventually he summoned up the courage to invite Jane to dine with him. She was initially reluctant to socialize with the boss, and he quickly found that there was a significant language barrier between them: She did not speak English well, and he knew little if any Korean, having grown up among Americans and speaking English. He was as foreign to her as any American GI would have been. Somehow they made it through their initial awkwardness to become friends. James made an effort to learn Korean and eventually obtain her parents' permission to court their daughter. The courtship continued after Jane and her family returned to Seoul upon its final liberation from Communist forces in early 1951.[5]

Jane's parents regarded James with the wariness that many Koreans held toward American soldiers, even those of Korean heritage. When he first called on them, they questioned him about his parents, and he could tell them little more than that his mother and father were originally from Pyongyang. He could tell them nothing about his grandparents, whom he had never met. Jane's parents consented to the marriage only reluctantly, concerned about the character of their foreign future son-in-law.[6]

James and Jane married on April 19, 1954. The mayor of Seoul, Kim Tai Sun, presided over the ceremony, reflecting James's stature in the U.S. mission in Korea.

Only four days later, James left Korea to take No Kum-Sok to the United States, leaving Jane behind in Seoul. Her mother, outraged at the apparent desertion, told Jane that she had made a mistake by marrying an untrustworthy American. She did not know that arrangements were in place for Jane to join her husband in the United States about a month later. Jane flew to Washington in May while James was busy there handling the North Korean defector's introduction to life in America. Now he had to do the same for his new bride.[7]

James was thirty-three years of age and starting what he considered to be his first real full-time job after having spent twelve years as a soldier in two wars and in college. He and Jane began their life together in modest surroundings on his meager government salary, supplemented by pay and benefits from his ongoing service as an army reserve officer. They moved into a small apartment on the farthest fringe of Southeast Washington, the lowest-rent area of the nation's capital then and now. The now world-famous CIA headquarters in Langley, Virginia, did not exist yet—its construction would not begin until 1959—so James commuted to the CIA's original offices in downtown Washington for training as an operations officer.[8]

His career path would send him to Europe and Africa, not back to Asia. His main foreign language was French, which he had first learned while living in Shanghai's French Concession as a child, not any Asian language.[9] Senior leadership of CIA operations assigned him to serve in Francophone countries in Europe, then in sub-Saharan Africa.[10]

Serving as an intelligence officer in Africa in the 1960s made James a pioneer in a hotly contested arena of the Cold War. As the European colonial empires in Africa ended and independent states emerged all over the continent, the Soviet Union and its Communist allies vied for influence over numerous newly created national governments—seventeen in 1960 alone—in a region where the United States had little history of involvement. James would spend more than a decade in Africa quietly advancing the interests of the United States in one recently established country after another, including Mali, Nigeria, and the Democratic Republic of the Congo, called Zaire from 1971 to 1997.[11]

James's superiors recognized his abilities by promoting him to the agency's senior leadership ranks in the early 1960s. The promotion preceded Congress's enacting the Civil Rights Act of 1964 that banned discrimination based on race or national origin. Without fanfare, the CIA made James Kim one of the agency's historic figures.

The CIA further acknowledged James's outstanding service by awarding him the Intelligence Medal of Merit, one of the agency's highest decorations.

James retired in 1975 after a quarter of a century with the CIA. He did consulting work in Europe and Africa for several years after his retirement before eventually settling into his second and final retirement. He and Jane then could enjoy their lives as competitive amateur golfers and fully retired grandparents, with their children and grandchildren not far from them in Northern Virginia.

James Kim passed away at the age of eighty in May 2001. He rests in the hallowed ground of Arlington National Cemetery, among veterans of more than a century of U.S. wars.[12] His headstone declares his final U.S. Army rank of lieutenant colonel and his service in World War II and the Korean War, but it can tell an observer nothing about his struggles to go to war as a normal American in World War II or to persuade members of Congress to take extraordinary action to admit his family into the United States at the beginning of the Korean War. Of course, it displays no reference to his career in the CIA from its early years in the Korean War to the height of the Cold War in Europe and Africa.

Millions of visitors to Arlington National Cemetery each year walk past James Kim's final resting place without even knowing that it is there, in the section closest to the visitors' parking lot and entrance. They are overlooking a memorial to a unique veteran of the Second World War in the Pacific and one of the pioneers of the modern U.S. intelligence community.

21

Lt. Col. and Rev. Richard Kim, Army Special Forces

AFTER THE END of the Korean War, Lt. Richard Kim found himself with a choice to make about his future. The CIA wanted him to remain with the agency as a civilian after his assignment to their field office in Tokyo ended in 1955.[1] Following in the footsteps of his older brother James tempted him, and he considered becoming a paramilitary operations officer for the CIA. The U.S. Army wanted him as well, though, and it had recently created a branch called the Special Forces in 1952. Founded to wage unconventional warfare against Communist forces worldwide, the Special Forces also needed soldiers with unusual backgrounds and skills.

Excited by the unconventional warfare mission of the Special Forces, Lieutenant Kim chose to stay in the army and become a career officer. The service separated him from the National Guard and integrated him into the regular army, setting him on a path to become one of the early leaders of the then little-known but soon-to-be-renowned Special Forces.[2]

After airborne training at Fort Benning, Georgia, Richard went to the Special Forces base at Fort Bragg, North Carolina, to join the 77th Special Forces Group (SFG), one of the branch's original two units.[3] He became the commander of an Operational Detachment Alpha, better known to the public as an A-team, the primary fighting unit of the Special Forces. Leading an

A-team put him in charge of twelve experienced noncommissioned officers, each trained in multiple skills for the variety of operations that the Special Forces were preparing to carry out all over the world.

One of his A-team's first training missions demonstrated the range of skills for unconventional warfare that the Special Forces were developing in these early years. For a winter mountaineering training exercise to prepare the men to survive in the harsh conditions of the Alps or Scandinavia and fight a Soviet invasion of Western Europe, they flew from Fort Bragg to Colorado in a c-119 transport to make a then-record high-altitude parachute jump into deep snow in the mountains around Camp Hale and Leadville. Richard led the team though weeks of training in mountain climbing, skiing, and a range of wilderness survival skills before they flew back to Fort Bragg, parachuting onto one of the base's drop zones.

His first overseas mission with the Special Forces came a year later in early 1957. Instead of going to Europe with his A-team, Richard went back to Asia with a military training team (MTT) in Taiwan. The team's mission was to train Chinese soldiers who would become the special forces of the Nationalist Chinese army. They were predominantly former prisoners of war from the Korean War who had refused repatriation to Communist China and had demanded to be sent to Taiwan. Richard was already linked to these now elite soldiers in the army of Nationalist China, as his younger brother Arthur was likely to have been the U.S. Army interrogator to whom they revealed their desire not to return to Communist China.

Richard's assignment with the MTT in Taiwan lasted for six months. Afterward he spent a brief period outside the Special Forces when the army sent him to the Infantry School at Fort Benning for its Infantry Officers Advanced Course and then assigned him to the 9th Infantry Division in Fort Carson, Colorado. As a company commander in an armored battalion, he supervised the training of newly drafted soldiers.

Richard returned to the Special Forces in 1959 when he received orders to join the 10th SFG in Germany, the other original Special Forces group. The 10th SFG was responsible for unconventional warfare all over Europe, including guerrilla operations in enemy-occupied territory in the event that the Soviet Union went to war with NATO and invaded and overran Western Europe. Richard again took command of an A-team, this time with the wartime mission of organizing resistance behind the "iron curtain" in Czechoslovakia.

In 1960 he was reassigned to the 10th SFG's headquarters staff. As the assistant plans officer (S-3 in U.S. Army parlance), he planned unconventional warfare field exercises across Europe. One was a 1961 theater-wide exercise code-named Devil Jump, which deployed the entire 10th SFG to the U.S. air base at Evreux, France, and parachuted its A-teams all over Germany to conduct joint guerrilla warfare exercises with other army forces, the navy, the air force, and the CIA.[4]

Richard's second role with 10th SFG's headquarters helped create the enduring public image of the U.S. Army's Special Forces. He became half of the 10th SFG's two-man briefing team when he was partnered with Capt. Michael Healy, an officer who had led U.S. Army Rangers in the Korean War and would later become a major general and a legendary figure in the Special Forces. The U.S. forces in Germany knew Healy and Kim as the "Huntley-Brinkley briefers," a play on the name of the NBC national news program *The Huntley-Brinkley Report*. Kim and Healy's briefings introduced the Special Forces to visiting political and media figures, including *New York Times* publisher Arthur Sulzberger, whose newspaper soon afterward reported on the up-and-coming service branch and its special relationship to the newly elected President Kennedy.

During his time in Germany, Richard pursued other activities outside his wide-ranging duties with the Special Forces. He learned German, which became his main foreign language following the Shanghainese and French that he had learned during his childhood in Shanghai's French Concession. He also trained as a ham radio operator and became a member of the Military Auxiliary Radio System, a mostly civilian organization that provided an emergency wartime backup for military communications.

His amateur radio skills became an asset to the Special Forces in July 1960 when the 10th SFG sent a team of three French-speaking operators to the Congo on a clandestine mission to rescue American citizens as civil war and lawlessness overwhelmed the newly independent country.[5] It was the first operation undertaken by the Special Forces for the U.S. Army in Europe, and it had a problem: No army field radio could transmit across the long distance between Germany and the Congo. Richard's ham radio served as the 10th SFG's communications link to its team in the field as the men moved around remote rural areas of the Congo.[6]

Another unusual task came when 10th SFG received a request for a French-speaking Asian to work with the Treasury Department. Being the only soldier in the entire 10th SFG who met this description, Capt. Richard Kim was given the mission of masquerading as a Chinese Communist official visiting Paris from Switzerland to buy millions of counterfeit U.S. dollars. He and an undercover agent from the Secret Service, which was formerly part of the Treasury Department and investigates counterfeiting along with protecting the nation's leaders, went to a café on the Champs Elysées to meet the sellers. The counterfeiters never showed up, however, apparently sensing that a trap had been set for them.[7]

In the summer of 1962, Captain Kim returned stateside to attend the Command and General Staff College at Fort Leavenworth, Kansas. Promoted to major after graduation in 1963, he returned to the Special Forces—by this time, colloquially known as the Green Berets—ready for higher responsibilities at the exact time when they were taking the leading role in the conflict that would define them for a generation.

The U.S. military's presence in Vietnam, which was divided in two at the conclusion of the war that ended French colonial rule in 1954, was rapidly becoming the primary responsibility of the U.S. Army Special Forces in 1963. After years of its operators acting as military advisers to the army of South Vietnam, the Special Forces took over a CIA program to organize and lead the mountain tribes of Vietnam's Central Highlands to fight the insurgency of the Vietcong. U.S. troops in Vietnam exceeded ten thousand personnel and kept rising as first the counterinsurgency campaign faltered, then protests against the government of South Vietnam began in May, and a military coup toppled the government in November.

Years before the U.S. Marines landed in March 1965 and escalated the war in Vietnam, which would involve hundreds of thousands of American servicemen, the Special Forces had been fighting Vietcong guerrillas and units of the army of North Vietnam in the Central Highlands. Maj. Richard Kim volunteered to go to Vietnam to join the provisional Special Forces group created to lead this campaign. He arrived soon after the newly created SFG took over responsibility for the local forces, named the Civilian Irregular Defense Group (CIDG), in a transfer called Operation Switchback.

For the next year, Major Kim served as the Special Forces group's intelligence officer, and Michael Healy, his friend from the 10th SFG in Germany, was its operations officer. As the SFG's intelligence officer, Richard's duty was to visit all of the Special Forces camps around the country and assess the intelligence they had gathered. The threat of surprise attack hung over each camp, and warning signs of Vietcong preparations rarely were found in time. More than one camp was attacked not long after a visit by the intelligence officer.

One of them was the camp at Nam Dong. Located in northern South Vietnam near the border with Laos, Nam Dong held more than three hundred CIDG troops along with a dozen Special Forces military advisers and an Australian adviser. Two weeks after Richard visited the camp and reviewed reports of nearby Vietcong supply caches, an attack early in the morning of July 5, 1964, took the lives of fifty Vietnamese, two Americans, and the Australian. The commander, Capt. Roger Donlon, would be awarded the Congressional Medal of Honor for leading the camp's defense despite being severely wounded. He became the war's first recipient of the Medal of Honor and was the first member of the Special Forces to be so honored. Richard helped write the recommendation that led to the award.

Richard was himself wounded after an attack on another camp. Visiting a camp that had been hit, he and the executive officer went outside the barbed wire perimeter to inspect the Vietcong's firing positions from the attack. After they found to their surprise that the Vietcong had cleverly used glowing June bugs attached to sticks to mark the direction of fire toward the camp's defensive positions, the executive officer stepped on a mine, and the explosion blew his foot off. The shrapnel superficially wounded Richard as well.

The Purple Heart from this wound was followed by numerous additional decorations. He had seen enough combat to receive the Combat Infantryman's

Badge and gone on enough helicopter-borne missions to receive two Air Medals.[8] He qualified as an aircrewman, receiving Aircrew Wings, and was awarded Vietnamese jump wings for training South Vietnam's paratroopers.

Senior officers of the U.S. military command in Vietnam were so impressed by Major Kim's actions in Vietnam that one recommended him for a position reflecting his high esteem among the army's leadership. The day before his departure from Vietnam in July 1964, Maj. Gen. Richard Stilwell, the chief of operations for Military Assistance Command, Vietnam, stated that he had personally written the Department of the Army to request that Major Kim receive an assignment to the U.S. Military Academy at West Point to serve as a tactical officer. In that position, he would have commanded a cadet company of approximately 125 young men, with the responsibility of instructing and mentoring future leaders of the U.S. Army.

The general's recommendation made an unequivocal statement that Richard Kim represented, as well as any officer, the values of the U.S. Army and the nation that it defends. It was comparable to the efforts of Gen. George Olmsted and Col. Marshall Carter to secure U.S. citizenship and a commission as an officer for Peter Kim two decades earlier.

With the war in Vietnam escalating and the Special Forces increasingly committed to the fight, the army needed Richard elsewhere in 1964. Rather than West Point, his next assignment was at the Pentagon with the U.S. Army General Staff in the Special Operations Division of the Office of the Deputy Chief of Staff. The head of the division was Brig. Gen. William Ray Peers, who had served with the OSS in Burma and China during the Second World War and with the CIA in the Korean War. Peers later rose to lieutenant general and became best known to the public as the head of the army's investigation of the 1968 My Lai Massacre.

Richard Kim was assigned to one of the most secretive covert operations of the Vietnam War in 1966. The U.S. Army, Air Force, and Navy created a highly classified joint task force to provide intelligence to support the interdiction of North Vietnamese supply lines through Laos and Cambodia that were known to Americans as the Ho Chi Minh Trail. Working under various names over time but ultimately known as Operation Igloo White, the task force used air force and navy electronic warfare aircraft to collect information from newly developed sensor devices dropped along the Ho Chi Minh Trail. An intelligence cell located far away in Washington DC, on the grounds of the U.S. Naval Observatory—better known as the residence of the vice president—analyzed and assessed the information to provide targeting data to air force and navy attack aircraft.

Maj. Richard Kim served with the intelligence cell, which was named the Defense Communications Planning Group (DCPG) and also called Joint Task Force 728. First, he was chief of the production branch of the DCPG, responsible for producing intelligence reports; then he became chief of the Intelligence Division. He voluntarily spent several months of his time with the DCPG in Vietnam in 1967–68, taking charge of the Igloo White intelligence collection program in the field.

In Washington, Richard represented the Igloo White program to officials at the highest levels of the intelligence community. The head of the DCPG, Lt. Gen. Alfred Starbird, brought Major Kim to the White House to brief the retired general Maxwell Taylor, the former chairman of the Joint Chiefs of Staff and ambassador to South Vietnam who had become the chairman of the President's Foreign Intelligence Advisory Board and the science adviser to the president. On another occasion, Richard accompanied General Starbird to Fort Meade, Maryland, to brief the director of the National Security Agency, Lt. Gen. Marshall Carter, who was delighted to see the younger brother of his comrade and best friend, Maj. Peter Kim.

Richard returned to the Special Forces in Asia for another field command, this time far from Vietnam, in the spring of 1968. Assigned to the 1st Special Forces Group in Okinawa, Major Kim became the commander of its Company A. The commander of the 1st SFG was Col. Robert Rheault, one of the best educated and most accomplished officers in the Special Forces. Educated at Philips Exeter Academy, West Point, and La Sorbonne, Rheault was considered a rising star and destined for promotion to general. Kim and Rheault had already served together in 1959 with the 10th SFG in Germany and in 1964 at the Pentagon with the Special Operations Division of the U.S. Army General Staff.

As commander of the 1st SFG's Company A, Richard led joint exercises in the Philippines and South Korea with the special forces of each nation.

The exercise in Korea in 1969 began with a parachute drop along the Han River outside of Seoul. When he hit the ground, it was the first time he had set foot on the soil of the country of his birth since his family had left it forty years earlier, when he was only a year old.

The year 1969 would be the peak of Richard Kim's career with the Special Forces. Colonel Rheault left the 1st Special Forces Group to command the 5th Special Forces Group in Vietnam, and his replacement was Col. Charles Simpson, another colleague from the 10th SFG in Germany and the Pentagon. Richard was promoted to lieutenant colonel and became the deputy commander of the 1st SFG. In the following year, the Special Forces planned to have Simpson and Kim become the commander and deputy commander, respectively, of the premier Special Forces formation in Vietnam—the 5th Special Forces Group.

This bright future suddenly clouded as a result of the most infamous event in the history of the Special Forces, one that became known to millions of people worldwide in a fictionalized form created by Hollywood: Colonel Rheault was arrested in July 1969 and charged with murder for the death of a Vietnamese double agent. Rheault later became the basis for the character Colonel Kurtz, an exceptionally talented Special Forces officer charged with murder for the death of a Vietnamese double agent, in the motion picture *Apocalypse Now*.

Although the charges against Rheault ultimately were dropped, the criminal case ended his military career. It also ruined the career of Colonel Simpson, a West Point classmate of Rheault's in the class of 1946. Wanting to support his friend in his time of crisis, Simpson had flown from Okinawa to Vietnam to visit Rheault in the stockade without first getting authorization or informing the U.S. commanding general in Vietnam, Gen. Creighton Abrams. A renowned armor officer who would later become chief of staff of the army, Abrams had ordered Rheault's arrest and was determined to rein in Special Forces officers whom he considered to have gone out of control during the long war in Vietnam.

Richard Kim's career survived the downfall of his commanding officer and friend, but his faith in the army did not. The treatment of Rheault and Simpson left him disillusioned and uncertain whether he wanted to continue to be part of the institution in which he had spent most of his adult life. After serving in three wars and excelling as a commander and an intelligence officer with the elite Special Forces, he had earned the respect of the army's senior leaders and achieved everything needed to join their ranks, but he now doubted that he wanted to be one of them.

At the same time, a new voice had begun calling out to him. It was from a far higher power than the army's generals, and it called him toward a new direction in life, one that he had never considered before then.

The Episcopal Church had long been an important part of Richard's life, playing a pivotal role in how he ended up in the army in the first place. As a college student in Pennsylvania two decades earlier, he had followed the advice of the rector of his church when he enlisted in the National Guard, with no intention of making a career in the army. In 1969, now a lieutenant colonel and the deputy commander of the 1st Special Forces Group, he was also a member of the vestry of the Episcopal Church in Okinawa and a friend of its bishop, Edmond Browning.

As doubts about whether he truly belonged in the army crept in, Richard Kim began to see in an entirely new light the religious faith that had come before his career as an army officer. Perhaps his life's work was in the church, not in the military service that world events had pushed him into as a young man.

Upon learning that his vestryman and friend was thinking about leaving the army for the church, Bishop Browning took the initiative to push Richard toward the new path that he had begun to consider. Browning urged him to go to a seminary and become a clergyman. When Richard expressed his uncertainty, saying that he did not feel worthy of such a calling, the bishop told him to cast aside his doubts. "Who was I to judge," Richard remembered him saying.

Heeding the bishop's advice, Richard decided to retire from the army and begin the next phase of his life.

Submitting his retirement papers brought a reminder of what he was leaving behind. A note from U.S. Army chief of staff Gen. William Westmoreland asked him to reconsider his decision and continue his career, informing him that he was on the promotion list for colonel and was being considered for further professional education at the Army War College. Coming at a time when his Special Forces peers from the 1950s were being elevated to the general officer ranks—among them Michael Healy, who was made a brigadier general in 1971—the prospect of further advancement in the army could have swayed others, but he had already made up his mind. On July 31, 1971, Lt. Col. Richard Kim officially retired from the U.S. Army, ending a journey that had begun more than quarter century earlier when he enlisted in Kunming, China, on December 7, 1944.

So he left his work with the Special Forces in Asia to become a seminary student at the University of the South in Sewanee, Tennessee. There he found himself in a different world, surrounded by seminarians who were avoiding the still-ongoing draft and the Vietnam War by using student deferments. One of them, a former football player who had played in the National Football League, provocatively asked Richard whether he had decided to go to a seminary to atone for the sins that he had committed in the military.[9]

A preview of how attitudes in the church were changing had come from his friend and mentor Edmond Browning, who had urged Richard and other senior military officers among his parishioners to sign a resolution calling on the United States to return Okinawa and the other Ryukyu Islands, which the United States had governed since 1945, to Japan. Richard had refused to sign the resolution. The incident did not affect their relationship, but it foreshadowed how the church would change along with much of American society in the years that followed. Browning would become the presiding bishop of the Episcopal Church in 1985 and lead the church to adopt liberal doctrines on a range of social issues that have prevailed into the twenty-first century.

Finding himself out of step with his new peers in the church did not change Richard's dedication to his new calling. After completing his studies at Sewanee, he became a postulant—a candidate for admission to the clergy—in Alabama, an arrangement that Browning had made for him with the bishop of the Episcopal Diocese of Alabama. In November 1973 he was ordained as a deacon at Canterbury Chapel in Tuscaloosa, Alabama, and in

May 1974 he was ordained into the priesthood at Grace Episcopal Church in Sheffield, Alabama.

When the time came for Rev. Richard Kim to become the priest in charge of a church, he was sent to Hawaii, where his mother and his siblings David and Betty still lived. In 1976 he became the rector of Good Shepherd Episcopal Church in Maui.

His journey around the United States with the church reached its final destination in the 1980s. In 1981 he moved to Michigan to become the priest in charge of Trinity Episcopal Church in Lexington, a town on the shore of Lake Huron, eighty miles north of Detroit. In 1987 he became the rector of St. John's Episcopal Church in Detroit. Dating back to 1859, the historic church on Woodward Avenue—the street synonymous with Detroit's heritage as the capital of the American automobile industry—placed him in the heart of the city as it was reviving after the riots of 1967 and 1968 and a long period of decline in the 1970s.

As the head of one of the leading religious and community institutions on Woodward Avenue, Reverend Kim led a coalition of ministers in downtown Detroit in advising campaigns to rebuild the city. They began with the renovation of the historic Fox Theater in 1988 by Detroit businessman Mike Ilitch, known nationally as the owner of the National Hockey League's Detroit Red Wings and Major League Baseball's Detroit Tigers. In the late 1990s, these efforts led to the construction of two stadiums near St. John's Church: Comerica Park for the Detroit Tigers and Ford Field for the National Football League's Detroit Lions.

Detroit Tigers fans who attended the first game at Comerica Park would have seen Reverend Kim in action. On April 11, 2000, he was the clergyman who blessed the field before the Tigers' first home game in their new ballpark.[10]

By then, he had already retired from active service in the church. He had retired in 1998, seventeen years after arriving in Michigan and twenty-six years after the end of his first career with the U.S. Army. He had been a priest longer than he had been a military officer, and in each role, he had distinguished himself and made his mark on the world.

The retired Rev. Richard Kim and his second wife, Helen—a former parishioner of his in Lexington, Michigan—live in the nearby city of Port

Huron on the U.S.-Canadian border. As a veteran parachutist with jump wings from four countries, he continued parachuting well into his eighties, making his 102nd jump in 2015 at the age of eighty-eight. He has returned regularly to Washington to serve as the chaplain of the OSS Society, an organization that preserves the heritage of the U.S. intelligence and special operations communities, and to minister at the funerals in Arlington National Cemetery of old comrades from the Special Forces who have been passing with increasing frequency.[11] He himself was still going strong at the age of ninety-seven in 2024, one of the last living links to the Second World War in China and the earliest years of the CIA and the Special Forces.

22

Arthur Kim, CIA Operations Officer and Businessman

ARTHUR KIM RETURNED from the Korean War as a sergeant in the U.S. Army with a future as an American ahead of him. U.S. citizenship was coming as a reward for his wartime military service, as it had for his brother Peter almost a decade earlier. Equally crucially, Peter, James, and Richard had provided him with a wealth of examples of what he could do with his wartime experience and his new identity as an American.

Following in his brothers' footsteps by becoming an officer in the U.S. Army was what he wanted to do, but their mother's opposition closed that door. After his struggle to enlist as an alien on a student visa a few years earlier, his wartime service had been an inspiring experience that made him interested in a military career. His mother, who had twice gone through the agony of seeing her sons go to war and already faced a future with Peter, James, and Richard serving in the army, forbade her youngest child from continuing to sign his life over to the service. Respecting her wishes, Arthur instead decided to accept demobilization at the end of his term of enlistment and return to civilian life in Hawaii before taking the oath of citizenship.

Arthur briefly went back to college on the GI Bill until the CIA came calling. James Kim's Chinese-speaking younger brother had come to the attention of the CIA station in Seoul during the war, so when the agency needed an intelligence officer in Korea with Chinese language skills, it hired Arthur as a civilian contractor. He ended up spending several months with the Seoul station, still called the JACK, just two blocks from his old army intelligence unit but forbidden to have any contact with it.

In April 1954 Arthur Kim became naturalized as a U.S. citizen in Honolulu. The CIA soon set about hiring him as a full-fledged member of its staff now that the barrier of his lacking U.S. citizenship was gone. In 1955 he became an intelligence officer in the CIA.

A long career as an operations officer in Asia followed. After training in surveillance, countersurveillance, and other espionage tradecraft, Arthur went to his first assignment at the CIA station in Hong Kong, then still a British colony on the fringe of China. There he used his understanding of the Shanghainese dialect in collecting intelligence on the People's Republic of China. At the end of his term in Hong Kong in 1961, he returned to CIA headquarters in Langley, Virginia; then he went on further assignments in Asia for the rest of the decade.

Arthur also married a woman working for the CIA in Korea, as his brother James had done almost a decade earlier, but unlike his older brother, Arthur married an American and did so in Korea because at the time it would have been illegal in their home state. Helen Goodnight, from the small town of Farmington, West Virginia, had been hired by the CIA as a secretary after her graduation from college. She and Arthur met at CIA headquarters in 1959 and got to know each other while she was stationed in Korea. When they became engaged in 1961, Virginia's Racial Integrity Act of 1924 not only criminalized marriages between "white" and "colored" persons but also prohibited interracial couples from marrying out of state and returning to live together in Virginia. Not until 1967 would the U.S. Supreme Court declare the law unconstitutional in a landmark decision on civil rights.[1]

Arthur and Helen decided to wed overseas to attempt to sidestep the law, whose language did not specifically mention interracial marriages conducted in foreign countries. They got married in Korea at the end of her assignment there in 1961 before returning to Virginia to begin their life together. Their marriage did not result in any problems with state authorities before the Racial Integrity Act was declared unconstitutional six years later.

The war in Vietnam sent Arthur to Southeast Asia as the conflict drew toward its end. In June 1974 he began a tour of duty at the CIA station in Vientiane, the capital of Laos. U.S. ground forces had withdrawn from Vietnam in 1972, and in the following year, the North Vietnamese army and Laotian Communist forces called the Pathet Lao coerced the U.S.-aligned government into a power-sharing agreement with the Pathet Lao. After the fall of South Vietnam in April 1975, the Pathet Lao seized Vientiane and took over the entire country, forcing the evacuation of the U.S. Embassy and the CIA station.

The closure of the CIA station in Vientiane sent Arthur on a lonely mission among hostile soldiers, the likes of which he had not experienced since he was a fourteen-year-old boy venturing by himself into the Japanese district of Shanghai to collect intelligence three decades earlier. After the hasty evacuation of the U.S. Embassy, Pathet Lao troops unexpectedly seized the embassy compound before the CIA station could finish destroying its papers. In an embassy annex building were fifteen safes filled with the station's classified files and scattered mail with the names and other personal details of CIA personnel and their Laotian allies. Arthur received orders to enter the building and destroy all of these papers while unarmed and with only two Laotian CIA operatives to help him.

Somehow, he would have to find a way into and around an embassy compound occupied by hostile armed men, shred all the documents, and further destroy the shreds to prevent their reconstruction—all overnight, without being detected. Then he would have to escape from the compound the next day.

Knowing that having an Asian face would by itself do little to make him blend in, Arthur wore locally bought clothes and put rocks into his shoes to try to force his feet into the shuffling steps of Laotians instead of the walk he learned in a lifetime among Americans and his years in the U.S. Army. An opportunity to enter the embassy compound emerged when a group of local employees appeared to demand their back pay, not knowing that the Americans had already abandoned the place. The angry mob entered unopposed by the Pathet Lao guards, and Arthur and his two Laotian aides walked in with them before sneaking away to the CIA station building.

There Arthur opened the fifteen safes while the Laotians emptied the desks of letters and other papers. The Laotians stuffed their findings into three large mail bags and then left, leaving Arthur alone to deal with the masses of paper and the bags. Working quietly in the dark all night, he shredded the classified documents and then further destroyed the shreds. The office's old-fashioned paper shredder left documents in quarter-inch-wide strips that could be easily reassembled, so normal protocol called for the pieces to be burned. Unable to risk starting a fire that would create smoke and attract attention, he instead soaked the shreds in water and mixed them up to make them too messy to piece together.

Early in the morning, the mission ended quietly. A U.S. Embassy car quietly drove into the compound, unchallenged by any Pathet Lao gunmen, and past the annex building at a prearranged time. Arthur emerged from a side door and threw the mail bags into the car's unlocked trunk. As the car accelerated and sped out of the compound, Arthur casually walked across the compound and out into the street, merging unseen into the crowds of Vientiane residents going about their normal business. In this way, without incident, the CIA presence in Laos during the Vietnam War era ended.[2]

Back at headquarters after returning from Laos, Arthur began a new period in his career that focused his work on Korea for the first time since he had joined the CIA full time twenty years earlier. The Directorate of Operations needed a new leader to revive its Korea branch, which had long faded in importance since the end of the Korean War. Asked to take over as head of the branch, Arthur at first was not interested, having had no professional or personal interest in North Korea, but he eventually decided to accept the challenge. Under his leadership, the Korea branch grew and began to score successes that it had not seen in years.

The peak and the end of Arthur's career in the CIA came at the same time a few years later. In 1977 Arthur learned that he was under consideration for appointment as the station chief in Seoul. It would have been a fitting reward for his years of service as an operations officer, and leading the CIA's presence in the country of his family's heritage would have made it even more meaningful. Turmoil in the CIA had turned him against accepting the promotion, however, and even against continuing to serve in the CIA at all.

Adm. Stansfield Turner, the new CIA director appointed by President Jimmy Carter, had begun a campaign to radically change the agency. Influenced by criticism of the CIA in the media and in Congress during the 1970s, Turner aimed to largely eliminate the CIA's Directorate of Operations and the human intelligence programs it conducted. Dismantling the CIA's clandestine operations would make it an agency dominated by analysts, who would rely mostly on signals intelligence, satellite and aerial photography, and other technical means of intelligence collection. Turner would eliminate more than eight hundred operations officers from the CIA by the end of his term in 1981.

Arthur chose to retire instead of experiencing the dismantling of the CIA division in which he had served as an operations officer for more than two decades. He submitted his retirement papers and ended his career at the CIA in December 1977, after twenty-two years at the agency.[3] He was only forty-seven years old, with no experience outside of military intelligence and the CIA for more than a quarter of a century, but as a matter of principle, he had to move on and find something else to do for the rest of his life.

Soon after his retirement, Arthur became one of the earliest members of the Association of Retired Intelligence Officers, now known as the Association of Former Intelligence Officers. Founded in 1975 by David Atlee Phillips, a former CIA operations officer who had been forced to defend himself against accusations of being involved in the assassination of President Kennedy, the association sought to counter the media's widespread negative portrayals of the U.S. intelligence community during the 1970s that had poisoned its reputation among the American public and in Congress. The association elevated Arthur to its board of directors for his contributions to its mission in its earliest years.

With a wife and three children to support, Arthur had to earn a living, and at first he started a modest handyman business. Just one man with tools and a van, his business was identical to countless others in Northern Virginia, but it had a key advantage: His recent former colleagues at the CIA knew that they could trust him to enter their houses while they were away at work. With this large base of clients, the handyman business did well, but Arthur still wanted to do something else, something that would use the skills that he had learned and mastered during his years in the CIA.

About a year later, Arthur thought of an idea that he decided was promising enough for him to take the leap of faith of starting a new business. Advancements in electronics were making wiretapping and other forms of electronic surveillance an increasingly widespread risk for people and businesses during the 1970s, and he saw a need for countersurveillance services that was unfilled at the time. So he sold his handyman business and started another one-man operation—this time as a private security company offering the expertise in surveillance and countersurveillance techniques that he had learned during his two decades in the CIA.

Arthur began his new business in a rented one-room office in McLean, Virginia. Starting with little capital and no clients, he could not afford to pay a secretary to answer the telephone or even the fees of the answering service that he hired instead, forcing him to rush to answer the phone whenever it rang to avoid the service's fee for each answered call. His first big break came when a major U.S. airline called. Concerned about eavesdropping on its company communications, the airline flew Arthur to its headquarters in Chicago and hired him to sweep its offices and telephones for bugs and to create communications security policies for the company. Saved by this first large client, Arthur's business began to expand and survived into the 1980s.[4]

A countersurveillance problem on a national scale, one that became infamous worldwide, created the greatest task that Arthur's security business would take on. In 1982 U.S. counterintelligence discovered that the half-completed new U.S. Embassy in Moscow had been thoroughly infested with electronic surveillance devices that Soviet construction workers had planted under the direction of the KGB. The fiasco compelled the State Department to cease construction of the embassy and reassess its security before tearing down the bugged buildings and constructing them anew. Arthur's company, already working as a security contractor for the State Department's headquarters in Washington, received the massive project of assessing the surveillance risks of the Moscow embassy and supervising the countersurveillance measures of the reconstruction project.

Working on the years-long task of rebuilding the U.S. Embassy in Moscow led to a contract to perform the same role at embassies worldwide for the State Department. Now with global responsibilities, Arthur hired large numbers of construction surveillance technicians (CSTs) who had learned their trades in the Seabees, the famous construction battalions (CBs) of the U.S. Navy that also supported the State Department overseas. Arthur's company would grow to have two hundred full-time employees at its peak. Its CSTs were present at every new construction or remodeling of a U.S. embassy for the rest of the 1980s and into the 1990s, ensuring the security of American diplomats and their operations against electronic surveillance.

Recognition as a national and worldwide leader in countersurveillance made Arthur's company the preferred contractor of a host of federal government agencies with domestic security concerns. Its clients would include the Federal Bureau of Investigation, the Defense Intelligence Agency, the Immigration and Naturalization Service, and the Federal Emergency Management Agency.

In April 2001, after twenty-three years in the private security business—a year longer than he had served in the CIA—Arthur sold his company and finally went into a well-earned retirement. Fifty years had passed since he had succeeded in getting himself drafted into the U.S. Army for the Korean War, and he had spent almost the entire half century serving the national security of the United States. In 2024 he was still living well in Northern Virginia at the age of ninety-four, another of the last living links to the Second World War in China and the formative years of the CIA.[5]

23

A Victory for America

A CENTURY AFTER a family from Korea began a journey to America that would span two generations, the success of its decades-long struggle was clearly a great victory for the nation, one made possible by leaders of the U.S. Army and intelligence services who recognized the family members as real Americans.

The sons of the Kim family had remained steadfastly loyal to the American people and the United States during their family's two decades of exclusion and the wartime years lived under enemy occupation in Shanghai. The commanders of the U.S. Army in China recognized Peter as the natural leader of the liberation of Shanghai and fought for the reward of U.S. citizenship for him, while James Kim, born an American, became a leader in the crucible of combat in the Pacific. Peter, James, Richard, and Arthur then served in defense of the nation during the Korean War and decades beyond it in the U.S Army and the CIA. The lives that they built in America were episodes to be proud of in the history of the armed forces and intelligence services of the United States.

Returned to America after the tireless efforts of James and righteous members of Congress, David, Betty, and their mother also fulfilled the long-deferred American dream of Kim Chang Sei. Each settled down in Hawaii, where David and Betty started families with native-born Americans. David became a U.S. citizen, and so did their mother, who passed her U.S. citizenship test with flying colors on her first try despite never having fully mastered the English language as her husband had.

The family has since enriched the country with three further generations of unquestionable Americans. From Hawaii to Virginia, where James and Arthur stayed after their CIA careers, more than a hundred children, grandchildren, and great-grandchildren have continued the Kim family's legacy into the twenty-first century.[1] At home in the country that their forebears struggled so hard to enter, only a few of them have reestablished ties to the old country.

One who did was David's grandson Jonathan Kim, who went to Korea for graduate study at Yonsei University, where in 1916 Kim Chang Sei earned the medical degree that made possible the start of the family's journey to America. A century after his great-grandfather thrilled the audience at Yonsei's commencement ceremony with his speech in English, Jonathan delivered a commencement address in Korean, which he had learned as a second language. His action brought the family's history at the university full circle.

In the twenty-first century, the still-living brothers reconnected with the country of their family's heritage, as Americans. They did so both as the sons of Kim Chang Sei and Lee Chung Sil and as the nephews of Ahn Chang Ho.

In 2001 a now-prosperous and confident Republic of Korea (ROK) reached out to the Kims as part of a campaign to recognize those patriots who had struggled for Korean independence in the early twentieth century. Kim Chang Sei received posthumous honors for his involvement in the 1920s and his activism in Washington in support of the imprisoned Ahn Chang Ho in 1932. Richard and Arthur received Korea's National Foundation Medal on behalf of their father in a ceremony at the ROK Embassy in Washington on September 7, 2001.[2]

In August 2021 Arthur went to Korea as a representative of the Ahn family at the commissioning of the ROK Navy submarine *Dosan Ahn Chang Ho*. The lead ship of Korea's first class of domestically designed attack submarines, the *Dosan Ahn Chang Ho* bears a name appropriate for a vessel representing a step forward in Korea's emergence as an independent power in Asia allied with the United States. With Ahn Chang Ho's descendants all living in the United States as U.S. citizens for multiple generations, as does the family of Kim Chang Sei, Arthur's presence at the commissioning ceremony represented not only the Ahn family but also the connection between the American and Korean peoples that the Ahns, Kims, and others built over the course of a century.

Having occurred in large part behind the barrier of secrecy shrouding the actions of U.S. intelligence and special operations, the history of the Kim family has long been hidden from the American public and even from most of the family itself. The Kim brothers' professional respect for secrets and their desire to shield their families from the hardships of the past, typical of the generation that fought the Second World War, almost kept their story hidden into eternity.

The barriers to immigration that excluded the Kim family from the United States and the events of the world war that brought them back have receded into the distant past, but a time of increasing divisiveness among Americans gives the family's story renewed importance. It reminds us both of the great sacrifices that many from all over the world have made to join the nation and of the decency that has always existed in the American people, regardless of the politics of their time. It harks back to famous words said in a time of even greater division, when Abraham Lincoln in his first inaugural address said: "The mystic chords of memory, stretching from every battlefield and patriot grave to every living heart and hearthstone all over this broad land, will yet swell the chorus of the Union, when again touched, as surely they will be, by the better angels of our nature."

May the story of the Kim family live on in the memory of the nation to remind future generations of the struggles of the past that have united them.

NOTES

2. FROM KOREA TO AMERICA

1. The Presbyterian Church counted 60,736 members in the Pyongyang area in 1910. See Brown, *Korean Conspiracy Case*, 7. The Methodist Church, the Catholic Church, and other denominations accounted for thousands of other Christians in Pyongyang. Kim Chang Sei and Lee Chung Sil were Seventh-day Adventists.

2. Kim, *Our Family History*, 1, Kim Chang Sei Family Papers, Hoover Institution Library & Archives, Stanford University, Stanford CA. (Collection hereafter as Kim Family Papers.)

3. Kim, *Our Family History*, 1, Kim Family Papers.

4. Kim, "Kim Family History," 2.

5. Kim, *Our Family History*, 1, Kim Family Papers.

6. Kim, *Our Family History*, 6, Kim Family Papers; and Kim, "Kim Family History," 4.

7. Kim, "Kim Family History," 4. Kim Chang Sei disembarked at San Francisco on arrival under his student visa, but the rest of the family had to wait approximately a week in detention at Angel Island, the West Coast immigration station in San Francisco Bay for the Chinese and other Asians.

8. Memorials to Ahn Chang Ho include the Dosan Memorial Park and the Dosan Ahn Chang Ho Memorial Hall in Seoul; the Dosan Ahn Chang Ho Memorial in Riverside, California; the Ahn family home preserved on the campus of the University of Southern California; Dosan Ahn Chang Ho Square in Los Angeles; and the Dosan Ahn Chang Ho Memorial Interchange where I-10 and I-110 intersect in downtown Los Angeles. In 2021 the Republic of Korea also named its navy's new class of attack submarines after Ahn Chang Ho, with the lead ship *Dosan Ahn Chang Ho* entering service on August 13, 2021.

9. Kim, *Our Family History*, 6, Kim Family Papers; and Kim, "Kim Family History," 4.

10. Kim, *Our Family History*, 8, Kim Family Papers.

11. Kim, *Our Family History*, 6, Kim Family Papers; and Kim, "Kim Family History," 9. A survivor of the Johnstown flood of 1889, which killed more than two thousand people including his parents and left him an orphan, Victor Heiser lived to

the age of ninety-nine, passing away in 1972. He described his early career in a 1936 autobiography, *An American Doctor's Odyssey: Adventures in Forty-Five Countries.*

12. Kim, "Kim Family History," 6–7. How Kim Chang Sei met Gustaf Adolf is unclear from the surviving accounts that the author found. Gustaf Adolf had an avid interest in East Asia and visited Korea, Japan, and China during his years as crown prince, but it is unclear whether Gustaf Adolf was introduced to Kim Chang Sei as a person of significance from Korea or China, or as a prominent medical doctor from America, or as a friend of a friend, or as all of these things at once.

13. Kim, *Our Family History*, 2–3, Kim Family Papers.

14. Kim, "Kim Family History," 7.

15. Kim, *Our Family History*, 2–3, Kim Family Papers; and Kim, "Kim Family History," 8.

16. Gustaf Adolf participated in the discovery of the gold crown in a tomb in Gyeongju, the capital of Korea's ancient Silla dynasty, that was later named the Seobongchong (Auspicious Phoenix) Tomb. The crown, now designated National Treasure No. 339, is held in the Gyeongju National Museum.

17. Kim, "Kim Family History," 7.

18. Kim, *Our Family History*, 4, Kim Family Papers; and American Consular Service Letter and Section Six Visa No. 118/1929—King Chang-Sei, dated December 31, 1929, Record Group 85, Immigration and Naturalization Service (INS), National Archives and Records Administration (NARA), San Bruno CA, courtesy of Grant Din, Angel Island Immigration Station Foundation. In the late 1920s and 1930s, Kim Chang Sei used the anglicized name "King" in official documentation. He also pronounced his given name as "Chauncey" and used that name in correspondence.

19. Application to Extend Time of Temporary Stay, Chang Sei King, dated December 8, 1930, and Affidavit of F. M. Pottinger, dated December 16, 1930, Record Group 85, INS, NARA, San Bruno CA, courtesy of Grant Din.

20. Application to Extend Time of Temporary Stay, Chang Sei King, dated November 20, 1931, and Affidavit of Iva M. Miller, M.D., dated November 25, 1931, Record Group 85, INS, NARA, San Bruno CA, courtesy of Grant Din.

21. Letter No. 22257 to U.S. Department of Labor, Immigration Service, District Director, Minneapolis, Minnesota, from W. G. Nyquist, Immigration Inspector, dated June 29, 1932, Record Group 85, INS, NARA, San Bruno CA, courtesy of Grant Din.

22. The leader of the bombing campaign was Kim Ku, a leader of the Korean liberation movement in Shanghai since 1919 and later the president of the Korean Provisional Government in exile during the Second World War.

23. Kim, *Our Family History*, 13–14, 21–22, Kim Family Papers. The McNairs' house was at 49 Route Winling, now called Wanping Road.

24. Letter from Victor Heiser, the Rockefeller Foundation, dated June 9, 1932; letter from W. H. Frost, dean, the Johns Hopkins University School of Hygiene and

Public Health, dated April 1, 1932; and letter from Kendall Emerson, M.D., managing director, National Tuberculosis Association—all in Record Group 85, INS, NARA, San Bruno CA, courtesy of Grant Din.

25. Kim Chang Sei's correspondence with U.S. immigration authorities about his own visa extension applications repeatedly referenced his family's situation in Shanghai, and one letter even mentioned specific plans to depart Shanghai for San Francisco on board the Japanese passenger liner *Chichibu Maru* on July 30, 1932. Letter to the Hon. W. W. Husband from C. S. Kim, dated July 19, 1932, Record Group 85, INS, NARA, San Bruno CA, courtesy of Grant Din.

26. Western Union telegram from Dr. C. S. Kim to P. Y. Kim, 3421 South Catalina Street, Los Angeles, May 4, 1932, 5:23 p.m., in Kim, *Our Family History*, 4, Kim Family Papers; and Hickcox, Kim, and Kim, *Brief History*, August 2015, 9, Kim Family Papers.

27. Kim, *Our Family History*, 4, Kim Family Papers.

28. Kim, *Our Family History*, 4, Kim Family Papers.

29. Kim, "Kim Family History," 19.

30. Kim, *Our Family History*, 4, Kim Family Papers.

31. In November 1932 Kim Chang Sei had been diagnosed at Johns Hopkins University's Henry Phipps Psychiatric Clinic as being in poor physical and mental condition. In December 1932 he traveled to Havana, Cuba, in an attempt to recuperate. Alexander Munsell, a wealthy Baltimorean who occasionally was Kim's benefactor during the early 1930s, paid for Kim's medical treatment at the Phipps Psychiatric Clinic and the trip to Cuba. Hickcox, Kim, and Kim, *Brief History*, 8–9, Kim Family Papers.

32. A grave for Kim Chang Sei is located in Ferncliff Cemetery and Mausoleum in Hartsdale, New York, in Westchester County. See "Dr Chang Sei Kim," Find a Grave, accessed October 28, 2024, https://www.findagrave.com/memorial /205486451/chang-sei-kim. According to Richard and Arthur Kim, their father was cremated, and his ashes were sent from the United States to their mother in Shanghai. What happened to the ashes between 1934 and their mother's final departure from Shanghai in 1950 is not known. Hickcox, Kim, and Kim, *Brief History*, 3, Kim Family Papers.

3. EXILE IN SHANGHAI

1. Letter from Peter Kim to Col. Paul J. B. Murphy, C.E., Chungking, 11 August 1945, Marshall S. Carter Collection, Peter Kim Papers, box 8, Central File: Selected Correspondence, George C. Marshall Research Library, Virginia Military Institute (VMI), Lexington VA.

2. Personnel Qualifications Questionnaire, question 21, 15 August 1945, Marshall S. Carter Collection, Peter Kim Papers, box 8, Central File: Selected Correspondence, George C. Marshall Research Library, VMI. Getz Brothers and Co. still exists today as the Getz Group, an international marketing, distribution, and

manufacturing company in the Asia-Pacific region. See getz.com, including the company history at https://www.getz.com/about-us/our-history.

3. The Lyceum Theater, built in 1931 and located at 57 South Maoming Road, had both a stage and a movie theater in the 1930s. Now called the Lanxin Theater, it is Shanghai's oldest theater. Renovations to restore the theater to its 1930s appearance began in 2020.

4. Kim, *Our Family History*, 9, Kim Family Papers.

5. Personnel Qualifications Questionnaire, question 17, 15 August 1945, Peter Kim Papers; and letter from Peter Kim to Col. Paul J. B. Murphy, C.E., 11 August 1945, Peter Kim Papers.

6. Kim, *Our Family History*, 10, Kim Family Papers.

7. David worked for Hollis H. Arnold, Inc., a company that provided lighting for offices, and served as the principal assistant to Hollis Arnold for over a decade. James worked as a gofer in the supply department in 1937 before leaving Shanghai during the Japanese invasion. Kim, *Our Family History*, 44, Kim Family Papers.

8. Conversation with Richard Kim, October 9, 2021.

9. Kim, *Our Family History*, 9–11, Kim Family Papers.

10. Kim, *Our Family History*, 2, Kim Family Papers.

11. Kim, *Our Family History*, 10, Kim Family Papers.

4. JAMES KIM, AMERICAN SOLDIER

1. The Ahn family house was designated a Historic-Cultural Monument by the city of Los Angeles in 2014. The building, relocated to West Thirty-Fourth Street in 2004, serves as a University of Southern California office building, which as of 2021 housed the university's Korean Studies Institute. See "Ahn Family House," USC Dornsife Korean Studies Institute, accessed October 28, 2024, https://dornsife.usc.edu/ksi/ahn-family-house/.

2. Philip Ahn's star is located at 6211 Hollywood Boulevard.

3. The middle brother, Philson, also worked as an actor in the 1930s and 1940s. See "Philson Ahn (1912–2001)," IMDb, accessed October 28, 2024, https://www.imdb.com/name/nm0014218/.

4. More information about the life and achievements of Susan Ahn Cuddy can be found in Katie Lange, "Navy Lt. Susan Ahn Cuddy Carved the Path for Asian American Women," *DOD News*, April 30, 2021, https://www.defense.gov/News/Feature-Stories/Story/Article/2586537/navy-lt-susan-ahn-cuddy-carved-the-path-for-asian-american-women/; the website "Susan Ahn Cuddy—Trailblazing Pioneer," accessed October 28, 2024, http://www.susanahncuddy.com/; and Cha, *Willow Tree Shade*.

5. According to his brother Arthur, part of the reason for the animosity between James and his cousins may have been an accident that occurred during their childhoods. The boys of the Kim and Ahn families had been playing with a loaded gun in the Ahns' house, and while they wrestled over it, it fired and sent a bullet into

Philson Ahn's shoulder that remained lodged there for the rest of his life. Conversation with Arthur Kim, October 30, 2021.

6. The YMCA was at 715 South Hope Street in Los Angeles. The eleven-story building built in 1907 has since been demolished.

7. James lived with two households in Beverly Hills: the Odd Youngs on San Ysidro Drive and Mr. Ruby Jenks at 439 Beverwil Drive.

8. Kim, *Our Family History*, 23–24, Kim Family Papers.

9. Kim, *Our Family History*, 25–26, Kim Family Papers.

10. An indication that James lacked anyone that he considered to be family in the United States is that his army records used the address of "Frank Holt (friend)" in Hollywood as his home address. GO No. 105, Hq 40th Inf Div, APO 40, 2 June 45, Award of Bronze Star, First Lieutenant James Kim, 01288069, Infantry, United States Army, personal papers of James Kim. It is possible that in the event of James Kim's death, the army would have informed Frank Holt.

11. Military Record and Report of Separation, Certificate of Service, James Kim, 01 288 069, Capt., Inf., AUS, 27 June 1947, personal papers of James Kim.

12. The 222nd Field Artillery still exists as the 2nd Battalion, 222nd Field Artillery Regiment of the Utah Army National Guard.

13. See *40th Infantry Division*, 82–90.

14. Kim, *Our Family History*, 29–30, Kim Family Papers. Maj. Leslie Cornaby, operations officer of the 222nd Field Artillery Battalion, informed James of his selection for Officer Candidate School. Cornaby later was promoted to lieutenant colonel and commanded the 640th Tank Destroyer Battalion, an antitank unit attached to the 40th Infantry Division that used towed antitank guns at first but transitioned to the self-propelled M-10 tank destroyer in 1944. See "Cornaby, Leslie H. (640th)," TankDestroyer, accessed October 28, 2024, https://tankdestroyer.net/honorees/c/507-cornaby-leslie-h-640th.

15. Kim, *Our Family History*, 30, Kim Family Papers.

16. The 160th Regiment State Armory, located in Exposition Park near the University of Southern California, served as the regiment's armory from 1912 to 1961. After the closure of the armory, the building became part of the Los Angeles Museum of Science and Industry and was later renamed the California Science Center.

17. Orders, Company "L," 160th Infantry, December 14, 1942, personal papers of James Kim. A Second World War–era U.S. Army infantry regiment had three infantry battalions; each had three infantry companies and one heavy weapons company that used letter designations with standardized words for each letter. The 1st Battalion had A(ble), B(aker), C(harlie), and weapons company D(og); 2nd Battalion, E(asy), F(ox), G(eorge), and weapons company H(ypo); and 3rd Battalion, I(tem), K(ing), L(ove), and weapons company M(ike). The letter *J* was skipped in this naming scheme. The name Love Company was often a source of amusement, unsurprisingly.

18. The SS *Lurline* was a Matson Lines passenger liner that had served routes from the West Coast to Hawaii and Australia and continued to do so as a troopship during the war. James Kim recalled that the ship retained its prewar crew and that it provided outstanding food service to the troops, including many luxury items such as baked Alaska, which he had never heard of before. After the war, the *Lurline* was sold to a Greek shipping line and renamed RHMS *Ellinis*. One of its postwar passengers was British rock star David Bowie, who in 1973 wrote the song "Aladdin Sane" while on board the *Ellinis* and credited the ship on the album of the same name. The ship was scrapped in 1987.
19. *40th Infantry Division*, 92–93.
20. *40th Infantry Division*, 94–98; and Kim, *Our Family History*, 31, Kim Family Papers.
21. *40th Infantry Division*, 98.
22. *40th Infantry Division*, 100–104.
23. *40th Infantry Division*, 99–100.
24. *40th Infantry Division*, 103–4; and Kim, *Our Family History*, 31, Kim Family Papers.

5. AMERICAN RESISTANCE

1. Rose, *Washington's Spies*. The television series *Turn: Washington's Spies*, broadcast on the AMC network for four seasons in 2014–17, told a fictionalized version of the story of the Culper Ring.
2. The Bridge House, located at 473 North Szechuan Road near the North Szechuan Road Bridge crossing Soochow Creek, originally was a seven-story apartment building built in 1934 that housed members of Shanghai's Western community.
3. Letter from Peter Kim to Col. Paul J. B. Murphy, C.E., Chungking, 11 August 1945, Peter Kim Papers.
4. Leck, *Captives of Empire*, 283–84.
5. Leck, *Captives of Empire*, 284.
6. Swiss Consulate General Shanghai, Section for Protection of American Interests, Accounts as at June 30, 1942. Dr. Charlotte Brooks found this document and other reports of the Swiss Consulate General Shanghai in the online resources of the Swiss Federal Archives, Bern, https://www.recherche.bar.admin.ch/.
7. Swiss Consulate General Shanghai, Section for Protection of American Interests, Accounts as at December 31, 1942; March 31, 1943; June 30, 1943; September 30, 1943; and December 31, 1943, Swiss Federal Archives. These reports itemize seven loans totaling 46,900 China Reserve Bank (CRB) dollars, equivalent to US$691.37. The March 31 report for the first quarter of 1943 itemizes two loans totaling 10,500 CRB dollars, equal to US$105. Subsequent reports from the second quarter of 1943 through the fourth quarter of 1945 itemize twenty loans totaling approximately 5.3 million CRB dollars, whose U.S. dollar value could not be provided because of hyperinflation in the Chinese puppet state. See also Swiss Consulate General

Shanghai, Section for Protection of American Interests, Accounts as at June 30, 1944; September 30, 1944; December 31, 1944; March 31, 1945; June 30, 1945; September 30, 1945; and December 31, 1945, Swiss Federal Archives.

8. The former 4th Marine Regiment barracks was located at 372 Haiphong Road, near the Jade Buddha Temple. Leck, *Captives of Empire*, 101–2, 449.

9. Leck, *Captives of Empire*, 121–36.

10. One of the British internees was a boy named James Graham Ballard, who after the war became a writer. As J. G. Ballard, he published a novel based on his experiences in the internment camps, *Empire of the Sun*, which was made into a 1987 motion picture of the same name. See Ballard, *Empire of the Sun*; and Ballard, *Miracles of Life*.

11. Letter from Peter Kim to Col. Paul J. B. Murphy, C.E., 11 August 1945, Peter Kim Papers. According to this letter, working for the Swiss consul provided Peter and his family with two sources of income: a salary for Peter from the consulate and the U.S. government allowance that Betty drew, being a U.S. citizen. The U.S.-funded loan program administered by the Swiss Consulate in practice gave out grants, since repayment was not expected.

12. For more information about the MS *Gripsholm* and its service as a wartime mercy ship, see Lars Hemingstam, "Drottningholm and Gripsholm: The Exchange and Repatriation Voyages during WWII," accessed October 28, 2024, https://www.salship.se/mercy.php.

13. The dog that the Hales gave to the Kims was named Raffie, after the Royal Air Force (RAF), as a gesture of defiance against the Japanese. The Hales were repatriated on the *Teia Maru* and *Gripsholm* in 1943. Email from Richard Kim, January 3, 2022; and interviews with Richard Kim and Arthur Kim from 2018 through 2024.

14. Email from Richard Kim, January 5, 2022.

15. Email from Richard Kim, January 2, 2022.

16. Don Chisholm, before the war had started, published the weekly Shanghai scandal sheet the *Shopping News*. He then worked under Japanese direction as an announcer for the radio station XMHA starting in February 1942. He eventually fell out of favor with the Japanese and ended up in the Chapei internment camp in December 1943. See Leck, *Captives of Empire*, 363–65. Another English-language broadcaster of Axis propaganda in Shanghai was Ernest Moy's brother, Herbert Moy, who worked for the German propaganda radio station XGRS. Herbert Moy had lost his U.S. citizenship in 1941 for his work for Nazi Germany. He stayed on the air until the surrender of Japan in August 1945 and committed suicide soon afterward. See Hayashi, *Asian American Spies*, 168–70.

17. Letter from Peter Kim to Col. Paul J. B. Murphy, C.E., 11 August 1945, Peter Kim Papers.

18. Rev. Richard (Dick) Kim, interview by Terry Shima and videographer Grant Jiro Hirabayashi, Japanese American Veterans Association, June 21, 2006, McLean VA, for Library of Congress Veterans History Project, accessed October 29, 2024, https://www.loc.gov/item/afc2001001.53062/ (hereafter VHP interview with

Richard Kim), 0:35:00–0:38:00; and correspondence and interviews with Richard Kim and Arthur Kim, 2018–24.

19. Letter from Peter Kim to Col. Paul J. B. Murphy, C.E., 11 August 1945, Peter Kim Papers.

20. Letter from Peter Kim to Col. Paul J. B. Murphy, C.E., 11 August 1945, Peter Kim Papers; and VHP interview with Richard Kim, 0:37:00–0:38:00.

21. Conversation with Richard Kim, October 16, 2021.

22. VHP interview with Richard Kim, 0:37:00–0:38:00; and interviews with Arthur Kim, 2018–24.

23. Letter from Peter Kim to Col. Paul J. B. Murphy, C.E., 11 August 1945, Peter Kim Papers.

24. VHP interview with Richard Kim, 0:37:30–0:39:00.

25. Letter from Peter Kim to Col. Paul J. B. Murphy, C.E., 11 August 1945, Peter Kim Papers.

26. Letter from Peter Kim to Col. Paul J. B. Murphy, C.E., 11 August 1945, Peter Kim Papers.

27. VHP interview with Richard Kim, 0:50:00–0:51:30.

28. VHP interview with Richard Kim, 0:37:30–0:39:00.

6. EXODUS FROM SHANGHAI

1. The black-and-white photograph, taken by Chinese photojournalist Wong Hai Sheng, has been called a variety of names including *Bloody Saturday* and *The Baby in the Shanghai Railroad Station*.

2. The *pao chia* (*baojia*) was an Imperial Chinese system of local authority, dating back to the eleventh century, that the Empire of Japan also implemented in the territories it occupied in China.

3. Letter from Peter Kim to Capt. Max Becker, Subject: Shanghai, Kweilin, June 12, 1944 (83,269), Record Group 226, Office of Strategic Services (OSS), entry 16, box 971, NARA, College Park MD.

4. A second Japanese name for Operation Ichigo, the Continent Cross-Through Operation (Tairiku Datsū Sakusen), reflected its goal of establishing an overland connection all the way across southern Asia.

5. Letter from Peter Kim to Capt. Max Becker, June 12, 1944, Record Group 226, OSS, NARA, College Park MD.

6. Letter from Peter Kim to Capt. Max Becker, June 12, 1944, Record Group 226, OSS, NARA, College Park MD.

7. Letter from Peter Kim to Capt. Max Becker, June 12, 1944, Record Group 226, OSS, NARA, College Park MD; and VHP interview with Richard Kim, 0:40:00–0:40:45.

8. Letter from Peter Kim to Capt. Max Becker, June 12, 1944, Record Group 226, OSS, NARA, College Park MD; and VHP interview with Richard Kim, 0:40:45–0:41:00.

9. VHP interview with Richard Kim, 0:41:30–0:42:00. Richard Kim later suspected that these guerrillas may have been working for U.S. and Chinese intelligence. A combined U.S. Navy–Nationalist Chinese organization named the Sino-American Cooperative Organization (SACO) trained and supported guerrillas in the areas of eastern China not controlled by Japanese forces.

10. VHP interview with Richard Kim, 0:41:30–0:42:00.

11. Letter from Peter Kim to Capt. Max Becker, June 12, 1944, Record Group 226, OSS, NARA, College Park MD; and VHP interview with Richard Kim, 0:40:45–0:41:30.

12. VHP interview with Richard Kim, 0:50:00–0:51:30.

13. VHP interview with Richard Kim, 0:42:15–0:43:00, 0:47:00–0:50:00. Peter and Richard Kim did not recall Morgan revealing the name of his intelligence organization when they met in Kukong. It was almost certainly the Sino-American Cooperative Organization, which was led by Nationalist Chinese intelligence chief Tai Li and trained and supported by U.S. Navy personnel under Capt. (later Vice Adm.) Milton Miles. SACO operated around Kukong, and the SACO veterans' organization database includes a Lt. (JG) George E. Morgan who served in the Kukong area. See SACO: Sino-American Cooperative Organization, U.S. Naval Group China Veterans, accessed October 28, 2024, https://saconavy.net. Peter and Richard Kim may have remembered Morgan's first name incorrectly as "Ralph."

14. VHP interview with Richard Kim, 0:44:30–0:47:00.

15. VHP interview with Richard Kim, 0:50:00–0:51:30.

16. VHP interview with Richard Kim, 0:51:30–0:52:30.

17. Peter Kim recorded the details in a memo a few days later. Letter from Peter Kim to Capt. Max Becker, June 12, 1944, Record Group 226, OSS, NARA, College Park MD.

18. Letter from Marshall S. Carter, Colonel, Subject: T/5 Peter Kim, ASN 10500015, 12 January 1945, Marshall S. Carter Collection, Peter Kim Papers, box 8, Central File: Selected Correspondence, George C. Marshall Research Library, VMI. The letter is dated January 12, 1945, but it appears to have actually been written in 1946 since it describes events up to January 7, 1946.

19. Kim, *Project Eagle*, 91–92. Colonel DePass completed this plan, named Project Olivia, on January 27, 1942.

20. VHP interview with Richard Kim, 0:53:00–0:54:00. Service, born in China to American missionary parents in 1909, attended high school in Shanghai at the same time as Peter. For additional biographical information about John Service, see his obituary: John Kifner, "John Service, a Purged 'China Hand,' Dies at 89," *New York Times*, February 4, 1999, https://www.nytimes.com/1999/02/04/world/john-service-a-purged-china-hand-dies-at-89.html.

21. A wartime newsreel covering the demolition of the air base at Kweilin is available to view at Army Pictorial Service, "Evacuation of Kweilin," YouTube, uploaded by HistoryFlicks4u, April 5, 2016, www.youtube.com/watch?v=a8h6pLd3NzY.

1. VHP interview with Richard Kim, 1:31:30–1:33:00.

2. The papers of H. Maxcy Smith, 1893–1945, Record Group 464, are at the Presbyterian Historical Society, Philadelphia, https://www.history.pcusa.org/collections/research-tools/guides-archival-collections/rg-464.

3. The founders of the GBT Group were Laurence Gordon, Harry Bernard, and Frank Tan. For the history of the GBT Group and its relationship to multiple British and U.S. intelligence organizations, see Yu, *OSS in China*, 203–7; and Bergin, "Three Amateur Spies."

4. Letter from Marshall S. Carter, Colonel, Subject: T/5 Peter Kim, ASN 10500015, 12 January 1945, Peter Kim Papers.

5. Special Order Number 188, 30 September 1944, Marshall S. Carter Collection, Peter Kim Papers, box 1, folder 7: Special Orders 1944–1946, George C. Marshall Research Library, VMI.

6. Letter from Marshall S. Carter, Colonel, Subject: T/5 Peter Kim, ASN 10500015, 12 January 1945, Peter Kim Papers.

7. Letter from Marshall S. Carter, Colonel, Subject: T/5 Peter Kim, ASN 10500015, 12 January 1945, Peter Kim Papers; and Special Order Number 38, 9 January 1945, Marshall S. Carter Collection, Peter Kim Papers, box 1, folder 7: Special Orders 1944–1946, George C. Marshall Research Library, VMI.

8. VHP interview with Richard Kim, 0:57:00–0:58:00.

9. VHP interview with Richard Kim, 0:58:00–0:59:00. Sister Mary Colombiere became a lifelong friend of Peter and Richard after their wartime experiences together. After the war, she remained in China until the Maryknoll sisters were expelled from the People's Republic of China in 1951. She served in New York City and Monrovia, California, until 1980 and passed away in 1983. See "Sister M. Colombiere Bradley, MM," accessed October 28, 2024, https://maryknollmissionarchives.org/deceased-sisters/sister-m-colombiere-bradley-mm/.

10. Letter from Marshall S. Carter, Colonel, Subject: T/5 Peter Kim, ASN 10500015, 12 January 1945, Peter Kim Papers.

11. Olmsted Scholars have included Gen. John Abizaid, commander of U.S. Central Command in 2003–7 and U.S. ambassador to Saudi Arabia in 2019–21; Adm. Carlisle Trost, chief of U.S. Naval Operations in 1986–90; Gen. George Butler, commander in chief of Strategic Air Command in 1991–94; and Robert McFarlane, marine lieutenant colonel and national security adviser to President Ronald Reagan in 1983–86. For more information about George Olmsted and the foundation and program that he created, see the Olmsted Foundation website at https://olmstedfoundation.org/.

12. Letter from Marshall S. Carter, Colonel, Subject: T/5 Peter Kim, ASN 10500015, 12 January 1945, Peter Kim Papers.

8. AMERICAN UNDERGROUND

1. Jack Young, "Hunting the Giant Panda with the Roosevelts in Central Asia," *China Weekly Review*, June 29, 1929, 195–208.
2. Burdsall, Emmons, Moore, and Young, *Men against the Clouds.*
3. After the Second World War, Captain Young served as an aide and interpreter to Gen. George C. Marshall during Marshall's mission to China from December 1945 to January 1947 that attempted to negotiate a reconciliation between the Nationalists and Communists. During the Korean War, Major Young served as the deputy chief of the G-2 intelligence section of the 2nd Infantry Division and organized and headed an intelligence unit of Korean volunteers named the Ivanhoe Security Force, which led the Eighth U.S. Army's intelligence exploitation team sent into Pyongyang in October 1950. See Briscoe, "Culture, Language & SPECIAL OPS," 30.
4. Ernest Moy is the only known personal connection between Peter Kim, Ruth Moy, and Jack Young in July 1944, so the role for him described here is a likely scenario. However, no documentary evidence of it has been found.
5. Interviews with Arthur Kim, 2018–24.

9. BAPTISM OF FIRE

1. James recalled years later that the navy had demanded that the soldiers from the 160th Infantry Regiment who had damaged their transport ship be punished, and the army had told them to try to find them at the front lines, with the result that nothing came of the incident. Kim, *Our Family History*, 32, Kim Family Papers.
2. Kim, *Our Family History*, 32, Kim Family Papers.
3. The 40th Infantry and 37th Infantry Divisions, under XIV Corps, assaulted the western landing areas around the towns of Lingayen and Dagupan. The 6th Infantry and 43rd Infantry Divisions, under XXX Corps, landed on the eastern beaches around the towns of San Fabian and Mangalden. They were under the Sixth Army led by Gen. Walter Krueger.
4. *40th Infantry Division*, 110–11.
5. *40th Infantry Division*, 110–12.
6. *40th Infantry Division*, 113; and Assistant Chief of Staff, G-2, 40th Infantry Division, Area Sketch, Storm King Mountain, personal papers of James Kim.
7. *40th Infantry Division*, 113; and Kim, *Our Family History*, 32, Kim Family Papers.
8. *40th Infantry Division*, 113–14.
9. General Order No. 105, Hq 40th Inf Div, APO 40, 2 June 45, Award of Bronze Star, First Lieutenant James Kim, 01288069, Infantry, United States Army, personal papers of James Kim; and James Kim, *Our Family History*, 33, Kim Family Papers.
10. *40th Infantry Division*, 113; and Kim, *Our Family History*, 33, Kim Family Papers.
11. *40th Infantry Division*, 113–14. The 40th Infantry Division's history states that the 108th Infantry Regiment encountered large numbers of 20mm automatic cannons

that had been scavenged from aircraft destroyed on Clark Field during battle in an area called the Seven Hills on February 2–19. These weapons were used as infantry weapons by Japanese airfield battalions that had withdrawn from Clark Field into the hills. The 108th Infantry claimed to have destroyed eight twin 20mm guns and five single 20mm guns on April 10 alone and to have captured sixty-three 20mm guns by the end of the battle. *40th Infantry Division*, 115–16.

12. Kim, *Our Family History*, 33–34, Kim Family Papers.
13. Kim, *Our Family History*, 34, Kim Family Papers.
14. *40th Infantry Division*, 118.
15. *40th Infantry Division*, 49.

10. ARMY INTELLIGENCE OFFICER

1. Separation Qualification Record, James Kim, 0-1288069, 27 June 1947; and Informal memo to S-2, 160th Infantry from James Kim, 1st Lt., Inf, S-2, Headquarters, 1st Battalion, 160th Infantry, 9 June 1945—both from personal papers of James Kim.
2. The 40th Infantry Division left one of its three infantry regiments, the 108th Infantry Regiment, behind on Luzon. The 160th Infantry Regiment left two of its battalions on Luzon, but they would rejoin the regiment and the division for the later operation on Negros. *40th Infantry Division*, 120.
3. Designated the Sixth Military District of the Philippine resistance forces, Colonel Peralta's command on Panay had approximately 1,500 officers and 21,000 enlisted men.
4. *40th Infantry Division*, 124.
5. *40th Infantry Division*, 124.
6. *40th Infantry Division*, 131–32.
7. *40th Infantry Division*, 132.
8. *40th Infantry Division*, 133.
9. Informal memo to S-2, 160th Infantry, from James Kim, personal papers of James Kim.
10. Kim, *Our Family History*, 34, Kim Family Papers.
11. *40th Infantry Division*, 133–34.
12. *40th Infantry Division*, 137. The division's 108th Infantry Regiment had operated separately from March to July, clearing remaining Japanese forces from Leyte in March and April, then landing on Mindanao to participate in the liberation of the second-largest Philippine island in May and June. The regiment rejoined the rest of the division on Panay in July.

11. VICTORY OVER JAPAN

1. *40th Infantry Division*, 144.
2. MacEachin, *The Final Months of the War with Japan*, 12–13.
3. *40th Infantry Division*, 144.
4. Kim, *Our Family History*, 35, Kim Family Papers.

5. *40th Infantry Division*, 144–45.
6. *40th Infantry Division*, 146.
7. For a detailed history of OSS interest in Korea and actions with the Korean liberation movement, see Kim, *Project Eagle*.
8. *40th Infantry Division*, 145–47.
9. *40th Infantry Division*, 147–51.
10. *40th Infantry Division*, 159–61.
11. *40th Infantry Division*, 166.
12. *40th Infantry Division*, 151–56.
13. James did not even bother mentioning anything he did in Korea in the personal history that he wrote for his family. All he had to say about his experience in Korea in 1945 was that his division was there to repatriate Japanese troops and that it processed them through the port of Pusan. Kim, *Our Family History*, 35, Kim Family Papers.

12. MISSION TO SHANGHAI

1. Operation Magpie, 13 August 1945, Record Group 226, OSS, entry 148, container 8, folder 111; Operation Flamingo, 13 August 1945, Record Group 226, OSS, entry 154, box 186, folder 3190; Operation Cardinal, Record Group 226, OSS, entry 154, box 187, folder 3194; Operation Duck, 13 August 1945, Record Group 226, OSS, entry 148, container 8, folder 153; outgoing radio message from Heppner to Bird, August 14, 1945, Record Group 226, OSS, entry 154, container 187; Operation Pigeon, 13 August 1945, Record Group 226, OSS, entry 154, container 174, folder 3014; outgoing message Nr. 586 to Heppner from Little, 14 August 1945, Record Group 226, OSS, entry 148, container 6, folder 82; and Operation Raven, 13 August 1945, Record Group 226, OSS, entry 154, container 174, folder 3019—all from NARA, College Park MD.
2. Operation Sparrow, 13 August 1945, Record Group 226, OSS, entry 154, container 186, folder 3191, NARA, College Park MD.
3. POW Camps, Record Group 226, OSS, entry 148, container 6, folder 89, NARA, College Park MD.
4. Emergency Liaison Teams for Allied Prisoners of War and Internee Camps upon Japanese Capitulation, 14 August 1945, Record Group 226, OSS, entry 154, container 186, folder 3185, NARA, College Park MD.
5. Kim, *Carter's One Man Army*, Kim Family Papers.
6. Kim, *Carter's One Man Army*, Kim Family Papers.
7. Kim, *Carter's One Man Army*, Kim Family Papers.
8. Travel orders from APO 879 to APO 627, 14 August 1945, Marshall S. Carter Collection, Peter Kim Papers, box 1, folder 1 (201 file), George C. Marshall Research Library, VMI.
9. Ellis Briggs had a distinguished thirty-six-year career as a U.S. diplomat that included serving as the U.S. ambassador to the Dominican Republic (1944–45),

Uruguay (1947–49), Czechoslovakia (1949–52), Republic of Korea (1952–55), Peru (1955–56), Brazil (1956–59), and Greece (1959–62). For his autobiography, see Briggs, *Proud Servant*.

10. Credentials, Embassy of the United States of America, Chungking, China, August 15, 1945, Marshall S. Carter Collection, Peter Kim Papers, 201 file, George C. Marshall Research Library, VMI.

11. Kim, *Carter's One Man Army*, Kim Family Papers; and VHP interview with Richard Kim, 1:06:00–1:10:00 (describing events similarly to the account in Kim, *Carter's One Man Army*; and reading a copy of the credentials signed by the U.S. ambassador and commanding general in China).

12. Shoemaker had been a stockbroker in New York before the war. Eaton was a teacher in New England prep schools, including Loomis Chaffee and Noble and Greenough. For a profile of Sidney Eaton, see "Sidney Lovett Eaton," Nobles Class of 1964, accessed October 29, 2024, https://nobles64.org/sidney-eaton-2/.

13. AGAS Emergency Liaison Team Mission to Shanghai, Record Group 319, Records of the Army Staff, entry 81, box 1, NARA, College Park MD; and Mission Report, box 3, folder 5, Papers of B. Preston Schoyer, Howard Gotlieb Archival Center, Boston University (hereafter Schoyer Papers).

14. AGAS Emergency Liaison Team Mission to Shanghai, NARA, College Park MD; and Mission Report, Schoyer Papers.

15. Operation Sparrow, 15 August 1945, Record Group 226, OSS, entry 154, container 186, folder 3191, NARA, College Park MD.

16. Operation Sparrow's C-46s were from the 11th Combat Cargo Squadron, one of the Fourteenth Air Force's transport plane units. Capt. Frank Haynie piloted C-46 tail number 478437, and Capt. Werter Drake piloted C-46 tail number 478433. AGAS Emergency Liaison Team Mission to Shanghai, NARA, College Park MD; and Mission Report, Schoyer Papers.

17. AGAS Emergency Liaison Team Mission to Shanghai, NARA, College Park MD; and Mission Report, Schoyer Papers.

18. AGAS Emergency Liaison Team Mission to Shanghai, NARA, College Park MD; Mission Report, Schoyer Papers; and Kim, *Carter's One Man Army*, Kim Family Papers.

19. AGAS Emergency Liaison Team Mission to Shanghai, NARA, College Park MD; Mission Report, Schoyer Papers; and Kim, *Carter's One Man Army*, Kim Family Papers.

20. AGAS Emergency Liaison Team Mission to Shanghai, NARA, College Park MD; and Mission Report, Schoyer Papers.

21. Leck, *Captives of Empire*, 391–93.

22. AGAS Emergency Liaison Team Mission to Shanghai, NARA, College Park MD; and Kim, *Carter's One Man Army*, Kim Family Papers.

23. AGAS Emergency Liaison Team Mission to Shanghai, NARA, College Park MD;

Mission Report, Schoyer Papers; and Kim, *Carter's One Man Army*, Kim Family Papers.

24. Kim, *Carter's One Man Army*, Kim Family Papers.

25. Interviews with Arthur Kim, 2018–24.

26. AGAS Emergency Liaison Team Mission to Shanghai, NARA, College Park MD; and Mission Report, Schoyer Papers.

27. AGAS Emergency Liaison Team Mission to Shanghai, NARA, College Park MD; Mission Report, Schoyer Papers; and Kim, *Carter's One Man Army*, Kim Family Papers.

28. AGAS Emergency Liaison Team Mission to Shanghai, NARA, College Park MD; and Mission Report, Schoyer Papers.

29. AGAS Emergency Liaison Team Mission to Shanghai, NARA, College Park MD; Mission Report, Schoyer Papers; Schoyer, *Uneasy Remembrance of Shanghai*, and personal papers, property of Lisa Schoyer.

30. AGAS Emergency Liaison Team Mission to Shanghai, NARA, College Park MD; Mission Report, Schoyer Papers; and Schoyer, *Uneasy Remembrance of Shanghai*.

31. AGAS Emergency Liaison Team Mission to Shanghai, NARA, College Park MD; Mission Report, Schoyer Papers; and Schoyer, *Uneasy Remembrance of Shanghai*.

32. AGAS Emergency Liaison Team Mission to Shanghai, NARA, College Park MD; Mission Report, Schoyer Papers; and Schoyer, *Uneasy Remembrance of Shanghai*.

33. AGAS Emergency Liaison Team Mission to Shanghai, NARA, College Park MD; Mission Report, Schoyer Papers; Schoyer, *Uneasy Remembrance of Shanghai*; and Kim, *Carter's One Man Army*, Kim Family Papers.

34. AGAS Emergency Liaison Team Mission to Shanghai, NARA, College Park MD; Mission Report, Schoyer Papers; Schoyer, *Uneasy Remembrance of Shanghai*; and Kim, *Carter's One Man Army*, Kim Family Papers.

35. AGAS Emergency Liaison Team Mission to Shanghai, NARA, College Park MD; Schoyer, *Uneasy Remembrance of Shanghai*; and Kim, *Carter's One Man Army*, Kim Family Papers.

36. Kim, *Carter's One Man Army*, Kim Family Papers. Peter Kim stated that Major Schoyer and Lieutenant Commander Shoemaker did not know about his diplomatic credentials until their presentation to the Japanese delegation at the Swiss Consulate and were surprised to learn of them at that moment.

37. This account is based on Peter Kim's detailed description of his initial actions at the Swiss Consulate in his *Carter's One Man Army*, Kim Family Papers. The quoted statements are taken word for word from it.

38. Mission Report, Schoyer Papers.

39. Kim, *Carter's One Man Army*, Kim Family Papers. The official reports of the mission do not mention the accommodations made for the team in the Swiss Consulate after the August 19 meeting with the Japanese. Its authors are likely to have been displeased by Fontanel's treatment of them relative to that shown Peter Kim.

40. Kim, *Carter's One Man Army*, Kim Family Papers.

1. AGAS Emergency Liaison Team Mission to Shanghai, NARA, College Park MD; Schoyer, *Uneasy Remembrance of Shanghai*; and Kim, *Carter's One Man Army*, Kim Family Papers.

2. AGAS Emergency Liaison Team Mission to Shanghai, NARA, College Park MD; and Mission Report, Schoyer Papers. A secret AGAS radio station set up in Shanghai evaded Japanese restrictions on Operation Sparrow's radio communications by transmitting reports from Shanghai and by receiving orders.

3. The official reports of Operation Sparrow do not explain how the invitation to move into the Marble Hall reached the Swiss Consulate. AGAS Emergency Liaison Team Mission to Shanghai, NARA, College Park MD; and Mission Report, Schoyer Papers.

4. The People's Republic of China took over the Marble Hall and made it the China Welfare Institute Children's Palace in 1953.

5. For more about the Kadoorie family members and their experience of internment, see Kaufman, *Last Kings of Shanghai*, 177–95.

6. Kaufman, *Last Kings of Shanghai*, 194–95.

7. Mission Report, Schoyer Papers.

8. Schoyer, *Uneasy Remembrance of Shanghai*.

9. AGAS Emergency Liaison Team Mission to Shanghai, NARA, College Park MD; and Mission Report, Schoyer Papers.

10. Schoyer, *Uneasy Remembrance of Shanghai*.

11. Mission Report, Schoyer Papers, and other accounts of Operation Sparrow do not state which camp, Chapei or Lincoln Avenue, the mission visited first on August 21.

12. Leck, *Captives of Empire*, 438–43.

13. Kim, *Carter's One Man Army*, Kim Family Papers.

14. Mission Report, Schoyer Papers.

15. Jimmy's Kitchen restaurants continued operating in Shanghai and Hong Kong into the twenty-first century, with the Hong Kong location closing in 2020. Jimmy James, after his repatriation to the United States, started a successful chain of chili parlors in Texas named Shanghai Jimmy's Chili Rice that lasted into the 1980s. He passed away in 1990.

16. Leck, *Captives of Empire*, 456–59.

17. Leck, *Captives of Empire*, 456–59.

18. For more information about the U.S. Marines captured in northern China in December 1941, see "Prisoners of War," North China Marines, accessed October 29, 2024, www.northchinamarines.com.

19. AGAS Emergency Liaison Team Mission to Shanghai, NARA, College Park MD; and Mission Report, Schoyer Papers.

20. AGAS Emergency Liaison Team Mission to Shanghai, NARA, College Park MD; and Mission Report, Schoyer Papers. According to the AGAS Emergency Liaison

Team Mission to Shanghai, the numbers of internees in each camp and hospital were as follows: Lincoln Road, 326; Chapei, 1,067; Yangtzepoo, 1,217; Pootung, 978; Longhua, 1,717; Ash, 462; St. Luke's Hospital, 65; and Shanghai General Hospital, 122.

21. Mission Report, Schoyer Papers. The mission log's entry on this meeting lists two additional persons, civilians not mentioned in other records of the mission: John Lau, a communications assistant, and LeRoy Healy, who had an array of responsibilities including supply procurement, security, and interviews. The report of the AGAS Emergency Liaison Team Mission to Shanghai, NARA, College Park MD, names a "John Lam" who worked for the secret AGAS radio station in Shanghai and a "Mr. E.L. Healey" who was a former Bridge House prisoner supporting the mission in various ways.

14. THE CARETAKER OF SHANGHAI

1. Radio Reports of Mission, box 3, folder 4, Schoyer Papers.

2. Status of American Properties in Shanghai, 28 September 1945, Marshall S. Carter Collection, Peter Kim Papers, box 8, Central File: Selected Correspondence, 1940–1971, Kim, Peter, 1945, tab 12, George C. Marshall Research Library, VMI.

3. Fragmentary descriptions of the actions of the Operation Sparrow team and Peter Kim to restore the property of interned civilians appear in the Mission Report, Schoyer Papers; the report of the AGAS Emergency Liaison Team Mission to Shanghai written by Preston Schoyer and Sidney Eaton, NARA, College Park MD; the report Peter Kim wrote September 28, 1945, on the status of American properties in Shanghai, Peter Kim Papers; and the Report of Activities of Capt. Robert L. Peaslee and Lt. Peter Kim, Theater G-5, Advance Liaison, Marshall S. Carter Collection, Peter Kim Papers, box 8, Central File: Selected Correspondence, 1940–1971, Kim, Peter, 1945, tab 5, George C. Marshall Research Library, VMI, describing both the work in September to maintain electricity and other essential services and the simultaneous efforts to restore the residences of internees. Peaslee's report, directed to General Olmsted and the G-5 (civil affairs) staff, attributes these actions to Peter Kim. Peter Kim's own report, directed to the U.S. consul general in Shanghai, does not claim credit for them. The report of the AGAS Emergency Liaison Team Mission to Shanghai, directed to AGAS, attributes these actions to "the AGAS Mission" or "we" without mentioning Peter Kim, although it specified the officers who performed other tasks and commended their work. It is possible that personal animosity between Preston Schoyer and Peter Kim, arising from the division of authority between Schoyer's commanding the mission and Kim's acting as the official representative of the U.S. supreme commander in China, as well as from the preferential treatment Swiss consul Emile Fontanel showed Kim, resulted in Schoyer's refusing to credit Kim specifically for his actions. Schoyer completely erased Peter Kim from his unofficial personal account of the mission, which named and described all U.S. military personnel and Chinese civilians in

Operation Sparrow except for Peter Kim. See Schoyer, *Uneasy Remembrance of Shanghai*.

4. Report of Activities of Capt. Robert L. Peaslee and Lt. Peter Kim, Theater G-5, Advance Liaison, Peter Kim Papers.

5. The foreign and Chinese communities had separate YMCAs in Shanghai. The Foreign YMCA became the Shanghai Sports Club in postwar China and has survived as a historic building.

6. AGAS Emergency Liaison Team Mission to Shanghai, NARA, College Park MD; and Mission Report, Schoyer Papers. The eight POWs were two U.S. Army Air Forces second lieutenants, a U.S. Army Air Forces sergeant, and five enlisted naval aviators.

7. Mission Report, Schoyer Papers. The mission log's reference to the move to the Park Hotel states that the mission also occupied the seventeenth floor, but the Mission Report in the Schoyer Papers and the unofficial accounts of Preston Schoyer and Peter Kim do not mention the mission's occupying a third floor of the hotel.

8. Kim, *Carter's One Man Army*, Kim Family Papers. The Japanese continued to confine the POWs held in the Foreign YMCA after Japan's formal surrender on September 2. On September 3 two POWs decided that it was not fun to stay at the YMCA and escaped to the Park Hotel next door, and Lieutenant Cox and Captain Levin had to persuade them to return to the YMCA. The POWs were not released and allowed to move into the Park Hotel until September 6. Mission Report, Schoyer Papers.

9. Lt. Cdr. David Fairbrother, a SACO intelligence officer working for AGAS, commanded the group that arrived on August 31. The OSS and the army POW team totaled thirty-seven officers and enlisted men. The Swiss Consulate sent a bus and a small convoy of cars and trucks to Longhua to pick them up and take them to the Park Hotel, the Marble Hall, and the Swiss Consulate. See Mission Report, Radio Reports of Mission, Schoyer Papers. In Miles, *Different Kind of War*, 528, the author mentioned Lieutenant Commander Fairbrother and his arrival in Shanghai but did not describe when or how Fairbrother got there.

10. Mission Report, Schoyer Papers.

11. The OSS team, with thirty-one officers and enlisted men under the command of Maj. Hamner Freeman, moved into the American Club on 209 Fuzhou Road, three blocks from the Bund. The Shanghai Mission, 30 September 1945, Report from Headquarters, Office of Strategic Services, China Theater, APO 627, reproduced in Kim, *Carter's One Man Army*, Kim Family Papers.

12. Mission Report, Schoyer Papers.

13. Report of Activities of Capt. Robert L. Peaslee and Lt. Peter Kim, Theater G-5, Advance Liaison, Peter Kim Papers.

14. Report of Activities of Capt. Robert L. Peaslee and Lt. Peter Kim, Theater G-5, Advance Liaison, Peter Kim Papers. A conflict emerged over the Shanghai Tele-

phone Company with Nationalist China's Ministry of Communications, which took over the company from the Japanese and nationalized it. Peaslee had to fly to Chongqing on September 17 to report to the U.S. ambassador and explain the situation. Ambassador Hurley's resulting démarche to Generalissimo Chiang Kai-Shek resulted in Chiang's ordering the immediate return of the Shanghai Telephone Company to its American owners. Peaslee returned to Shanghai on September 20.

15. Report of Activities of Capt. Robert L. Peaslee and Lt. Peter Kim, Theater G-5, Advance Liaison, Peter Kim Papers. Some British citizens in Shanghai were dissatisfied with the work of the American Military Relief Mission and Peter Kim in returning them to their homes. On September 9 the British Residents' Association and the Shanghai Chamber of Commerce sent a telegram to the British Embassy in Chongqing that complained, "The delay in releasing internees in camps where conditions are unhealthy and humiliating is deplorable and damaging to self respect of all persons concerned. This problem must be tackled in a big way and requires financing for relief of unemployed and purchase of clothing et cetera." The British ambassador responded to the British Residents' Association and the Shanghai Chamber of Commerce that they had "failed to appreciate that in bringing you relief before Japanese surrender in China has taken place, American forces in this theatre have carried out a hazardous operation specifically for the welfare of all prisoners of war and internees in this theatre." Leck, *Captives of Empire*, 403–4.

16. James Graham Ballard based the main character in *Empire of the Sun*, Jim Graham, on himself and his experiences as a boy in the Longhua prison camp, adding features of other children in Longhua and further fictionalizing the character and his actions. For example, Ballard lived with his parents in Longhua, while Jim Graham was separated from his parents and lived with another married couple in a cubicle that he made for himself. Ballard modeled Jim Graham's living situation after that of a real person interned in Longhua—a boy named Bobby Henderson. See Ballard, *Miracles of Life*, 63.

17. Ballard claimed years afterward to have taken matters into his own hands and reclaimed his family's house himself. In his autobiography, he stated that after being revived by eating airdropped Spam and chocolate, he abandoned his parents—with whom he had grown disillusioned during their internment—and left Longhua alone to walk the several miles from the internment camp to their home at 31 Amherst Avenue. He found the house unscathed, with all of his family's furniture and other property still intact inside. The house had been occupied by a general of the Chinese puppet army, who left it guarded by a young soldier. When Ballard arrived and told the soldier that the house was his, the soldier fled. Ballard, *Miracles of Life*, 94–100.

15. REUNION IN SHANGHAI

1. Kim, *Carter's One Man Army*, n. 12, Kim Family Papers.
2. Emails with Richard Kim and Arthur Kim, September 12–14, 2022.

3. VHP interview with Richard Kim, 1:26:30–1:30:50.

4. Emails with Richard Kim and Arthur Kim, September 12–14, 2022.

5. Navy Day was not the same as the U.S. Navy's birthday, which was observed on October 13. Navy Day was an unofficial commemorative event that the U.S. Navy celebrated from 1922 to 1949 on October 27, the birthday of the former assistant secretary of the navy and president Theodore Roosevelt.

6. According to U.S. Navy records, USS *Nashville* was the flagship of Task Force 73 that hosted the Navy Day celebration in Shanghai on October 27, 1945. "Log Book, USS Nashville, Saturday, 27 October, 1945," Record Group 24, Records of the Bureau of Naval Personnel, Deck Logs, 1941–1950, Nashville (CL-43), June 1945 to June 24, 1946, box 6485, NARA, College Park MD. Arthur Kim remembered the USS *St. Louis* as the ship that hosted the event, but on that date the *St. Louis* was steaming to Pearl Harbor. "Log Book, USS St. Louis, Saturday, 27 October, 1945," Record Group 24, Records of the Bureau of Naval Personnel, Deck Logs, 1941–1950, Saint Louis (CL-49), November 1944 to October 1945, box 8367, NARA, College Park MD. The *Nashville* and *St. Louis* were identical *Brooklyn*-class light cruisers, and *St. Louis* had been anchored on the Shanghai Bund until October 12, when it departed to participate in the transportation of Nationalist Chinese troops to the island of Formosa. "Log Book, USS St. Louis, Friday, 12 October, 1945," Record Group 24, NARA, College Park MD.

7. The 40th Infantry Division sent more than a thousand officers and enlisted men home from August 18 to September 14, 1945. The entire division received orders to leave Korea and return to the United States for demobilization in February 1946. *40th Infantry Division*, 171–72.

8. Conversation with Arthur Kim, October 30, 2021.

9. Emails with Richard Kim and Arthur Kim, September 12–14, 2022.

10. VHP interview with Richard Kim, 1:31:00–1:41:00.

16. AMERICANS AT LAST

1. Letter from George Olmsted, Brig. Gen., to Mrs. Ruth B. Shipley, Chief, Passport Division, Department of State, 19 October 1945, Marshall S. Carter Collection, Peter Kim Papers, box 2, folder 1, Correspondence Related to Naturalization 1945–1950, George C. Marshall Research Library, VMI.

2. Letter from A. C. Wedemeyer, Lieutenant General, United States Army, To Whom It May Concern, 27 October 1945, Marshall S. Carter Collection, Peter Kim Papers, box 2, folder 1, Correspondence Related to Naturalization 1945–1950, George C. Marshall Research Library, VMI.

3. Letter from Robert Peaslee to Peter Kim, 31 October 1945, Marshall S. Carter Collection, Peter Kim Papers, box 2, folder 1, Correspondence Related to Naturalization 1945–1950, George C. Marshall Research Library, VMI.

4. Letter from Robert Peaslee to Peter Kim, 31 October 1945, Peter Kim Papers. Peaslee wrote the letter to Peter reporting the results of his meetings on the letter-

head of the Hotel Twenty-Four Hundred Sixteenth Street, a hotel and apartment building located at 2400 Sixteenth Street Northwest in Washington on the edge of the Adams Morgan neighborhood. Opened in 1918 under the name Meridian Mansions, the building was the Washington residence of numerous U.S. senators and foreign diplomats. It was also the home of the future first president of Czechoslovakia, Tomáš Masaryk, during his 1918 discussions with President Woodrow Wilson and members of his administration on the creation of an independent Czechoslovakia. The building was added to the National Register of Historic Places in 1983 and currently is an apartment building called the Envoy.

5. Letter from Robert Peaslee to Peter Kim, 31 October 1945, Peter Kim Papers.
6. A bill to provide for the naturalization of Peter Kim, S. 1607, 79th Congress (1945), *Congressional Record*, November 19, 1945, 10788, https://www.govinfo.gov/content/pkg/GPO-CRECB-1945-pt8/pdf/GPO-CRECB-1945-pt8-22-1.pdf.
7. Memorandum from Marshall S. Carter, Colonel, to the Commanding General, Headquarters, United States Forces, China Theater, 29 November 1945, Marshall S. Carter Collection, Peter Kim Papers, box 2, folder 1, Correspondence Related to Naturalization 1945–1950, George C. Marshall Research Library, VMI.
8. Swiss Consulate General Shanghai, Section for Protection of American Interests, Accounts as at December 31, 1945, Swiss Federal Archives.
9. Memorandum from Paul J. B. Murphy, Colonel, to Assistant Chief of Staff G-5, 20 November 1945, Marshall S. Carter Collection, Peter Kim Papers, box 2, folder 1, Correspondence Related to Naturalization 1945–1950, George C. Marshall Research Library, VMI.
10. Kim, *Carter's One Man Army*, Kim Family Papers.
11. Permission to live in Separate Quarters, letter from James Kim, Captain, Infantry to Commanding General, United States Forces, China Theater, 9 March 1946; and letter to Capt. James Kim, Headquarters, United States Forces, China Theater, 14 March 1946, personal papers of James Kim.
12. Kim, *Our Family History*, 35, Kim Family Papers.
13. Officer's and Warrant Officer's Qualification Card Copy, Kim, Peter, Marshall S. Carter Collection, Peter Kim Papers, box 1, folder 1 (201 File), George C. Marshall Research Library, VMI.
14. Letter from Marshall S. Carter, Colonel, to 2nd Lt. Peter Kim, 7 March 1946, Marshall S. Carter Collection, Peter Kim Papers, box 2, folder 2, Correspondence with Lt. Gen. Marshall S. Carter, 1945–69, George C. Marshall Research Library, VMI. While Colonel Carter used his position at the War Department in Washington to support Peter Kim's cause during the summer of 1946, a counterintelligence officer with the Shanghai office of the Strategic Services Unit (SSU), a postwar continuation of the OSS under the War Department, was filing reports of allegations by Chinese informants that Peter Kim was working for Nationalist Chinese intelligence and the Shanghai criminal underworld, and that he possessed more money than the informants thought was normal for a lieutenant. Whether any of these

reports were considered credible at the time is not apparent. One included the obviously erroneous information that "[the informant] states that Peter Kim was employed at the Swiss Consulate during the war but did not wear an alien armband even though he was an American citizen." Peter Kim, Espionage, Shanghai, 10 May 1946, Report No. YEX-2067, Record Group 226, OSS, entry 109, box 110, NARA, College Park MD. Another stated that the "X-2 [SSU's counterintelligence branch] files states [*sic*] that Peter Kim is familiar with a certain Chinese family called Moy who are believed to be related to the infamous Herbert Moy who worked for the Germans and Japanese and who committed suicide shortly after V-J Day." Peter's fiancée, Ruth Moy, was related to Herbert Moy, but the U.S. Forces–China Theater command had already nominated her for the Presidential Medal of Freedom for operating a safe house in Shanghai for U.S. Army intelligence during the war. Peter Kim, Espionage, Shanghai, 20 June 1946, Record Group 226, OSS, entry 109, box 112, NARA, College Park MD.

15. Representative Judd's House bill was H.R. 7049, A bill to provide for the naturalization of Peter Kim. See "Private Bills and Resolutions," *Congressional Record*, July 16, 1946, 9058, https://www.govinfo.gov/content/pkg/GPO-CRECB-1946-pt7/pdf/GPO-CRECB-1946-pt7-11.pdf.

16. An act to provide for the naturalization of Peter Kim, Private Law 808, S. 1607, 79th Congress, August 2, 1946, in U.S. Congress, *United States Statutes at Large*, vol. 60, part 1, chap. 749, 1288.

17. "Approval of Senate Bills and Joint Resolutions after Sine Die Adjournment," *Congressional Record*, August 2, 1946, 10740.

18. Anker Henningsen and H. Maxcy Smith, Peter Kim's friends from prewar Shanghai who had stayed in free China during the war, stood as witnesses when Peter swore the oath of allegiance to the United States before an Immigration and Naturalization Service officer. See Kim, *Carter's One Man Army*, Kim Family Papers.

19. Officer's and Warrant Officer's Qualification Card Copy, Kim, Peter, Peter Kim Papers.

20. Movement Order, Casual Group RDD 34-2, 3, 7, 10, 14, 14, and 4 (USAT *David Shanks*), 11 August 1946, personal papers of James Kim.

21. Kim, *Our Family History*, 35, Kim Family Papers.

22. For a biography of Philip Potter, see Philip Potter, "I Was Born Lucky: The Autobiography of John Philip Potter of the Baltimore Sun," edited by John Black, accessed October 29, 2024, https://philippotter.net/pdf/Bio.pdf.

23. General Wedemeyer gave a verbal commitment that he would support a bill granting citizenship for Richard but later wrote to Philip Potter on November 27 that he could not support it because he did not know Richard personally. Kim, *Private Law No. 11*, 1, Kim Family Papers.

24. Kim, *Private Law No. 11*, 1–2, Kim Family Papers.

25. VHP interview with Richard Kim, 1:41:00–1:42:00.

26. VHP interview with Richard Kim, 1:42:00–1:43:00; and Kim, *Private Law No. 11*, 2, Kim Family Papers.

27. A bill to provide for the naturalization of Richard Kim, S. 108, 80th Congress (1947), Kim Family Papers.

28. "Naturalization of Richard Kim," *Congressional Record*, June 10, 1948, 7700, https://www.govinfo.gov/content/pkg/GPO-CRECB-1948-pt6/pdf/GPO -CRECB-1948-pt6-6.pdf.

29. Kim, *Private Law No. 11*, 2, Kim Family Papers; and email with Richard Kim, October 12, 2022.

30. Email with Richard Kim, October 12, 2022. St. Thomas' Episcopal Church later burned down in 1970. Its site became a park on the grounds of St. Thomas' Parish in the Dupont Circle neighborhood of Washington.

31. Special Orders Number 192, War Department, 4 September 1946; Special Orders Number 8, Headquarters Special Troops Sixth Army, Presidio of San Francisco California, 18 November 1946; Special Orders Number 185, Headquarters Special Troops Sixth Army, Presidio of San Francisco California, 9 January 1947—all in personal papers of James Kim.

32. Special Orders Number 8, Headquarters Special Troops Sixth Army, Presidio of San Francisco California, 10 January 1947; Special Orders Number 10, Headquarters Special Troops Sixth Army, Presidio of San Francisco California, 13 January 1947—in personal papers of James Kim.

33. The leader of the U.S. Department of State team accompanying the Saudi delegation was Raymond Muir, who had been the State Department representative on board the MS *Gripsholm* during the voyages to exchange Japanese and American civilians in 1942–43. Party Accompanying His Royal Highness Amir Saud, Crown Prince of Saudi Arabia, on Visit to United States, personal papers of James Kim.

34. Memorandum for the Chief of Staff, Synopsis of conference held 30 January 1947 between Mr. Ted Huggins, Public Relations Department, Standard Oil Company of California, San Francisco, and Colonel S. M. Montesinos, G-2 Section, 30 January 1947; Letter from George P. Hays, Major General, USA, to Captain James O. Kim, Officer's Club, Presidio of San Francisco, 10 February 1947; Letter from James Kim, Captain, Infantry, to Mr. Raphael Chabaury, Catering Department, City of Paris, Geary and Stockton, San Francisco, California, 12 February 1947— all in personal papers of James Kim.

35. Kim, *Our Family History*, 35, Kim Family Papers.

36. Richard received the letter at some point in 1948 that he could not recall almost seventy-five years later. Emails with Richard Kim and Arthur Kim, October 12, 2022.

37. Homer Ferguson, a Republican who served in the Senate from 1943 to 1955, later served as the U.S. ambassador to the Philippines in 1955–56 and as a federal judge of the U.S. Court of Appeals for the Armed Forces from 1956 to 1976.

38. Kim, *Private Law No. 11*, 3–4, Kim Family Papers.

39. "Bills and Joint Resolutions Introduced, by Mr. Ferguson," *Congressional Record*, January 5, 1949, 39–40, https://www.congress.gov/81/crecb/1949/01/05/GPO-CRECB-1949-pt1-2.pdf.

40. "Richard Kim," *Congressional Record*, February 8, 1949, 944, https://www.govinfo.gov/content/pkg/GPO-CRECB-1949-pt1/pdf/GPO-CRECB-1949-pt1-17-1.pdf.

41. "Message from the House," *Congressional Record*, March 16, 1949, 2554; and An act to provide for permanent residence status of Richard Kim, Private Law 11, March 29, 1949, in U.S. Congress, *United States Statutes at Large*, vol. 63, part 1, 1078.

42. James had corresponded regularly with Senator Ferguson during the process of passing the bill; then he called the White House on the telephone "almost daily" to get updates on whether President Truman was about to sign the act into law. The last call was a few minutes after Truman signed the bill in the evening of March 29. An ordinary citizen having this kind of access to a senator and to the office of the president was possible in 1949 but would soon be consigned to history. Kim, *Private Law No. 11*, 4, Kim Family Papers.

17. REUNITED BY THE KOREAN WAR

1. Jack Young also went to Korea as an army intelligence officer. For more about Major Young's actions in the Korean War, see Briscoe, "Culture, Language & SPECIAL OPS."

2. Kim, *Our Family History*, 35, Kim Family Papers.

3. David still worked for Hollis H. Arnold, Inc. Kim, *Our Family History*, 44, Kim Family Papers. Betty worked as a buyer in Shanghai for Ming's, Inc., a prominent Hawaii-based jewelry retailer. Ming's was in business from the 1940s to 1999 and had stores in Hawaii and in multiple states on the mainland. See "Crowds Pack Ming's Jewelers' Final Days," *Honolulu Star-Bulletin*, February 29, 1999, http://archives.starbulletin.com/1999/02/27/news/story3.html. Email with Arthur Kim, October 11, 2022; and letter from James Kim, Captain, Infantry, USAR, to the president, July 10, 1950, Kim Family Papers.

4. Kim, *Our Family History*, 44, Kim Family Papers.

5. Kim, *Our Family History*, 44, Kim Family Papers. They left the house and a bundle of U.S. dollars in the possession of a family friend who was serving as the caretaker of property belonging to David's employer, Hollis H. Arnold, Inc. In the 1990s James, Richard, and Arthur traveled to Shanghai to rediscover places that they had known in their youth, and when they visited the house, they found the caretaker was still living there. After recovering from the shock of recognizing them, the now-elderly man revealed that since 1950 he had continued to live in the house after it had been divided into apartments for Communist Party members, and he had kept their money and left-behind family heirlooms safely hidden in a compartment that he had built into a wall. He offered to return the house, the money,

and everything else immediately, but moved by the man's astounding integrity and loyalty for so many years, they told him to consider the house and everything in it as his from then onward. Years later, when Arthur traveled to Shanghai again and visited the house, he found that Chow had passed away, but his widow was still living there. Arthur took a single teacup and saucer from the family's china set as mementoes from the house. Interviews with Arthur Kim and Richard Kim, 2018–24; and Hickcox, Kim, and Kim, *Brief History*, 5, Kim Family Papers.

6. Kim, *Private Law 1028*, 1, Kim Family Papers. David's former office manager eventually immigrated to the United States with his family.

7. Kim, *Private Law 1028*, Kim Family Papers.

8. Kim, *Private Law 1028*, Kim Family Papers.

9. Hickerson later served as the U.S. ambassador to Finland (1955–59) and the Philippines (1960–61). See Office of the Historian, "John Dewey Hickerson (1898–1989)," Department of State, last updated March 14, 2024, https://history.state.gov/departmenthistory/people/hickerson-john-dewey.

10. Richard Pearson, "Jules Davids, Lauded Professor of Diplomatic History, Dies at 75," *Washington Post*, December 11, 1996, https://www.washingtonpost.com/archive/local/1996/12/11/jules-davids-lauded-professor-of-diplomatic-history-dies-at-75/9673dff0-bce1-448a-9fb0-399a16639901/; and Robert Thomas Jr., "Jules Davids Dies at 75; Helped Kennedy with 'Profiles' Book," *New York Times*, December 12, 1996, https://www.nytimes.com/1996/12/12/us/jules-davids-dies-at-75-helped-kennedy-with-profiles-book.html.

11. Kim, *Private Law 1028*, 1, Kim Family Papers.

12. Kim, *Private Law 1028*, Kim Family Papers. The vice president of Dickinson College, Dr. Gilbert Malcolm, also put James in touch with several members of the U.S. House and Senate, including Senators Francis Myers and Edward Martin and Representatives John Kunkel, Robert Rich, and Daniel Flood of Pennsylvania; Lansdale Sasscer of Maryland; and T. Millet Hand of New Jersey. Dr. Malcolm knew Richard and his wife, who worked as a secretary to the dean of Dickinson College, and he became involved at the request of the headmaster of the Mount Hermon School, Howard Rubendall, after James wrote to him asking for help. See also Kim, *Private Law 1028*, 3–5, Kim Family Papers.

13. Representative Judd's House bill was H.R. 7049, A bill to provide for the naturalization of Peter Kim. See chapter 16, note 15.

14. Kim, *Private Law 1028*, 3, Kim Family Papers.

15. W. H. McMains worked for the Distilled Spirits Institute, which later merged with other organizations to form the Distilled Spirits Council of the United States. Distilled Spirits Council of the United States, "History of the Distilled Spirits Council," accessed October 29, 2024, https://www.distilledspirits.org/our-heritage/.

16. Kim, *Private Law 1028*, 3, Kim Family Papers.

17. Letter from James Kim, Captain, Infantry, USAR, to the president, July 10, 1950, Kim Family Papers; and email with Arthur Kim, October 11, 2022.

18. A bill for the relief of Mrs. Chang-Sei Kim and David Kim, H.R. 9082, 81st Congress, 2nd session (1950), *Congressional Record*, August 7, 1950, 11882, https://www.govinfo.gov/content/pkg/GPO-CRECB-1950-pt9/pdf/GPO-CRECB-1950-pt9-5.pdf.

19. A bill for the relief of Mrs. Chang-Sei Kim, David Kim, and Arthur Kim, S. 3914, 81st Congress, 2nd session (1950), *Congressional Record*, July 31, 1950, 10043, https://www.congress.gov/bound-congressional-record/1950/07/13/senate-section.

20. Kim, *Private Law 1028*, 3, 5, Kim Family Papers.

21. Kim, *Private Law 1028*, 5–6, Kim Family Papers.

22. Kim, *Private Law 1028*, 6–7, Kim Family Papers.

23. Kim, *Private Law 1028*, 7, Kim Family Papers; and "Message from the House," *Congressional Record*, August 16, 1950, 12573.

24. "Message from the Senate," *Congressional Record*, September 14, 1950, 14830.

25. An act for the relief of Mrs. Chang-Sei Kim, David Kim, and Arthur Kim, Private Law 1028, September 27, 1950, in U.S. Congress, *United States Statutes at Large*, vol. 64, part 2, A251.

26. Kim, *Private Law 1028*, 7, Kim Family Papers.

27. Kim, *Private Law 1028*, 7, Kim Family Papers.

28. An act for the relief of Mrs. Chang-Sei Kim, David Kim, and Arthur Kim, in U.S. Congress, *United States Statutes at Large*, vol. 64, part 2, A251.

29. Kim, *Private Law 1028*, 7–8, Kim Family Papers.

30. Kim, *Private Law 1028*, 8, Kim Family Papers.

31. Kim, *Private Law 1028*, 8, Kim Family Papers. ss *President Wilson* was an American President Lines passenger liner that operated on a transpacific route from San Francisco to Los Angeles, Hawaii, the Philippines, China, Japan, and back during the 1950s. The *President Wilson* was sold to a Hong Kong–based shipping line in 1973 and eventually scrapped in 1984.

32. Lee Chung Sil became a U.S. citizen in 1955, passing her citizenship test on her first attempt despite taking it in English, which she had not fully mastered. She died at Arthur's house in McLean, Virginia, in 1985, surrounded by her children and grandchildren. She is buried in Honolulu in Valley of the Temples Memorial Park. Betty married a man named Sherman Dahl and raised a family of eight children. She died in 2012 and is also buried in Honolulu. Hickcox, Kim, and Kim, *Brief History*, 3, Kim Family Papers; and interviews with Arthur Kim, 2018–24.

33. Hickcox, Kim, and Kim, *Brief History*, 8, Kim Family Papers.

34. Hickcox, Kim, and Kim, *Brief History*, 5, Kim Family Papers.

35. Hickcox, Kim, and Kim, *Brief History*, 8, Kim Family Papers.

36. Hickcox, Kim, and Kim, *Brief History*, 8, Kim Family Papers. This letter was not the first time that David had informed James that he intended to leave Hong Kong and return to Shanghai. In a letter dated June 5, David had written that he intended to return to Shanghai to liquidate the business and sell the family house,

having received a Hong Kong residence card that would permit him to reenter the city. Alarmed, James immediately sent David a telegram urging him to remain in Hong Kong. Hickcox, Kim, and Kim, *Brief History*, 1–2, Kim Family Papers.

37. McMains had remained actively involved in lobbying for the Kim family throughout the legislative effort in the summer and autumn of 1950. In July–August he had corresponded with President Truman's secretary, Matthew Connelly, regarding reports from the State Department's Visa Division and the Immigration and Naturalization Service. Connelly had recommended to McMains that the executive branch could not help and that going to Congress was the right course of action. Hickcox, Kim, and Kim, *Brief History*, 7, Kim Family Papers.

38. David settled down in Hawaii and worked for a time as a car salesman, then as an office manager for a construction company. He died in 1986 and is buried beside his mother in Valley of the Temples Memorial Park in Honolulu. Hickcox, Kim, and Kim, *Brief History*, 5, Kim Family Papers.

39. Hickcox, Kim, and Kim, *Brief History*, 8–9, Kim Family Papers.

18. AMERICAN INTELLIGENCE OFFICERS

1. The CIA detachment in Pusan was located in the Tongnae district, and James's title was chief of base, Tongnae.

2. Kim, *Our Family History*, 36–37, Kim Family Papers.

3. VHP interview with Richard Kim, 1:43:30–1:45:30; and email with Richard Kim and Arthur Kim, October 12, 2022.

4. The four National Guard divisions federalized in September 1950 were the 28th Infantry Division from Pennsylvania; the 40th Infantry Division from California (James Kim's former division); the 43rd Infantry Division from Connecticut, Rhode Island, and Vermont; and the 45th Infantry Division from Oklahoma. The 40th and 45th Infantry Divisions went to Korea; the 28th and 43rd Infantry Divisions instead deployed to Germany to reinforce NATO's forces.

5. The 525th Military Intelligence Group continues to exist into the twenty-first century as the 525th Expeditionary Military Intelligence Brigade, stationed at Fort Bragg, North Carolina.

6. VHP interview with Richard Kim, 1:45:30–1:47:30.

7. While waiting in Honolulu, Arthur lived with David, Betty, and his mother and worked as a salesman for Kirby vacuum cleaners to pay back the dairy farmer who had loaned him the ninety-nine dollars. Email with Arthur Kim, September 11, 2023.

8. Email with Arthur Kim, October 11, 2022.

9. This historic building, named Gyeonggyojang, also served as the Embassy of the Republic of China from 1949 to 1952. It became a hospital building in 1967, then a museum of the Korean Provisional Government and Kim Ku in 2005.

10. Interviews with Arthur Kim, 2018–24.

11. Interview with Arthur Kim, April 30, 2024.

12. The JACK's office in the Traymore Hotel in Seoul also was located only a short distance from a house that the Kim family had rented in the late 1920s while their father was in Shanghai. He had sent remittances to the grandfather, who embezzled all the money. Kim, *Our Family History*, 8–9, Kim Family Papers.

13. Kim, *Our Family History*, 36–37, Kim Family Papers.

19. MAJ. PETER KIM

1. Letter of Appreciation from Marshall Carter, Major General, to Capt. Peter Kim, Aide de Camp, Marshall S. Carter Collection, Peter Kim Papers, box 2, folder 2, Correspondence with Lt. Gen. Marshall S. Carter, 1945–69, George C. Marshall Research Library, VMI.

2. Medal of Freedom Citation, Mrs. Peter Kim (then Mrs. Ruth K. Moy), Marshall S. Carter Collection, Peter Kim Papers, box 2, folder 23, Scrapbook: Presentation of Medal of Freedom to Ruth Kim, 9/51, George C. Marshall Research Library, VMI.

3. Peter Kim married Althea Nadine Reeves on April 25, 1981, when he was sixty-eight years old and she was sixty-three.

4. For additional biographical information about Marshall Carter, see his obituary: Bart Barnes, "Gen. Marshall S. Carter Dies at 83," *Washington Post*, February 19, 1993, https://www.washingtonpost.com/archive/local/1993/02/20/gen-marshall -s-carter-dies-at-83/7b67c573-1c01-4a11-9f4a-89f6663b5c6d/.

5. The George C. Marshall Foundation lists the personal papers of Peter Kim and Marshall Carter as separate collections on its website, https://www .marshallfoundation.org/research-library/library-collections/ (accessed August 17, 2023).

20. JAMES KIM, CIA PIONEER

1. No and Osterholm, *MiG-15 to Freedom*, 139–57.

2. Representative Joseph Holt, a Republican from California who had been a high school classmate of James in Los Angeles, introduced No to Vice President Nixon and to the House of Representatives. See No and Osterholm, *MiG-15 to Freedom*, 168.

3. No and Osterholm, *MiG-15 to Freedom*, 170.

4. No and Osterholm, *MiG-15 to Freedom*, 170–71.

5. Kim, *Our Family History*, 37, Kim Family Papers.

6. Kim, *Our Family History*, 37, Kim Family Papers. James's only knowledge of his grandparents was that his father had entrusted James's paternal grandfather with handling remittances to the family from his work overseas in Shanghai, but the grandfather had taken all of the money to spend on himself and his concubine. Kim, *Our Family History*, 3, 8, Kim Family Papers.

7. Kim, *Our Family History*, 37–38, Kim Family Papers.

8. Kim, *Our Family History*, 38, Kim Family Papers.

9. Kim, *Our Family History*, 2, Kim Family Papers.

10. Kim, *Our Family History*, 38, Kim Family Papers.
11. Kim, *Our Family History*, 40–42, Kim Family Papers.
12. The location of James Kim's grave in Arlington National Cemetery is section 54, site 4093. Veterans interred in the same section include Lt. Cdr. Richard Best, the dive-bomber squadron commander whose aircraft sank two of the Japanese aircraft carriers destroyed in the Battle of Midway, in site 3192; and Martin Conboy, a second lieutenant in the 37th New York Volunteer Infantry during the Civil War who was awarded the Medal of Honor for his actions during the Battle of Williamsburg in 1862, in site 3841.

21. LT. COL. AND REV. RICHARD KIM

1. When Richard Kim left the CIA field office in Tokyo in 1955, his replacement was James Lilley, who would serve with the CIA in Asia for a quarter of a century and then become a distinguished diplomat. Lilley served as the U.S. ambassador to South Korea in 1986–89 and the U.S. ambassador to China in 1989–91. For more about the life and career of James Lilley, see his autobiography: Lilley and Lilley, *China Hands*.
2. VHP interview with Richard Kim, 1:47:00–1:48:30.
3. Fort Benning and Fort Bragg became two of the ten U.S. Army bases named after Confederate generals that received new names in 2023. In 2025 Fort Bragg's name was restored, but it is now named after Pfc. Roland L. Bragg, who earned a Silver Star and Purple Heart in World War II.
4. At the end of Devil Jump, Capt. Richard Kim received a letter from Lt. Gen. Marshall Carter, deputy director of the CIA, requesting that he stop by CIA headquarters in Langley, Virginia, to discuss the exercise. After a decade and a half as Peter Kim's benefactor and friend, Carter was interested in the progress of Peter's younger brothers.
5. For a detailed history of this operation, see Briscoe, "Congo Rescue 1960."
6. Briscoe, "Congo Rescue 1960," 15.
7. Hickcox, Kim, and Kim, *Brief History*, 12, Kim Family Papers.
8. Up to 1968, the awarding of an Air Medal by the U.S. Army required twenty-five hours of combat assault flights, fifty hours of combat support flights (e.g., reconnaissance, resupply, and medical evacuation), or a hundred hours of noncombat service flights.
9. VHP interview with Richard Kim, 1:48:30–1:50:00.
10. Exactly twenty-two years later, on April 11, 2022, Rev. Richard Kim officiated the author's wedding to his wife, Kelley Sievert.
11. They have included the late Maj. Gen. Michael Healy, interred in Arlington National Cemetery in 2018. See "Arlington—Full Military Honors for a Green Beret Legend, MG 'Iron Mike' Healy, October 5, 2018," YouTube, uploaded by Kirk Healy, November 19, 2018, https://www.youtube.com/watch?v=JjEI624xGsk, 10:15–11:50.

22. ARTHUR KIM

1. Loving v. Virginia, 388 U.S. 1 (1967).
2. Hickcox, Kim, and Kim, *Brief History*, 13, Kim Family Papers; and interviews with Arthur Kim, 2018–24.
3. Some relief from financial hardship came from the ability to collect a pension immediately upon retirement in 1977. The CIA's retirement policies in the late 1970s required twenty-five years of service for eligibility for a pension, but they also permitted prior military service to count toward those years of service. Arthur Kim's twenty-two years of service in the CIA (1955–77) and three years of service in the army (1951–54) just barely qualified him for a CIA pension.
4. The company was originally created by James Kim and subsequently acquired by Arthur Kim to save the cost of incorporating a new entity when starting his new business. The author confirmed the identity and history of the company on the online database of the Virginia State Corporation Commission.
5. The sources for this chapter include discussions with Arthur Kim, 2018–24; and Hickcox, Kim, and Kim, *Brief History*, Kim Family Papers.

23. A VICTORY FOR AMERICA

1. David had three children; James, four; Betty, eight; Richard, eight (including two adopted in Japan); and Arthur, three. As of 2024, Richard alone had forty-seven children, grandchildren, and great-grandchildren.
2. Kim Chang-Sei (22 February 1893–15 March 1934), State Administration for Patriots and Veterans Affairs, Records of Distinguished Services of Independence Patriots, Vol. 15 (Awardees 2001–2003), pp. 139–40, in the Kims' possession; and Lee Jong Guk, "The National Foundation Medal for Mr. Kim Chang-Sei Conveyed to Family," *Korea Times*, September 7, 2001. The National Foundation Medal is second in precedence behind Korea's highest award for contributors to Korean independence, the Order of Merit for National Foundation.

BIBLIOGRAPHY

ARCHIVES AND MANUSCRIPT MATERIALS

Kim, James. Personal papers. Property of the family of James Kim.

Kim, Peter. Papers. Marshall S. Carter Collection, George C. Marshall Research Library, Virginia Military Institute, Lexington VA.

Kim Chang Sei Family Papers. Hoover Institution Library & Archives, Stanford University, Stanford CA.

  Hickcox, Edward Lee, Arthur Kim, and Richard Kim. *A Brief History of the Family of Dr. Kim Chang-Sei.*

  Kim, James. *How Private Law No. 11 (S. 90), 81st Congress (Dick's) Came to Be Enacted.*

  ———. *How Private Law 1028 (81st Congress) (1950) for the Relief of Mom, David and Arthur Came to Be Enacted.*

  ———. *Our Family History.*

  Kim, Peter. *Carter's One Man Army, a "Vignette": A "Vignette" of His Long and Cherished Friendship with the Late Lt General Marshall Sylvester Carter (US Army Ret).*

National Archives and Records Administration, College Park MD.

  Record Group 24, Records of the Bureau of Naval Personnel.

  Record Group 226, the declassified records of the Office of Strategic Services.

  Record Group 319, Records of the Army Staff.

National Archives and Records Administration, San Bruno CA.

  Record Group 85, Immigration and Naturalization Service.

Schoyer, B. Preston. Papers. Howard Gotlieb Archival Center, Boston University, Boston.

  ———. *An Uneasy Remembrance of Shanghai.* Property of Lisa Schoyer.

PUBLISHED WORKS

Ballard, J. G. *Empire of the Sun.* London: Victor Gollancz, 1984.

———. *Miracles of Life: Shanghai to Shepperton: An Autobiography.* New York: Liveright, 2008.

Bergin, Bob. "Three Amateur Spies and the Intelligence Organization They Created in

Occupied WWII Indochina." *Studies in Intelligence* 63, no. 1 (March 2019). https://www.cia.gov/resources/csi/static/Three-Amateur-Spies.pdf.

Briggs, Ellis. *Proud Servant: The Memoirs of a Career Ambassador*. Kent OH: Kent State University Press, 1998.

Briscoe, Charles H. "Congo Rescue 1960." *Veritas* 14, no. 1 (2018): 6–24. https://arsof -history.org/pdf/v14n1.pdf.

———. "Culture, Language & SPECIAL OPS: Recruiting & Training 'Turncoat' Agents in Korea." *Veritas* 9, no. 1 (2013): 30–40. https://arsof-history.org/pdf/v9n1.pdf.

Brown, Arthur. *The Korean Conspiracy Case*. Northfield MA: Northfield, 1912.

Burdsall, Richard, Arthur Emmons, Terris Moore, and Jack Young. *Men against the Clouds: The Conquest of Minya Konka*. New York: Harper & Brothers, 1935.

Cha, John. *Willow Tree Shade: The Susan Ahn Cuddy Story*. New York: Korean American Heritage Foundation, 2002.

40th Infantry Division: The Years of World War II, 7 December 1941–7 April 1946. Baton Rouge: Army & Navy Publishing, 1946; Nashville: Battery Press, Inc., 1995. Also available at https://worldwartwoveterans.org/wp-content/uploads/2020/09/40th -Infantry-Division-Unit-history-PDF-Book.pdf.

Hayashi, Brian. *Asian American Spies: How Asian Americans Helped Win the Allied Victory*. New York: Oxford University Press, 2021.

Heiser, Victor. *An American Doctor's Odyssey: Adventures in Forty-Five Countries*. New York: W. W. Norton, 1936.

Kaufman, Jonathan. *The Last Kings of Shanghai: The Rival Jewish Dynasties That Helped Create Modern China*. New York: Viking, 2020.

Kim, James. "Kim Family History." In *Kim Chang Sei Gwan Ryeon Ja Ryo Jib*. Seoul: Department of Medical History, Yonsei University College of Medicine, 2006.

Kim, Robert S. *Project Eagle: The American Christians of North Korea in World War II*. Lincoln NE: Potomac Books, 2017.

Kum-Sok, No, and J. Roger Osterholm. *A MiG-15 to Freedom*. Jefferson NC: McFarland, 1996.

Leck, Greg. *Captives of Empire: The Japanese Internment of Allied Civilians in China, 1941–1945*. Bangor PA: Shandy Press, 2007.

Lilley, James R., and Jeffrey Lilley. *China Hands: Nine Decades of Adventure, Espionage, and Diplomacy in Asia*. New York: PublicAffairs, 2004.

MacEachin, Douglas J. *The Final Months of the War with Japan: Signals Intelligence, U.S. Invasion Planning, and the A-Bomb Decision*. Washington DC: Center for the Study of Intelligence, 1998.

Miles, Vice Adm. Milton E. *A Different Kind of War: The Unknown Story of the U.S. Navy's Guerrilla Forces in World War II China*. New York: Doubleday, 1967.

Rose, Alexander. *Washington's Spies: The Story of America's First Spy Ring*. New York: Bantam, 2006.

U.S. Congress. *United States Statutes at Large, Containing the Laws and Concurrent*

Resolutions Enacted during the First Session of the Eighty-First Congress of the United States of America, 1949, and Proclamations, Treaties, International Agreements Other than Treaties, and Reorganization Plans. Vol. 63, part 1, Public Laws, Reorganization Plans, Private Laws, Concurrent Resolutions, and Proclamations. Washington DC: U.S. Government Printing Office, 1950.

———. United States Statutes at Large, Containing the Laws and Concurrent Resolutions Enacted during the Second Session of the Eighty-First Congress of the United States of America, 1950–1951, and Proclamations, Treaties, International Agreements Other than Treaties, and Reorganization Plans. Vol. 64, part 2, Private Laws, Concurrent Resolutions, and Proclamations. Washington DC: U.S. Government Printing Office, 1952.

———. United States Statutes at Large, Containing the Laws and Concurrent Resolutions Enacted during the Second Session of the Seventy-Ninth Congress of the United States of America, 1946, and Proclamations, Treaties, International Agreements Other than Treaties, and Reorganization Plans. Vol. 60, part 1, Public Laws and Reorganization Plans. Washington DC: U.S. Government Printing Office, 1947.

Yu, Maochun. OSS in China: Prelude to Cold War. Annapolis: Naval Institute Press, 1996.

INDEX

Judd, Walter, 151, 153–54. *See also* legislation

Kadoorie, Eleazar, 113
Kadoorie, Horace, 113–14
Kadoorie, Lawrence, 113–14
Kadoorie, Muriel, 113–14
kamikazes (Divine Wind Special Attack Units), 74, 90
Kefauver, Estes, 153
Kempeitai, 39, 41, 45–48, 103, 108, 121–22
Kim, Arthur: birth of, 15; childhood of, 19; CIA career of, 193–97, 232n3; and CIA station in Vientiane, 195–96; defying Japanese indoctrination, 44; education of, 24; enlisting in the U.S. Army, 167–68, 229n7; and intelligence collection in Shanghai, 71–73; and James Kim's return, 128–31, 166; Korean War service of, 168–70; living in Hawaii and California, 166–67; marriage of, to Helen Goodnight, 194–95; and Operation Sparrow, 106; and Peter Kim's return, 125–26; post-CIA career of, 197–99; private security business of, 198–99, 232n4; representing the Ahn family in Korea (2021), 201–2; retirement of, 199; U.S. citizenship of, 193–94
Kim, Betty: birth of, 12; childhood of, 19; defying Japanese occupation policies, 42; evacuation of, from Shanghai (1937), 23, 29; leaving Hong Kong (1950), 156–58; living in Hawaii, 175, 191, 200, 226n3; living in postwar Shanghai, 148–49; marriage of, 228n32; passing of, 228n32; returning to Shanghai (1939), 24, 30; and wartime U.S. financial assistance, 40–41, 208n7, 208n11
Kim, Chang Sei: early life of, in Korea, 7–8; education of, at Yonsei University (Chosun Christian College), 9, 201; living in Korea (1926–28), 13–14; living in Shanghai (1917–20), 10–11; living in Shanghai (1928–30), 14–15; living in the United States (1920–26), 11–13, 203n7; living in the United States (1930–34),

15–18; lobbying for Ahn Chang Ho (1932), 17, 201; mental health of, 205n31; Republic of Korea's National Foundation Medal awarded to, 201; suicide of, 18, 205n32
Kim, David: birth of, 10; childhood of, 19; education of, 21; employment of, 21, 24, 206n7, 226n3; and intelligence collection in Shanghai, 71–73; leaving Hong Kong, 156–61, 228n36; living in Hawaii, 175, 191, 200, 229n38; living in postwar Shanghai, 148–49; living under Japanese occupation, 40, 44, 48; passing of, 229n38; and Shanghai Volunteer Corps, 21, 22
Kim, James: and 160th Infantry Regiment, 34–37, 74–82, 83–87, 89–92, 95–96; and 222nd Field Artillery Battalion, 33; Arlington National Cemetery interment of, 180, 231n12; army discharge resisted by, 32–33; as army intelligence officer, 83, 86–87; birth of, 11; Bronze Star and Purple Heart awarded to, 82; childhood of, 19, 21; CIA career of, 177–80; in combat at Storm King Mountain, 79–80; commissioned as a U.S. Army officer, 34; contacted by Peter and Richard Kim (1944), 64; education of, 21, 30–31; enlisting in the U.S. Army, 31; evacuating family from Hong Kong, 156–62; evacuation of, from Shanghai, 23, 29; and family reunion (October 1945), 129–31; and father's suicide, 18; at Georgetown University, 145, 148–50, 163, 164; in Korea (September–October 1945), 95–96, 215n13; Korean War service of, 163–64, 170, 229n1; living alone in Los Angeles (1938–41), 30–31, 207nn6–7, 207n10; living with the Ahn family (1937–38), 29–30, 206n5; lobbying of, for Lee Chung Sil, David Kim, and Arthur Kim, 149–56, 226n42; lobbying of, for Richard Kim, 141–44; marriage of, to Jane Yang, 178–79, 180; retirement of, 180; U.S. Army Reserve service of, 148, 163